19th. Dec. '95.

THE FORTUNATE WEED

To.

David and Anne.

With all Best Wishes

IAN.

ME

Ian May

THE FORTUNATE WEED

Ian J. May

The Book Guild Ltd
Sussex, England

The Book Guild Ltd
25 High Street,
Lewes, Sussex

First published 1996

Set in Times
Typesetting by Raven Typesetters, Chester

Printed in Great Britain by
Antony Rowe Ltd.
Chippenham, Wiltshire.

A catalogue record for this book is available from the British Library

ISBN 1 85776 050 6

I was simply going to dedicate this book to Audrey. Then I thought she would have wanted to share it with others she knew who had also lived with a terminal illness; therefore I have chosen two of her friends, Jennifer and Rita.

They enriched the lives of those they came in contact with and saw their children grow up to become fine adults. Jennifer's youngest, David, who is one of our godchildren, was a teenage schoolboy when his mother died.

They suffered long distressing illness with courage. Jennifer died thirteen years before Audrey and Rita, who both died within a few months of each other. All three constantly thought of their families and friends.

PREFACE

There are probably a lot more people than generally imagined who have a story or a poem somewhere at the back of their mind that they would like one day to put down on paper. Perhaps, like me, some find there are occasions when verse form can produce a particular 'something' that translates with deeper truth a poignant feeling or restless conscience. At such moments, to one less than a talented writer the response of logically placed prose sentences hardly ever seems sufficient and leaves the printed content dull and lifeless. For that reason I insert now and again a simple poem or short story into my writing in an attempt to underline a particular event, scene or thought.

It has long been established that there is a difference between one who writes and a writer, and one who produces rhyme verse and a poet. I thought it wisest to get that in before someone else does. Perhaps I could describe myself as a slide rule writer and poet who works on the principal that 'if the results looks right – that's near enough.'

I have written of my early impression and influences covering the period in my life from the late thirties, when I was a young schoolboy, up to 1950 when I was a junior engineering draughtsman.

1

weed: 1 Any of various usually common, or abundantly growing plants.
2 A plant considered undesirable, unattractive or troublesome, especially one growing where it is not wanted in cultivated ground.

At one time or another during those turbulent years I should imagine the whole of my European generation was in some way slotted somewherc into one of the above derivations through either political or wartime fortune. Some, sadly, did a lot worse than others.

It must have been a hurtful and distressing time for mothers who were present at the school assembly points in the latter part of 1939, watching the young evacuees forming into their respective classroom lines in the playground. It ended with them waving an encouraging 'goodbye' to their own and the other children who had all quite suddenly been uprooted from their homes and were now being marched away to the railway station under the supervision of teachers, some of whom were virtual strangers. Their destination was not known.

The watching grandmothers and mothers must have also known that in a very short time many of their fathers would also be marching off in a not unsimilar fashion.

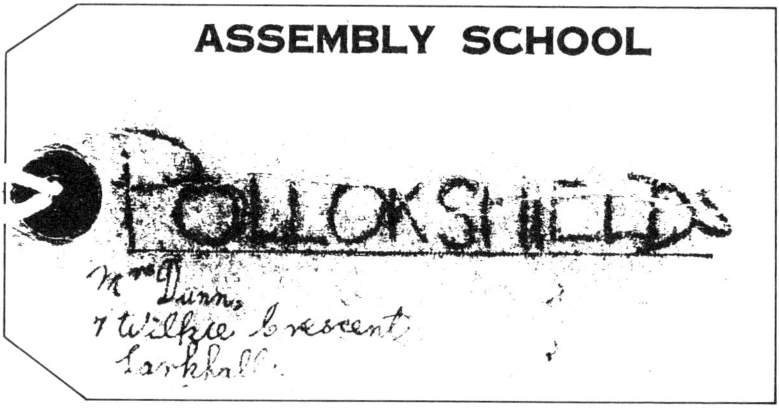
ASSEMBLY SCHOOL

POLLOKSHIELDS

Mrs Dunn,
7 Wilkie Crescent
Larkhall.

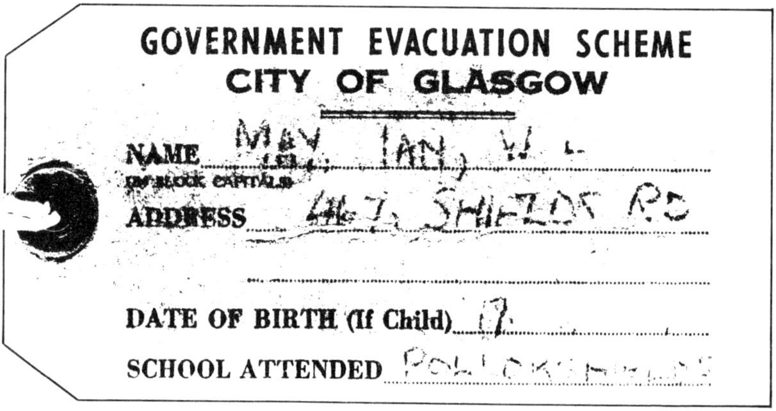
GOVERNMENT EVACUATION SCHEME
CITY OF GLASGOW

NAME (in BLOCK CAPITALS) MAY, IAN, W. L.

ADDRESS ....

....

DATE OF BIRTH (If Child) ....

SCHOOL ATTENDED POLLOKSHIELDS

My very first personal ID document.

The parents had been told by the Government Evacuation Scheme officials that, providing the children were healthy and hardy, then they should be in no doubt that they were doing the best possible thing for them to survive the expected imminent wartime bombings. They were further assured that the countryside was the ideal place to sustain healthy growth in town children, even though it might well be in a living environment much different from what they had been used to.

Many of these young mothers would carry the hopeless dread that their child would land somewhere quite alien to it and where it would be unwanted, troublesome and unattractive when compared with other people's children.

I had heard the same thing said about weeds.

Every adult is aware that in this world the yet unborn child, like a tiny wafting seed, has no choice either in where it will land for its birth or in the area it will grow up in. Most will land on fertile ground that will immediately receive and nurture the helpless thing, and will welcome the first signs of minute wriggling roots by both feeding and securing them. These are the fortunate ones. There are others who arrive at a place where they are not wanted. They will be lonely, insecure and extremely vulnerable.

Human nature does not improve with warring governments nor in fighting fringe causes. It is during such times that children become, more than usual, the defenceless victims of Chance with its varying degrees of adversity, depending merely on where they were at a particular time.

It is a sad fact about our civilised world that a child at any time and in any place can suddenly become a little human war-weed. It's not the small frightened fingers or the tiny trembling toes, or even the turbulent tears that cannot always flow. It must surely be the terrible mixture of all these things battling inside a small body, and anyone trying to justify any part of that torment is wanton and wrong. Our Evacuation Scheme was well planned and with a degree of understanding. The same could not be said of some other countries.

I was one of the children taken to a Schoolchild's Evacuation Assembly Point a few days before the start of the war. I had an orange coloured label attached to my coat with my name and address, date of birth and the school I attended on one side, and on the reverse was the name of the assembly school. I had to bring my gas mask and a hand case which I would have to manage by myself; therefore it must have been fairly light, and probably contained a change of underwear, a pair of socks, a clean shirt, a pair of pyjamas, a towel, hair brush and comb, toothbrush and paste, a pair of slippers, and with the onset of winter a warm jersey. Amongst this was packed the basic school requirements, exercise jotters, pencils and ruler. I also had a stamped PC addressed to my parents.

I am starting my story at the beginning of 1940, simply because it will make a good basic marker to keep my timing of events as tidy as possible, and allows me to group the years neatly together, one decade at a time.

Past memories can be taken from a stratum of time lying between two straight lines of known dates where remembered highlights can be strictly placed. Such logic seems all very well, but my recall of those early years is that they were made up from some colourful jigsaw with large curved shaped pieces of episodes that bubbled well over any set edges. There were no jagged corners or straight lines on any of them and thankfully all the parts somehow fitted idyllically together. It is because of this that I will be found guilty at times of ranging between my evacuee days and the immediate pre-war years.

Here, then, is my first ten years commencing from the first winter of the war. At that time I was a twelve-year-old evacuee from the city of Glasgow, and living in the mining village of Larkhall in Lanarkshire.

We were told by our teachers and parents at the very start of the evacuation to keep in contact with the other evacuees whom we knew, and not to wander off on our own. We had to write the name and address of where we were staying on our evacuation label in our pocket when we went out anywhere until we had become familiar with our new locality and above all we had to behave ourselves.

I was lucky to be fostered to a Mrs Dunn who had thrown open her home to two boys she knew nothing about. The other evacuee was called Gordon Foster, whom I had known previously, having been in the same class at Melville Street School and who had also been in the same Wolf Cub pack a year or so earlier. (I was then a Boy Scout and can't remember if Gordon was or not.) We now shared an upstairs room between the pair of us.

After the initial adventure feeling was over and the excitement began to die down, came the realisation that I was actually going to sleep in another house and share a bed with someone other than my brother, and that was probably the time when the first cracks started to appear on the sham brave front. These feelings would have been shared by many children who were learner evacuees.

I had already been away from home on two occasions by myself. The first was a lengthy stay in the Glasgow Victoria Infirmary which was followed by a one week holiday with Mother at a farm near Rothesay on the Isle of Bute in the Firth of Clyde, that turned out to be a two week sojourn for me. I was allowed to stay on by myself to be well and truly spoilt by the farmer's wife and another lady who worked on the farm. The memory I have of the first event were bath times after an operation where the tender area had to be submerged every few days. The memory I carry from the second stay was how high it was between the ground and sitting on the bare back of a Clydesdale horse. These were the only times I had been on my own away from the family and I mention them to inform the reader that I was hardly the molly-coddled type of young boy.

Just before leaving home at the start of the evacuation my older brother Eric gave me a Wizard and a Dixon Hawke detective book and Mum packed my favourite Dinky toy car which was a red open topped MG, along with some toffee and tablet she and my sisters had made the night before. It didn't all total up to an awful lot to remind me of home, but it was all I had.

Mrs Dunn welcomed both of us with a friendly attitude and a kindly smile which we were to see a lot of, and treated each of her two war waifs as one of her own. She was a widow with two sons and a daughter. Her eldest son worked in the local bus service and was a very quiet-natured, silent type of person. I don't remember much about him, although I seem to think that I was told he had a slight heart condition which had prevented him passing his call-up medical examination. John was the eldest of the family.

The daughter was married and lived nearby, and had recently had her first baby. Her husband was away serving in the Army during the whole time I was staying in Larkhall, which were two good reasons why she spent a lot of her time at her mother's home.

The youngest son, Jim, was a student attending the Motherwell Polytechnic and I cannot remember what he was studying to be. He was the one nearest to my age, which probably explains why I can remember him more that I can his brother and sister. He must also have shown a lot of patience towards the two in-comers who probably now pestered him more than his own family did.

It is not easy for a child to determine how old someone is, and to put an age to a grown lady is impossible by assessing her general wear and tear. He must therefore slot her into being as old as a more familiar female figure like a mother, grandmother or aunt, perhaps even a neighbour. By that method Mrs Dunn was about the same age as my mother. After that wealth of reasoning I will now tell of a more accurate method of knowing how old she was. She told me one day that she shared the same birthday and year as Adolf Hitler, 20th April 1889. My birthday was just three days away from that, but many years later.

Mrs Dunn's elderly father had an upstairs room where he spent all his time and I only saw him on the very few occasions when I passed his room and the door was open. I often heard him talk to himself when I went upstairs to the bathroom or the room I shared with Gordon. Mrs Dunn told both of us that her father spent much of his time reading aloud from the Bible.

I liked the whole family for they had made me welcome, and I was allowed to ride Jim's adult-sized bicycle providing I kept to the quiet streets in the vicinity of the neighbourhood. Looking back I do not think there was such a thing as a busy street anywhere outside city centres.

Quite often when I was out on the bike or on foot I would pass the customary quota of miners walking their whippet dogs, and I can remember a particular grassed area, just a little bit off the pavement, where a group of them used to gather to play Pitch and Toss, which was a popular gambling game. Usually these were the only times I saw or met any of the miners, and that was because of the shift working system used in the pits. Whenever I called at a friend's house where there was a pitman, he was either sleeping, working or not at home. I did hear them most early mornings before we were called, tramping along the pavement with their heavy boots loudly sounding their masters' presence on their way to the pit.

Many of them were pigeon fanciers, and this showed in the number of pigeon lofts there were scattered around the gardens at the back of their houses. The care and concern shown over these birds was truly remarkable, and many of the owners were accepted experts on the breeding and handling of these homing pigeons.

I used to wonder what the miners got from releasing those birds and watching them fly upwards to freedom, sunlight and fresh air before finding their way back to their home loft. But then! I was only a very young boy who only thought that they could carry secret messages attached to their legs.

I didn't meet any of the miners that I can recall but somehow or another I remember occasionally speaking to some older retired men. They would talk about the dangers of explosions or of the roofs suddenly caving in and the water they had to walk about in. I already knew about the sea and how fishermen went about their task; I had often been told of the countryside where animals grazed and crops grew and were harvested, but all I knew about coal was that it came out from the ground and that canaries had been once used to detect gas and that the coal was delivered to our home by a horse-drawn cart.

Bit by bit the horizons of all the evacuees were slowly widening.

I can remember quite clearly the Sunday morning when Prime Minister Chamberlain spoke on the wireless telling the people of the country that the German Government had not replied to a note handed to them earlier in the day by the British Ambassador in Berlin, and that we were now at war with Germany.

It was not long after the declaration of war when Mother told me in one of her letters that the *Athenia* had been sunk by a U-boat, and how providential it had been for the family that my Aunt Clara had been spared by returning to Canada prematurely on board her on the voyage before she was sunk. It is strange how an incident or disaster affects a person when there is a personal link between that someone and the event.

The *Athenia* was the first big ocean-going ship I had ever been on board and the experience was still fresh in my mind. The whole family had wandered around her as visitors prior to seeing Aunt Clara (Mother's sister) off on her return voyage across the Atlantic which would carry her half the way back to her home and Uncle John in Vancouver after having spent a holiday with us in Glasgow.

One ritual both Eric and I carried out in Glasgow was to dubbin our football boots regularly, which was probably each week during the football season. When I was evacuated there was, of course, no room for football boots in my case. Funnily enough, I never really missed them and have never worn a pair since. I couldn't even tell what happened to the ones I left behind. I don't think Mrs Dunn bought any Sunday papers because I must have asked my Mother in a letter how 'Wullie', 'The Broons' and 'Nero and Zero, the Rollicking Romans' were getting on. Anyway whatever the reason or reasons were, I received regular Sunday Post comic pages.

On 10th May 1940 a Mr Winston Churchill became Prime Minister. I had never heard of him.

There were quite a number of local boys of my age group living in and near Wilkie Crescent, and it didn't take Gordon or myself very long to establish ourselves among a group of friends. There were plenty of outdoor games to play at as well as mischief to get up to, both being part of the magical make-belief world that all young boys can create for themselves. At the school I was now attending in Larkhall there were plenty of familiar faces from the Pollokshields School, and the teachers, with one exception, were very nice. Looking back, the odd one out seemed to have an appetite for 'handing out the belt' to the boys for the least possible thing and no-one liked him. To make matters worse he bore a strong resemblance to the German SS leader Himmler, and I'm sure he revelled in the likeness.

The winter of 1940/41 was very cold and during it there were times when both Gordon and myself kept on some of our clothes under our pyjamas when we went to bed. At such times we slept under the sheet we were supposed to lie on for extra warmth. It was through no fault of Mrs Dunn as she had no control over the weather, and in any case both the wireless and public information weather forecast centres had long since stopped giving predictions as a wartime security measure. Being warned would not have made much difference during that particularly severe icy spell because of the rationing and shortages which affected every commodity that could have made the winter months more comfortable. Downstairs there was always a bright fire burning in the dining room-cum-lounge each day when it was in any way cold or chilly out of doors. The only trouble was, that when there was a cold spell outside then the warm room downstairs greatly added to the contrast of the low temperature upstairs. I recall being told at some time that with the onset of winter it had been known for children in the poorer districts of Glasgow to be sewn into their underclothes after alterations had been made to the garments. This ensured that the youngsters had another 'skin' at all times until the milder weather arrived.

I suppose, being removed from a secure environment and not fully understanding the reason why, could quite easily have planted a seed in a young mind that pointed towards betrayal. Childhood minds act on instinct rather than logic. At such a time the former of these processes works in some mysterious manner that deletes from the conscious memory what it wants to. I would not be surprised if one consequence of the love or preference for animals in a person came about as a spin-off from some forgotten true or imaginary deep feeling of rejection. Animals are refreshingly honest in their feelings and give no such sense of deception. That is one of their characteristics which, no doubt, is one of the attractions for many young people entering the veterinary colleges and animal care centres.

I must state in full honesty that I have no recollection at or around that time of being unwanted in any way, and I am very fond of animals. I must confess that much later on, during the postwar years, I developed a feeling about some types of people such that if I were given the choice of snatching one of them or an animal from the raging torrents – I would grab the creature.

As far as I can recall Mrs Dunn was not a churchgoer, but having said that I might very well be doing her an injustice. Perhaps I should say that she never offered me the opportunity to accompany her to a service. Hers was a Protestant household and she might well have had a close church connection but did not want to influence either of her two evacuees in religious matters. Religion was never mentioned under her roof and there were no clerical visits when I was in the house that I can recall.

Mrs Dunn's house was council-owned and had a garden both front and back which was new to me, though to be honest I did not give it much thought at the time. Children quickly accept such differences. Coming from a tenement building type of home I was used to a back green that everyone in the same close shared but didn't often use. Its only function that I can recall was to hang out washing in or beating carpets that were hung over the washing lines. There was a covered-in area beside a door that opened into the back lane and this was where the dustbins were kept for the residents' refuse which always included the ashes from the coal fires, and to keep the dust from them to a minimum they were always wrapped up in newspaper. Why I know about this was because it was my job to take the remains of the previous day's fire out to the bin.

Somehow or another my clothes caught up with me at my new home. Probably bits arrived by post or Mother contrived a method to get them to me. I remember being the owner of a leather helmet which were commonly worn by boys during the winter. Whether I was wearing it when I left home or if it was forwarded to me, I do not know, though it was probably the former. I wonder how some evacuees managed for their everyday wear when they were taken a long way from their home town. The very young evacuees could not have carried very much with them on their departure.

I was conscious of not being associated with any boys' groups during my evacuee days, at least not so that I would complain about it. I had moved up from the Wolf Cubs into the Boy Scouts earlier in the year before the evacuation of children started. I took my Scout's Oath with the 134th Glasgow Pack in St Ninian's Church Hall. My brother Eric was already a member of the troop, which made me feel as though I was now in the Big League for young boys.

Apart from the Cubs and the Scouts I was also in the church choir which meant attending a choir practice once a week, and at least two Sunday choir services.

In steps of seniority my sisters had started to receive piano lessons from a Mr Hunter who came to the house, and from what I heard from my siblings, was a very strict teacher. Father played the piano quite often in those days, always verging towards the classics or traditional pieces. He was to stop playing completely during the war due to arthritis in his fingers. It did not stop him playing golf. I cannot remember who taught me the scales with the correct fingering. It might have been Father, but more probably a sister doing an impersonation of Mr Hunter. I do not think that Eric had an inclination for music and I think it quite likely I was being tested out on the scales to find out if I should be put forward for lessons.

There must have been two stools for our piano. One was the usual rectangular seated type that Father and Aunt Clara used. The other, which must have been acquired for the children, had a circular padded seat connected to its base by a heavy wooden threaded spindle, and depending on which direction the seat was turned it was either raised or lowered. I used to like sitting on it and giving myself a wee birl (spin). It's a pity 'piano stool birling' wasn't an Olympic event as I might have won a gold medal when I was old – at say, twenty.

There was no piano in Mrs Dunn's home, which made it then quite irrelevant whether I had started tuition. Being evacuated at that time in my life really meant I had lost the last opportunity of having lessons, and in any case many men and women teachers would have been called-up.

By June of the first summer of the war what had remained of the Allied fighting force in Europe had been evacuated from the beaches of Dunkirk, and I remember seeing the film of the men wading out and climbing onto any one of the assortment of small craft that had crossed the Channel from our side to bring our soldiers home.

I still think to this day that I saw that film a few days after the evacuation had finished, but that could not have been, as I never went to a picture house during the whole of my stay in Larkhall;

in fact I do not recollect if there was a cinema there.

I must have gained that vivid impression of having practically been there at Dunkirk from the daily newspaper articles and their pictures as well as the accounts given out over the air waves of the BBC and what people told me about it at the time.

I did, of course, like everyone else, see the actual pictures shown in the Pathé newsreels, but in my case at a later time than I had thought.

Adolf Hitler must have gone berserk after the dust had settled on the sands of Dunkirk over the final outcome of the evacuation because that was when he started to shout about the total annihilation of his enemies. I do not remember being told about him saying that. I just knew. I also knew that the war was not going too well for us at that time, but to me it was something that would sort itself out. One didn't have to be a grown-up to know that They were the baddies and We were the goodies and of course there had to be the cliff-hangers where the Goodies had their backs to the wall against tremendous odds, but the outcome was always the same in the end. Heaven's above! Everyone knew that Good always triumphs over Evil.

As though to drive home the reality of what happened at Dunkirk the school air raid, gas attacks and fire drills were held more often and with greater discipline. We all became quite used to hearing the air raid warning siren which as far as I was aware, had been more for testing purposes than anything else. The part of the sound that I disliked most about the siren was when it stopped its wailing and its sound died slowly away. It seemed to take such a long time before it was completely silent and for some reason or another I was very much aware of those last few seconds.

What I yearned most for during the time I was away from the family home was, I think, my mother's kitchen. Had I been asked in 1939 what I missed most, and I can't recall any such enquiry, though it was highly probable it was put to me at least a thousand times, my answer would have been something about missing my chums and enjoying the games we had played at together in familiar places. Oh, there were lots of boyhood priorities I could have mentioned. The kitchen very slowly sifted out from my subconscious over a long period, yet there must have been moments during my early stay at Larkhall when I really must have missed it. No doubt one of those occasions must have been on bath night during that first winter when it was straight from a chilly bathroom to dry my hair in front of the open fire before retracing my steps back to the unheated bedroom. At home the ritual changed slightly inasmuch as there was a mad scramble from an icy bathroom into a warm kitchen, and then to bed with a hot stone bottle and the added heat of a brother.

Mrs Dunn's kitchen was very much smaller than Mother's and I don't think there was an open fire in it. All the cooking was done on a gas stove. The one other downstairs room was the lounge where there was always an open coal fire burning. Upstairs there were three bedrooms and a bathroom. I do not think there were any fireplaces upstairs and I seem to remember seeing an electric fire in her father's room.

My mother's kitchen was always warm with a fire burning in the grate, but it was not only that. There were the familiar tempting smells of home-made soup and mouthwatering odours of baking. My clothes were warmed for me there and during the cold spells the 'boys' stone hot water bottle was always filled from a kettle boiled over its homely fire. Every time I entered my home it was the kitchen I first headed for because I always knew someone would be there. It was a very much occupied place. The family ate in the kitchen with the boys sitting with their backs to the fire and the three girls facing them. Behind my sisters was the dresser, part of which was the coal bunker. Father's place was at one end of the table with his back to the kitchen sink and window. Mother sat at the opposite end facing him.

I had played on the kitchen floor where my imagination could stretch to any length, and I had listened quietly to the BBC wireless programmes there. The parts of my neck and behind my ears which I had skilfully avoided washing in the bathroom had more than often merely preceded a more thorough repeat performance at the kitchen sink in front of family witnesses. I have never heard of any child's neck being broken in this common room, but the nearest it ever came to happening to me on many occasions was a few years earlier when I would usually be seated on a sister's knee and facing her. Two intent eyes would bore into mine and a voice would intone:

Away down deep at the bottom of the sea,
catching fishes for Ian (or whoever) and me,
how many will you catch?

Depending on how many I gave in my reply, probably two or three, then I would be thrown back until my head was almost touching the floor and both my arms would be shaken rather violently, through each count of the number I had given.

I was taught my first steps in table manners in the kitchen, and I must have learnt how to read the time from the clock on the mantelpiece over the fire. My first lesson in simple science was patiently explained to me after I had enquired why the sun should shine when the little lady in the small cottage beside the clock came out, and why it rained when the little man came out. My education started in that room and a major part of my personality must have been shaped there as well.

Sometimes in these pre-war days Father would fall asleep in his chair beside the fire. He was probably lulled into that condition by something on the wireless. It wouldn't be very long before he would begin snoring loudly, which would start the younger members of the family giggling with mischievous intent, and then we would make all sorts of noises to waken him without making it look too obvious what we had done. Later on when Cappy the cat came into the family circle we used to miaow loudly in Father's ear. He wasn't at his best when he awoke and instinctively knew what we had been up to. Mother always scolded us but at times I'm sure she enjoyed it every bit as we had.

The kitchen was the busy household hub of the home where everyone in the family had an equal share, at least that's the way it seemed to me. It was the centre of my world. When I scraped my knee or cut my finger the first move towards the healing process started there with carbolic soap and iodine and a reservoir of tears must have been soothed away in that area and all within the warmth of its fire, set within its shiny black leaded surrounds.

Our cat Cappy must have shared the same sentiments as the rest of the family, for he spent most of his time there. I don't know whether he was a he or she, but I remember how his name came about. Sister Joey had an accident where she broke her leg during a fall down the close stairs just about a year or so before the war started. During her convalescence and as a special treat Joey, in a wheelchair and pushed by Sybil and myself, was allowed to go to the Waverley picture house in Shawlands. The film was about a circus and an escaped lion called Caprice. What the dastardly plot was about I cannot remember but not long after that visit to the cinema a member of the family (I do not remember who it was) won a kitten in the church raffle, organised by a rather smart minister whose cat had just had a litter of kittens. The name Caprice was shortened to Cappy, and our kitchen had a new permanent occupier.

I could not have been a little angel all or perhaps even any of the time because one day I decided to leave home. I suppose a man really has to do what a man has to do even at the tender age of nine or ten. I remember seeing some older boys playing cricket of all things on a spare piece of ground which probably places the day as a Saturday sometime during the summer. I must have wandered quite a distance away from home as it was late (for me) when Sybil found me on the landing outside our front door. Amongst other things it has to be borne in mind that a man has also to eat and sleep in his own bed. I don't remember if anyone was overjoyed to see the return of the run-away though the part of the Welcome Home I do remember was the smacking I received on my bottom with a slipper wielded by Father. No doubt that was the closing scene of one more family trauma before the next one appeared.

The distance from where I was evacuated to from my home was in the region of twenty or twenty-five miles, which wasn't very far compared with the distances that other children were from theirs, yet I do not recall the subject of mileage cropping up amongst evacuees. We were at an age where one was either at home or not at home. We were well aware, however, that if anyone did decide to go home on their own it was imperative to be doubly sure that he or she knew the way because all the sign posts had been removed. We were also warned not to attempt eating any chocolates that any one of us might find lying around on the open ground as they were probably poisoned ones dropped by the Germans to spread panic. Strangely enough I never heard of anyone ever finding any. Not really surprising.

Talking about sweets makes me wonder why I do not remember much about shops. I suppose that is quite normal for a young boy. I can only think of one corner shop on the way to school where I must have obtained something at some time. Mrs Dunn used the Co-op, so there must have been a branch in Larkhall. I must have had my hair cut somewhere, but for the life of me I can't remember. I can only draw the conclusion that if a barber there was, then he must have been a good one.

Every child uprooted like a weed from a garden must have suffered some effect of being suddenly removed from his or her family and home. I was the youngest of a family of five children. That meant seven people sitting around the kitchen table for a meal with a warm glowing fire in the grate. I was used to having warm, trusted people around me; therefore I can say that I started out from the beginning as a fortunate and secure war-weed-to-be in my foster home.

I recall seeing large pieces of ice flowing fairly fast down the River Avon (Larkhall) one freezing snowy afternoon during a cold spell during the winter. The river runs quite close to the main thoroughfare. I was amongst a group of boys discovering and exploring the river's Arctic banks at the time and knew we only had until dark to do it in. It was all so very new to me as I had never in real life watched such a bleak wintry scene like it before.

Weather is about the most difficult thing there is to recall from my childhood. At certain times of the year I was probably told about one hundred times in a single week to put on a scarf and wrap up well against the elements, but quite honestly I cannot remember once hearing anyone telling me to do so. I cannot even remember sheltering from rain, which I must have done many times in a city like Glasgow, which is renowned for its summer, autumn, winter and spring showers. Memory in a child is very often remembering only the parts that fitted into the child's world at the time.

I will give one example, though in order to do so I must jump back again to a pre-war day and recall a family picnic to Loch Lomond. I remember the beach, which I thought to be wide and spacious. There was also an average-size shop with plenty of goods to sell and where I spent the tuppence Father had given me before leaving home. Father never came on any of these outings. The Loch itself could not have impressed me too much because I remember it as a small waterway.

When I returned to the same spot many years later the first thing that amazed me was the great length of Loch Lomond. The shore line around it is a mere ribbon in size compared with the impression I had carried in my mental memory box over the years. The shop where I spent my tuppence turned out to be the local post office, and a very small one indeed. The biggest surprise turned out to be the magnificent breathtaking scenery of the whole area, a fact that had not registered in the slightest way on me as a child. I am afraid I have to confess that at that early age, if I could not touch it, walk in it or taste it, then it was of little consequence.

During these same years just prior to the war I remember the Sunday school trips which meant a steam train journey to some station with a park or field nearby. I might be right in saying that I seem to remember that Cardross was one such place. Once we had all arrived and been counted there were the usual games, and if I can say that the sack race was a sort of one-legged affair, then we all joined in running races of the one, two and three-legged types. I certainly do recall enjoying my 'piece' (bread sandwich and not very dainty) and sometimes did a sandwich roll (a soft round bread roll) swop with someone else, but I had to be careful that Eric didn't con me out of anything as he had a very healthy appetite. Each child brought his or her own 'piece' to the outing along with a cup which was usually a white enamel mug for drinking whatever beverage was being served.

Going out for the day meant just that; there was never a time when the picnic party would leave early to return home. The weather must have turned bad at times but it could only have been a matter of seeking shelter until it passed.

I used to wonder what happened to Lucy. She was a German refugee who had been in my class before I was evacuated. She lived with a Scottish Jewish family that stayed close to where we lived in Shields Road. I seem to have been elected to accompany her to and from the nearby Shields Road/Darnley Street corner and the school by some power or powers that I have long since forgotten. Being the same age and with her English being a bit better than my German, we didn't have any trouble understanding each other. I carried her case until we were in the vicinity of the school playground; then she had to carry it herself; then I sort of disowned her and she went over and was lost amongst the girls.

Sometimes the time taken going home with Lucy from school would take a bit longer because I might have got myself involved with a game of 'jorries', perhaps better known as marbles, with some of the other schoolboys. This was a game we played along the roadside gutter. There were two types of marbles with one being made of a hard clay substance and the other being made from glass and called 'glassies'. The idea and purpose of the game was that you tried to hit your opponents 'jorrie' or 'glassie'. The rule was, if you were using a 'jorrie' and hit another 'jorrie' then it was yours. However, you had to hit a 'glassie' three times before you won it. With a 'glassie' whatever you hit was yours. I'm sure all this became very clear to Lucy. Mother always insisted that my brother and I washed our hands with red carbolic soap when she learnt that any of the two of us had been playing marbles in the street, which incidentally meant the marbles had to be washed as well. All this was done much to the consternation of our hygienic sisters. I'm afraid that all the warnings flung at the two young males from their antiseptic siblings went over their heads, as both continued playing 'jorries' in and with their gutter friends until the evacuation started.

During one of these homeward 'jorrie' sessions I'm sure I explained to Lucy that boys wore their schoolbags strapped to their backs in order that they can use their arms and hands to play such games. With her little knowledge of English and our youthful capacity to understand each other, I don't think she was too confused with some of my explanations, such as the one I have just mentioned. I certainly hope I never passed on any germs to her through her schoolcase handle.

I had been told about Lucy and why she was with us, but it was going to take a few years before I even started to begin to realise what she had been through. She, and others like her, must have had the tough survival stuff that weeds are made of, having been plucked up from somewhere to land somewhere else, only to be plucked up again, and always praying that some grim gardener's finger didn't close too tightly around her.

The distinction between refugee and evacuee was not known to me then. How could any young person know the difference between fleeing with nothing from persecution inside your community, against the orderly departure of being moved away from a threat from outside your community with the almost sure certainty you would return when the threat was removed?

I am not absolutely sure whether Lucy was my first love, or if it was just because I had been told to take her to school, but I did not have to carry her case, did I? Perhaps it was two schoolchildren in the same class that gave us something in common.

Moving forward again to the wartime days at Larkhall, I remember it as being a quiet and pleasant place, yet for the boys at least there seemed plenty to do. It would probably be nearer the truth to say that it was just that we had a bit of open space to play in and the rest was what our imaginations contrived. The countryside was on our doorstep and offered all kinds of scenery, including coal bings, which I had never seen before. They were the heaps of mining refuse that looked like large upturned cones and most of them were covered with grass, giving them a miniature hill appearance. I became quite used to seeing them. Nearby would be the pit with its huge winding wheel that spun so effortless telling the world that men were either going into or returning from the ground directly below it. In so many ways I was still a city boy who knew little of hedges and birds and 'things'.

It wasn't until many years later that I wondered what other people had thought of us. After all, every type of child from every background was included in the evacuation scheme. There must have been times when Mrs Dunn and/or her family talked in private about me. If I had tried I'm sure I could have been a little angel perhaps for five minutes, but for almost a year would be asking too much for any darling little boy. Looking back, I find there was a lot of piffling snobbishness among middle class children and young people can say things in all innocence that might offend only because they said what they heard inside the privacy of their own home. The foster homes couldn't pick and chose who they would take, apart from the gender. For them it was literally what they found on their doorstep. Fortunately I cannot look back and recall anyone I wanted to get away from.

Regarding family contact I seem to hazily remember labouring over the writing of post cards which I have a feeling Mother fed to me when she could, having pre-written my home address on each. Such was our method of communication.

I had visits from my mother and sometimes Eric or one of my sisters would accompany her. It could not have been a very easy time for her as these visits covered the winters and springs of 1940 and 1941. Later on, during the summer school holidays and the long light evenings, I made several trips home at the weekend by bus into Buchanan Street Bus Station where I was met by one of the family before boarding a White No. 3 tram to Shields Road.

In 1940 it was still considered wisest to have the children out of the cities and major towns as the war was still going badly for the Allies. There was a general disappointment amongst our group of evacuees that we were not returning home for the summer of 1940. We were to stay on for a further year to complete our schooling without another change and for me it was an important year that would decide whether I 'qualified' on to secondary education. There was another reason too: my family might be moving down to stay in Prestwick with an aunt.

Quite a lot of evacuees managed home for a few days at that time, and as the weeks passed their numbers became fewer as more returned permanently home.

Gordon returned home for good during that summer, which left me with a bedroom all to myself for the first time in my life.

Of course Larkhall did not have the gardens or parks that Glasgow had, and with so much countryside around there was not the need for them. At home I had Queen's Park and Maxwell Park more or less on the doorstep and I had visited them quite often, although more usually at weekends. On Sundays the children's swings were chained up so that they could not be used, and the round-a-bouts were secured by order of the powers-that-were at the time, who believed it sinful for children to play in any public place during the Sabbath.

It was a world where Sundays brought out everyone wearing their best clothes, and woe betide the child who dirtied or damaged anything worn on that day. Good clothes usually meant brighter clothes that added a pleasant touch of colour to an otherwise colourless day. One story told me by my sisters was how the poorer little girls wore their darned or patched jerseys inside their satin dresses on that day, which says something for their mothers who helped to make the Sunday a little brighter.

The peace and quiet of rural Larkhall was disturbed by rumour and gossip that travelled as fast as the fiery cross could carry it. It was all because Rudolph Hess had dropped out of the sky in the vicinity of the Duke of Hamilton's country seat, Dungavel House. It was probably the most talked about secret of the war at that particular time, and the ex-Local Defence Volunteers (LDV), then recently renamed the Home Guard, had a field day, or month, over it and no doubt wives and families did the same.

Everyone seemed to know how he did it, but no-one seemed to know why. Putting politics aside, and regardless of what Hess had done or condoned in the past, or his strange behaviour pattern during the later Nuremburg Trials, it was no faint-hearted stupid man who flew across the North Sea on the evening of Saturday, 10th May 1941, and then continued his flight, crossing Scotland over the Cheviot Hills in darkness under wartime conditions, finally to parachute from his plane, landing with such accuracy in his preselected area and apparently all from memory, without the aid of charts.

Thinking back to the first few days as an evacuee I never gave a thought to the upheaval it must have caused the whole household where I was billeted. The very fact of one of their rooms being prepared and then handed over to young strangers, along with the freedom of the house, must have caused a lot of inconvenience, for as I recollect from my own experience, Mrs Dunn's son Jim slept on a bed-settee downstairs. It could hardly be expected of me to be aware at the time that a payment was made by the Government, which was not unreasonable. I did not consider whether it was compulsory or would become so to take in evacuees. Even so, I am certain that by far most foster mothers took in their young boarders voluntarily and through kindness splashed with patriotism.

One morning an evacuee classmate was sick in the classroom and I suppose it makes sense to think that different feeding times or foods could bring about upsets in young tummies. I seem to recall, or was left with the impression that, the janitor had a bucket of sawdust always at hand for this contingency. I don't know if this was a wartime measure during the evacuee scheme or whether the bucket of sawdust had always been readily available and perhaps still is at the time of writing. A child being sick during the time of losing a mother's presence and her familiar cooking style seems to be a fair probability, especially with the added stress ingredient of the father being away in one of the Forces.

I had found myself in another world. A world where I passed most of the day outside school hours in a foster home. Most of the time there was spent in the type of room that in my own home was reserved for visitors and was without the usual relaxed family warmth of the kitchen. It always made me feel that I had continually to be on my best behaviour. I do not want to sound ungrateful but the shared bedroom was too grown-up for me and was a constant reminder that it was not mine. The black-out did not help any as it operated through the hours of darkness. This meant curtains being drawn before going to bed, and the luxury of seeing the night sky, not knowing what the weather was like on a dark morning, had to be discovered by some means that would not assist the enemy. I missed Cappy a lot too – even though it was no secret in my family that he only loved the fire and the fish.

I think the biggest change for me was the weekends. My previous Saturdays and Sundays had been reasonably predictable in comings and goings. Saturday meant general play in the morning with pictures or football in the afternoon and some sort of board game at home in the evening. Sundays meant best clothes with best behaviour that always included a church service followed by attendance at Sunday school and a walk. Not a bad life really. During my evacuee non-schooldays it was either play or just passing time. Still, not a bad life for a growing lad.

During the first year of the war the events that were attractive to a young person and that were normally looked forward to were played out on a much lower key. A birthday no longer merited a party with friends. There were no, or very few choc eggs at Easter, and bonfires with fireworks on or around 5th November was out of the question. I cannot recall as an evacuee having a string of chestnuts and doing battle with someone else's or roasting them for eating. Christmas was a sentimental time that carried the message of being grateful for what you had. (How did one send a card to a friend's home where one of its members had been lost or killed in action, and wishing that someone a Happy Easter or a Merry Christmas?)

Mrs Dunn must have used some sort of discipline over me in some sort or another. It must have been cleverly done because I cannot remember any form of restraint. I do not think I was any better than the average boy of my age, and hopefully no worse, but I think most mothers would agree that a child seems by nature to be able to exploit most situations to its advantage.

It was not compulsory for me to stay where I was placed, and I could have returned home at any time, but like most evacuees I remained until my parents decided it was the safe and proper time for me to do so. I was lucky because I still had both parents and a good home to return to. I had been exceptionally well-treated and cared for during the whole of my stay with Mrs Dunn, or as the matured married ladies of Larkhall addressed themselves, Mistress Dunn.

I don't think that full recognition was given to the women who fostered wartime evacuees; probably because, as the war moved more in our favour, the children slowly returned to their own homes and the evacuation scheme slowly petered away from being a concerned priority at its beginning to a quiet satisfied completion with varied belated memories at its finish.

I must have been a healthy brat because I cannot tell whether there was a doctor or a dentist in Larkhall during my stay there. The same logic applies to girls of my own age. I remember three girls who used to watch us play in the street and whom we knew, so presumably they were sisters of the neighbourhood boys. There must also have been girls in my class. The village therefore must have comprised a lot of grown-ups, an adequate number of boys and about ten or eleven girls which would have made a fairly normal place. On the other hand, maybe I was still living in a boy's world during the tail-end of the blissful years of absolute innocence.

Thinking back as an adult, questions do arise. For instance I cannot remember if I had any pocket money. Now I know full well that I probably did have a few pennies but for the life of me I cannot recall being given any pocket money. Whether Mother sent a postal order to me or left me a shilling or half-a-crown during her visits I just do not know.

I stayed with Mrs Dunn for ten months, by which time I had passed my qualifying exam at school and my parents had moved from Pollokshields and were now living down in Prestwick, waiting for their long-lost child. They were staying in the house of my Aunt Bell, (Father's sister) at the airport end where I was to join them. Father would have to travel each working day to and from Glasgow by train.

During my days at Larkhall I had only seen my father during a handful of visits home, which were non-existent at the beginning, rare during the middle and a bit more frequent towards the end of 1940.

Around that time it was perfectly safe for a young person to travel without an adult in attendance. It was quite in order for a child to ask a grown-up for assistance or help in regard to any travel arrangement. There was not always a policeman around then, but at the same time it was safe for a young boy to approach a stranger and ask him for cigarette cards.

It would be hard for me to think that a young human body could be created without some form of built-in protective device to cover most contingencies outside the malevolence of the deranged and corrupt. It is something which is probably very scientific, but let me simply call it a guardian angel or some make-belief barrier against fear. Or let me put it another way:

THE IMPOSSIBLE FENCE.

(Have I Now Been Partly Stolen? Or Perhaps Just Slightly
Sold?
Or Maybe I'm Not Young Enough? Or By Chance I'm Not
Too Old?)

Slight puzzled and total trusting, lapsed-lone since scheme had begun,
When familiar family aren't with you, is the time for wanting just one.
Yet something fly-flits around me, singing starlings tell they can see,
It often talks through one of them, though seems it never speaks to me.
It might be the size of an eagle, or crabbit crow that's not too small,
And there wasn't one back in the city, least not from what I can recall.
Its vague shape size I've never known, and designed with ghostly skill,
From a mystic matter's secret store, flowing fine from its magic quill.

(A Wee Hand Case And Gas Mask With An Orange Label Telling I'm Me! An Unsure Wartime-Migrant City Child, That's Now Called An Evacuee.)

The bewitching bead-eyed blackbird's prance, to forewarn of perils near,
A raucous shriek to call 'Alert' and soft squawk to sound 'all clear.'
A pre-war coloured butterfly, flutter-fetches a past picnic reflection,
And downed doves coo calm-comforts, removing nightmares of rejection.
The dusk owl's hoot tells banished child, the watchful shield is there,
That tired tender eyes made heavier still sleep sure beneath its care.
And dreamed the calling wind did sound, like a known voice on the wing,
That carried the memory message, with words someone special would sing.

(I Know Why My Parents Sent Me To Be Safe From A Bomb Blitz At Home,
Can't I Fall With The Rest From My Family Nest, Than Flutter On Alone?)

Those trees and fields and hedgerows must mean more work for the rain
Yet falling it sounds no heavier, when tip-tapped a town's window pane
From weaving branches overhead, thrush-trilled this care cautious sound,
'Unlike a tree your roots roam free, not tight tethered to the ground,'
Then quiet quacked warned the duckling, wary retold by a warbling-reed,
'When alone near dark deep water, then take heed! take heed! take heed!
A coy cygnet made some ripples run, and from each their message wends,
'Sensing danger keep with company, don't swan single from safe friends.'

(Sometimes I Feel Quite Uneasy, And Make The Same Wish Each Day,
That What I Hope Remains Near Me, Will Not-Never Be Too Far Away.)

On seeing the red breast of a robin, dressed fine in his waist-coat attire,
Broke stern spell of weary wartime, with warm glow of a far family fire.
Then nightingale perched beside cuckoo, and a duet was heard from the pair,
The first sang a sweet cradle love song, and the other echoed 'take care'.
Same summer sun and winter winds, shared past peace with war weather scene,
As the necks and faces of children, all still remained chirpy bright clean.

But with rural school and country home, amongst so much
else that was new,
Where moments of child's lingering envy, of what homing
pigeons could do.

(By Living Now In A Second Home, Makes An Anxious
Doubt Persist,
That When I'm Gone From Any One, Will I Then Be Only
Half Missed?)

It warned when play roughened to harmful, seemed nowhere
hid a hide place,
And then in a dream it spoke again, this time from a wise
sparrow's face.
'Your fence is mere one amongst many, that outnumber the
birds in the sky,
"Spread further afield" was twitter-sung, "than sharp-eye
swallows can spy.
Penned and netted with homing hopes." cheep-chirped the
old feathered sage
"Having mingled plead-prayers of a mother, left at home
with an empty cage,
And although you've been given good shelter, and been well
watered and fed,
You wish only this war is soon ended, and return home to
your own city bed." '

(Locked Away Are My Unheard Wished, Of A Waif's Fear
Of Being Forgot,
With Each Distress That Never Showed, Now Sealed In
Mind And Thought.)

Inevitably the time came for me to say goodbye to my Larkhall home, friends and school. I liked Mrs Dunn who had treated me as one of her own, and I also detested fond farewells, but as it was, she was the one who did all the crying at the bus stop, which I don't think was entirely due to her relief at my final departure. She had made a promise to my mother during a recent visit she had made to Wilkie Crescent that she would visit us at Prestwick as soon as she could manage the trip, which she did.

It had seemed no time at all since I was wandering amongst a group of wide-eyed, slightly bewildered children being directed along strange roads leading away from Larkhall Railway Station, each with an orange-coloured label attached to our coats, and some of us still clutching the bar of dark chocolate we had been given. I did not know it then, but when my name was called out in front of a certain council house at No. 7 Wilkie Crescent, I was to be one of the luckiest war-weeds of the war.

Looking back over my evacuee days I must be honest and say that I cannot recall any particular 'up' or 'down', but if I were to highlight a particular aspect I would have to say with hindsight that I would like to give thanks for having been allotted to the billet I was placed in. One of the few clear memories I have is of Mrs Dunn making Christmas as happy as possible for her two young boarders. I cannot recall a festival party at school.

I did not make any lasting friendships either with the local boys or with any other evacuee, and I do not think I did very well at school.

I might be deluding myself, but it would be nice to think that the experience taught me in some measure how to cope on my own. I do not think it left me with any psychological hang-ups, or at least none more than was usual anywhere at that age.

My time spent as an evacuee could be summed up in the one word 'repetitious'. It was a period in my life where I had to imitate my life style and at the same time blend into a situation that I could only vaguely understand. I went to school and back to Wilkie Crescent, then back to school again. The boys I played with all lived within a few doors from No. 7 and the area we played in was nearby. I could not direct anyone to a place outside the immediate area of my stated weekday route, nor could I tell of any landmarks or buildings inside the village. In Glasgow I had been used to travelling in a tramcar, taking me this way or that way to where, or near to where I was being taken, but in Larkhall I lived within the parameters of Mrs Dunn's and the Crescent, apart from going to and from school and a few limited forays from off the beaten track. It was not in any way a hardship and I passed my evacuee days quite happily.

I had now reached the stage to start secondary school learning and was leaving behind the time when the necessary basic maths times-tables had been committed to memory. Such was the fashion in those days to exercise and develop the youthful memory cells and raise the concentration threshold, and one that did me no harm.

And now, between bringing this chapter to a close and before the reader peruses the following few pages, let me leave you with this thought.

There were three and a half million children evacuated from towns and cities throughout Britain at the outbreak of war, and if I assume the average height of those boys and girls was four feet and the height of a person is roughly the same length as the distance between the fingertips of the outstretched hands when both arms are lifted outwards parallel to the ground – if all the evacuees had stood side by side with arms outspread and the fingertips touching, they could have formed a line 2,500 statute miles long.

The distance between London and Berlin is 592 statute miles and the distance from London to Cairo is 2,194 statute miles. As I mentioned, just a thought.

Looking out over the estuary of the River Forth and lying side by side along its Northern Bank are the two small Fife towns of Charlestown and Limekilns.

By leaving Limekilns and walking Eastward along Coffin Road that runs more or less alongside the water's edge you will shortly arrive at the now deserted, Rosyth Churchyard where a number of my kinfolk found their last resting place.

One of the gravestones, (B145), bears the following inscription:

> To the memory of Andrew May for many
> years coachman at Broomhall who died at
> Charlestown January 19th 1883 aged 92. This
> stone was erected by the Earl of Elgin in
> grateful remembrance of his long and
> faithful service and kindly intercourse
> with many members of the family.

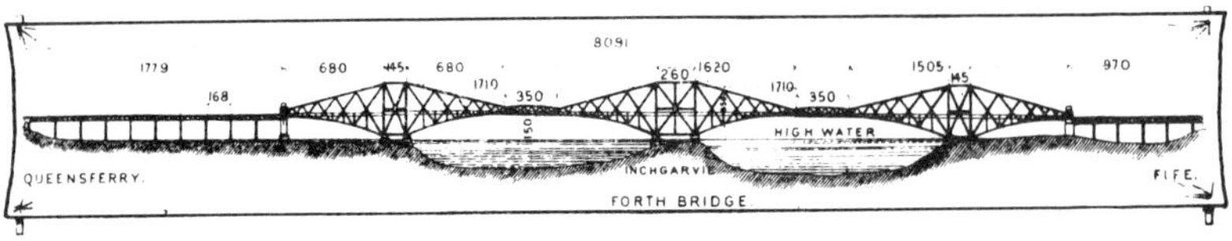

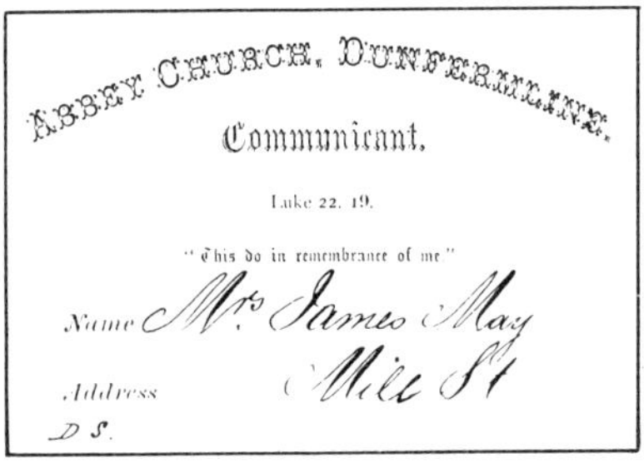

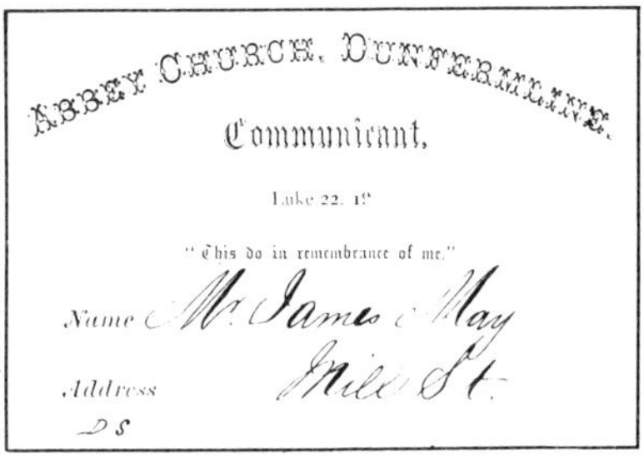

From amongst the locks of hair and book markers in the family bible.

The following short story was written by Andrew's engineer brother James who held Andrew Carnegie to be one amongst his friends and which might explain the involvement of both the method of transport and the scenario it contains.

James designed many of the patterns required for the iron castings used in the building of the Forth Bridge that became the first ever cantilever bridge to be built, and which was completed in 1890. He died in 1899.

I am assuming that my grandfather wrote *The Family Coach*. It was in a wooden box belonging to him and which finally passed into my hands. Someone had a reason for keeping it. It is undated by hand but the paper bears the clear watermark of – A. Pirie & Son, 1859.

What the story was written for or who was supposed to have read it is anyone's guess. It was obviously written by one who was interested in the details and workings of a coach to ensure as much as possible the safety and care of its passengers and horses – but had no control over the weather. It appears to be a draft copy that is very theatrical in substance with pantomime names, yet nevertheless might well have been the writer's conception of America and of its way of life as it was then. I'm sure it was written in a light hearted Punch and Judy style even with its drama-of-the-day conclusion. I would like to know the reasons for the underlining and the obvious repetitions, and who were Mr and Mrs Didler? It is almost as though questions were going to be asked of the reader. It's all rather confusing, but strangely enough his grandson is also an engineer whose nearest and dearest has told him that he has much in common with the author of *The Family Coach*.

It was written at the time when families and social groups gained their pleasure in what and how they entertained themselves and that would entail a degree of preparation on someone's part. It may be something along these lines. If thirty readers read it there will probably be - well, maybe one or two who can imagine the circumstances in which it was probably written or what would induce the reader to write a similar story. Anyway please read on:

The Family Coach

Dramatis Personae

1 Box, 2 Rumble Tumble,
3 Axle-tree, 4 Door, 5 Springs,
6 Windows, 7 Perch, 8 Horses,
9 Reins, 10 Whip, 11 Wheels,
12 Steps, 13 Dog, 14 Aunt
Ellen, 15 Capt. Tobacco,
16 Master Jonathan, 17 Miss
Jemima, 8 Juba, 19 Chloe,
20 Coachman —

A party of pleasure was made to go from New York to the Falls of Niagara, consisting of Mr & Mrs Diddle

Aunt Ellen, her dear little
Dog, Miss Jemima & Capn
Jobbens inside the Family
Coach. Master Jonathan,
on the box, Jubba & Chloe,
two black servants on the
Rumble Tumble — This
meeting the wishes of the
whole party, the axeltree
and Springs were examined
And the luggage was packed
into the Family Coach —
The door was opened and the
steps let down, the windows
shut — The Coachman
taking the whip & reins
mounted the box, and

Jonathan beside him,
and the rest - including the
dog, got into the Family
Coach — The Dog placed
himself upon the cushion,
Aunt Ellen said, the dog
was not comfortable; pooh!
the dog, said Capt. Tobacco;
dont abuse the dear little
dog, said Aunt Ellen.
There's a fuss about a dog,
said Miss Jemima; throw
the dog out of the window,
reiterated Capt. Tobacco, let
the dear little dog alone, said
Aunt Ellen — Capt. Tobacco
hoped the springs of the

family Coach would stand,
And that the perch & Axletree
would bear the weight —
Miss Jemima was too warm,
Let down the window, said
Miss Jemima, not that
window, the other window,
Oh! no not that side window
said Aunt Ellen, the other
side window; no, no, the front
window, & put up the side
window, said Miss Jemima
There's a breeze said Capn.
Tobacco, I wish they'd let the
windows alone. The dog
got uneasy & barked —
Stop the family Coach said
Aunt Ellen, open the door,
Which door said Jeeba from

the Rumble tumble, at
the same time jumping
down to let down the steps —
Not that door, said Aunt
Ellen, the other door, — Capt.
Tobacco begged Aunt Ellen
not to put her feet on the
wheel, & the dear little dog
followed Aunt Ellen out
of the family Coach. Put
the dog beside Jonathan on
the box, said Capt Tobacco, and
tell the Coachman to see the
whip does not touch him, said
Aunt Ellen. — Jonathan
protested against having
the dog at all; the dog was
therefore ordered off the box
to sit on the Rumble tumble,

with Juba & Chloe. There's
a fuss about a dog said Capt.
Tobacco. No yours Massa
dog, inside Rumble Tumble
cried Juba & Chloe. Peace
being again restored in
the family coach and
all were seated in said fa-
mily coach. The dear little
dog barked with delight, &
Juba & Chloe grinned from
the Rumble Tumble. The
Coachman again cracked
his whip, & cautioned Master
Jonathan to sit still — when
trotting down a steep hill,
the horses ran away, &
the reins broke, the whip

fell, & the fore wheel came off

the hind wheel followed,

the perch broke, the [illegible]

gave way, and the dog

fell out of the window. The

dog will be killed said Aunt

Ellen, Oh! do take care of the dog,

& with that the family coach

upset. The box was smashed

to pieces, & the dear little

dog fainted. Take care of

my dear little dog, said

Aunt Ellen, as she crawled

with the rest out of the family

coach. The following morn-

ing a bill was brought

upon the repairs of the family

coach. Searching out for the

for the horse's knees, bleeding one horse, blistering the wheel horse, mending the reins, an entire new whip, two spokes in the fore wheel, three spokes in the hind wheel, fastening the Rumble Tumble, varnishing the axle tree & perch, glass for the windows, linings for the right door, repairing the steps & springs, physic for the poor dear little dog, making for the whole repairs of the family Coach £10.17.2 3/4.

And now the family Coach once more in order, set off & all arrived safely in the hand[?] family Coach at the

Niagara Falls. — La!! cried Master Jonathan from the box, how grand!!! The Ladies looked out of the window, Aunt Ellen from the other side window, Juba & Chloe from the Rumble Tumble. The dog was alarmed. Keep that brute quiet said Capt. Tobacco. The dog is no brute I guess, said Aunt Ellen. — All was now harmony and delight in the family Coach at the majestic view the Coachman seemed to forget he —

hold the reins. — When sud-
denly!!! a blast — of wind
blew — the — Family
Coach down the Falls!!
Box, Steps, Rumble
Tumble, — axeltree,
perch, — Horses, Reins,
Whip, Wheels, Steps,
Aunt Ellen, Capt. Tobacco
Miss Jemima — Master
Jonathan, — Juba, — Chloe
Coachman, and all
were swept away, together
with the dear Kittledog
in the Family Coach

And here ends the Story
of the Family Coach.

THE FAMILY COACH.

Dramatis Personae

1) Box, 2) Rumble Tumble, 3) Axletree, 4) Door, 5) Spring, 6) Windows, 7) Perch, 8) Horses 9) Reins, 10) Whip, 11) Wheels, 12) Steps, 13) Dog, 14) Aunt Ellen, 15) Capt. Tobacco 16) Master Jonathan, 17) Miss Jemina and Juba, 19) Chloe, 20) Coachman.

A party of pleasure was made to go from New York to the Falls of Niagara, consisting of Mr and Mrs Didler, Aunt Ellen, her dear little dog, Miss Jemima and Capt. Tobacco inside the family Coach. Master Jonathan on the box, Juba and Chloe, two black servants on the Rumble Tumble. This meeting the wishes of the whole family, the axletree and springs were examined and the luggage was packed into the Family Coach. The door was open and steps let down, the windows shut. The Coachman taking the whip and reins mounted the box – and Jonathan beside him, and the rest - including the dog, got into the Family Coach. The dog placed himself upon the cushion Aunt Ellen said the dog was not comfortable.

'Pooh the dog,' said Capt. Tobacco.

'Don't abuse the dear little dog,' said Aunt Ellen.

'There's a fuss about a dog,' said Miss Jemima

'Throw the dog out of the window,' reiterated Capt. Tobacco.

'Let the dear little dog alone,' said Aunt Ellen.

Capt. Tobacco hoped that the springs of the Family Coach would stand and that the Perch and Axletree would bear the weights.

Miss Jemima was too warm. 'Let down the window,' said Miss Jemima. 'Not that window. The other window.'

'Ah! No, not that side window,' said Aunt Ellen. 'The other side window.'

'No! No! The front window and put up the side windows,' said Miss Jemima.

'There's a breeze,' said Capt. Tobacco. 'I wish they'd let the windows alone.'

The dog got weasy and barked.

'Stop the Family Coach,' said Aunt Ellen. 'Open the door.'

'Which door,' said Juba from the Rumble Tumble, at the same

time jumping down to let down the step.

'Not that door,' said Aunt Ellen. 'The other door.'

Capt. Tobacco begged Aunt Ellen not to put her feet on the wheel, and the dear little dog followed Aunt Ellen out of the Family Coach.

'Put the dog beside Jonathan on the box,' said Capt Tobacco.

'And tell the Coachman to see the whip does not touch him,' said Aunt Ellen.

Jonathan protested against having the dog at all. The dog was therefore ordered off the box to sit on the Rumble Tumble, with Juba and Chloe.

'There's a fuss about a dog,' said Capt. Tobacco.

'No room Masser dog inside the Rumble Tumble,' cried Juba and Chloe.

Peace being again restored in the Family Coach – and all were elated in said Family Coach. The dear little dog barked with delight, and Juba and Chloe grinned from the Rumble Tumble. The Coachman again cracked his whip and cautioned Master Jonathan to sit still – when trotting down a steep hill, the horses ran away – and the reins broke, the whip fell, the fore wheel came off, the hind wheel followed, the perch broke, the axletree gave way and the dog fell out of the window.

'The dog will be killed,' said Aunt Ellen. 'Oh! Do take care of the dog.' And with that the Family Coach upset. The box was smashed to pieces, and the dear little dog blamed.

'Take care of the dear little dog,' said Aunt Ellen, who crawled with the rest out of the Family Coach. The following morning a bill was brought in for the repair of the Family Coach. Searching oil for the horses knees, bleeding one horse, blistering the wheel horse, mending the reins, an entire new whip, two spokes in the fore wheels, three spokes in the hind wheel, fastening the Rumble Tumble, ironing the Axletree and Perch, glass of the windows, hinges for the right door, repairing the steps and springs, Physic on the dog – making the whole repairs of the Family Coach £10.19.2$\frac{3}{4}$

And now the Family Coach once more in order set off and all arrived in the said Family Coach at the Niagara Falls.

'Ha!!' cried Master Jonathan from the box. 'How grand!!!'

The ladies looked out of the windows, Aunt Ellen from the other side window, Juba and Chloe from the Rumble Tumble.

The dog was alarmed.

'Keep that brute quiet,' said Capt. Tobacco.

'The dog is no brute I guess,' said Aunt Ellen.

All was now harmony and delight in the Family Coach. At the majestic view the Coachman seemed to forget. He held the reins. – When suddenly!!! A blast – of – wind - blew – the- Family Coach down the Falls!! Box, steps, Rumble Tumble, – Axletree, Perch, horses, Reins, Whip, Wheels, Steps, Aunt Ellen, Capt. Tobacco, Miss Jemima – Master Jonathan, – Juba, – Chloe, – Coachman and all were all swept away, together with the dear little dog in the Family Coach.

And here ends the Story of the Family Coach.

2

I had stayed at my Aunt Bell's house several times before on holidays, so that part of it was not new to me. I had always liked my trips down to Prestwick although I don't think I can say the same for my sisters. My Aunt was old and must have been very pernickety about how young girls should behave. She was very much of a recluse, spending most of her time in her bedroom, only venturing out occasionally, and that was usually to attempt to cut the front lawn with a pair of scissors and at the same time taking a good look around to check that nothing had changed in any area she could not view from her window. She was one of many of her age group who saw their world and lived out their lives through net curtains. Aunt Bell lived at a time when grandmas and grandads and most elderly maiden aunts wore a style of clothes traditionally worn by the older members of the family. This fashion made them look old and was compounded by them acting as though they were infirm. I think it was called respectability but the sad fact was that many of these respectably clad so-called old people could very well have been only in their sixties or even fifties.

In most of my friends' homes there was an elderly relative sitting permanently in a chair in front of the fire. On the merit side this meant that there was always someone in the house to welcome the children at all times. It was also a rich source of unsolicited advice regarding dress, noise and the general decadent behaviour of the young.

I was glad to be in Prestwick and once again staying under the same roof as Mum and Dad were. It also meant knowing what was going on in the family and when whatever was going on in the family happened, instead of having to read about it in a letter or during some quick visit between homes.

Each Sunday morning I went with Mother to St Ninian's Church. All the May children were Episcopalians from their mother's side. She was a regular church-goer, whereas, to present my father's religious beliefs and activities in the optimum light I can only say to the best of my knowledge that he had been a member of the Church of Scotland at one time, and that I cannot remember him ever attending any religious service apart from marriages, christenings and funerals. One thing he never did was to either condemn or ridicule any faith or person, which is a very special quality in itself. I was, therefore, a Protestant simply because I was born into a home where my parents were Protestants, and for no other reason.

Our church had been built at the southern part of Prestwick, better known as the Ayr end, and as we lived in the northern area it meant a bus journey to get there. Sometimes after the service, if the weather permitted, we would both walk back along the seafront, and at certain times we would watch seals playing in the water from the end of St Ninian's Road. The town's promenade is built alongside a fine sandy beach for the main part with a few very small ripples or traces of fine shingle. The beach was always clean and I cannot even remember seeing a lot of seaweed at any time, even after a storm. This doesn't seem to be very plausible, but I do not honestly recollect seeing any litter or debris along the length of the beach. During the early part of the war large goal-post-shaped obstacles had been erected at irregular intervals on the shore to deter any chance of the Germans attempting to land troop carrying gliders on it. This precaution was carried out on all flat areas at the coast around the whole country.

The war didn't change the seaside habits. People still swam and children still paddled under the watchful eye of someone huddled in a deck chair. Sand castles were still being built, and from the

Sunshine Corner young voices could be heard singing their clap-happy songs. In amongst the sand dunes young bathers were furtively drying themselves or changing into or out of a bathing costume. In those days it was a tricky business dressing in public after a swim. Somehow it meant hopping and staggering about while clutching a towel around your body. The average person was no more ungainly then than they are today, but the garments worn were. There was a lack of fathers and young men; otherwise it was just the same to me as it had always been when I stayed with my Aunt Bell before the war.

The beach and the row of houses and hotels facing on to it were separated by a green strip that had a flower arrangement and a putting course. Further along where the residential buildings stopped at the northern end, the famous Prestwick golf course took over. Between the Club House and the water was a large carpark and at its furthest end could be seen the open-air swimming pool, standing in tasteful isolation on the beach and shared between sand and sea.

Both Eric and I had the advantage of an early coaching in golf from Father who had religiously taught us how to hold a club, keep our heads down as in prayer and how to power a shot down through a straight left leg. He was always critical of our performance when we played a round with him, but we were none the worse for it. Eric and I had been given the basic golf clubs when each of us reached the age of eleven or twelve and by the time I had reached the age of fourteen we both had a thin pencil-like golf bag containing a wooden driver, wooden spoon, a number four and seven iron and a putter.

To play over a golf course costs money and to subsidise the expense of this activity I used to 'hunt' for lost golf balls along with some friends, either after school or during holidays, or simply just whenever we thought it would be a good time to do it. It wasn't hard work by any stretch of the imagination as we knew where to look and at the very worst we may have managed to get our feet as wet as our arms. We sold the retrieved golf balls mostly to the American servicemen who paid well for them. Most probably they were buying back their own goods.

Mum and I would continue our walk homewards by leaving the

seafront and passing the station then crossing the main street and cutting up by the side of the Red Lion. From there we walked along to the bottom of Berelands Road and up to McNeill Avenue. It was quite a long walk and we only did it when the weather permitted; otherwise it was travel by bus both ways on Sundays when we attended the kirk.

The reader may wonder why I seem to be the only one amongst the children who now accompanies Mother to and from church. It would be easy for me to say that I had no difficulty in getting up and out of my bed in the morning but there was probably another reason in that it was a sign the family were growing up. It certainly was not because I was any holier that they were. Mother's greatest strength was gentleness, and although she persuaded her children to do certain things she never forced anything on any one of them. Example and patience was her natural method of getting things done. No doubt through her influence we were a very tolerant family in religious matters. There were times I went to the Presbyterian church with my friends and I'm quite sure my siblings did the same. Sister Sybil and Frank, whom you will learn about later, certainly did.

I cannot remember doing any particular chore as a punishment for misbehaviour. Some people claim that they learnt to peel potatoes expertly or develop some other gift because it had been the standard task meted out to them by a parent for some wrongdoing.

I wonder how I was admonished as a little boy. I cannot remember, but it must have been for my own safety. Looking, or more accurately thinking back, children in general lived in a pretty dangerous environment. I can't remember my mother ever smacking me, but surely she must have done so when my fingers strayed towards burning coals, sharp knives or boiling water in kettle or pan and, of course, anything electrical was an absolute hazard in any household.

With my later knowledge about the movement of electrons I absolutely shudder to think of these first generation fires, manufactured from sheets of planished steel where the heat was generated through a length of unprotected coiled wire that became red-hot when the current flowed and sometimes burnt itself through, which broke the circuit. To get the thing working again one waited until the wire cooled down, then merely coupled up the two coil ends by intertwining then; but this is providing the two-pin (unearthed) plug had been removed from its wall socket. If the plug had not been pulled out then there would have been a severe shock to the amateur electrician when contact was made between the parted ends of the heating coil.

Another hazard that I remember was when the only convenient source of power was from the light bulb socket suspended from the ceiling which meant someone standing on chairs or table and removing or replacing the light bulb in full view of little watching eyes. There were also the many needles and pins within easy reach from the continuous dressmaking and alterations or repairing that seemed to have gone on endlessly with clothes and curtains. Such an environment was not a safe place for small children intent on copying much of what they saw.

I can assure anyone reading this that neither my brother or I were angels, but whatever our parents made us do or did to us when we misbehaved I just cannot recall. Around the cheeky age of pre and post ten years of age when Dad got real mad at either of his sons he would on rare occasions give the offender a flick smack across the face with the back of his hand, but more than often the threat of such action would suffice, and it was merely a matter of getting and keeping out of his way for the rest of the evening. When a smack did land it was always with an open hand, and with a lot less force than would knock you off your feet. There were never any black eyes or cuts or weals. Looking back I suppose it could be likened to the slap that the girl in the movies at some time or another gave to the man she finally married. One big difference between the Hollywood hero and Eric and I was that we both had a mother and three sisters to run to for sympathy, and we didn't end up having to marry someone.

A child has to learn its family touch language and translate it into either a caress, an encouraging pat, a spank or a hard smack. Each is a clear expression of family feeling and concern.

Different words used by different temperaments about the same incident seen through different eyes will always remain to be argued over. Everyone with the responsibility of bringing up a child allows their conduct to range between the boundary edges of acceptable behaviour. We had a flexible conduct line in the family which could not be crossed with impunity. It taught us to develop our sense of timing in matters relating to others.

I remember taking the brunt of a smack on the face on two occasions as a pre-war schoolboy and I honestly believe that I must have deserved each one of them. The contact was more than a clip but less than a clout; perhaps greater than a cuff and certainly nothing that could be described anywhere near a thrashing or a beating, so I will use the word 'slap' for across my face and 'smack' for across my bottom. At least I talk about something I personally experienced. I will add in here a sort of afterthought. On the very few occasions Father struck us it was always across the face. It was never a body punch or a push to knock us away from him and perhaps there was something in that.

Neither Eric nor I were were ever struck by our father through drink, drugs or pique. It never happened out of the blue for we already knew more or less what was coming. I think in fairness that it must be remembered that where people lived together (tenements) where there were a lot of children there was a chain of command which was usually headed by the widowed grandmothers who sat enthroned in their kitchen chairs or in the legacy they left their own offsprings. These ladies had a freemasonry of their own over the control of their grandchildren's behaviour, which was usually reflected in the degree of sternness of any punishment dosed out. It is therefore not very surprising that even the most gentle of mothers and fathers gave a smack when the occasion arose.

I am not rushing to defend or decry that Father smacked his sons when they crossed that flexible line. It was probably as a last resort for a variety of reasons that culminated after a gentle chastisement, then a lecture, followed by a stern reprimand, leading on to a disciplining of some sorts. It also taught a stubborn young lad that in this life there were certain limits on how far you could go. There was never any shouting nor screaming or the issuing of dire threats, nor was I scarred mentally with any frightening attitude and bewildering argument which I could not understand that could be interpreted as mental cruelty or conditioning towards me or anyone else within my earshot during the whole of my young life. I am therefore not in the position to place blame on anyone else's personality shortfalls for my mis-doing. On the contrary if I now have the right amount of animal cunning or what is otherwise called diplomacy, then I have my mother to thank, and if I am nimble of foot by not being in the wrong place at the wrong time then I have my father to thank. It seemed to work for me. After all, nobody knew that I would soon be away, living in another home without my mother and father, yet somehow I had been trained how to conduct myself.

Could it not be argued that some children have a greater sense of security in each cuddle when such an endearment could be balanced against a smack? The bringing up of a child is most certainly a skill involving a lot of patience and a modicum of chance. It is mostly done through a combination of sight, sound and touch with each having its limit and although I did not appreciate it at the time I ranked amongst the most fortunate children in the world, having no impaired sense and being born into the family that would have still been my choice had I been given it. The argument for or against smacking will go on no doubt until the cows come home. I think we would all agree that if there must be smacking then the smack given a small child should be much, much less than one given to an impudent young pre-adolescent boy. Is it then so very wrong for the personality for feeling not to find an outlet across reasonable bounds of physical contact? One might even wonder from whence the physician, the artist or the musician first learnt of touch and the importance of its meaning.

My first smack was probably on my bottom, by a midwife instructing me to take my first breath and make my first audible sound. A mother with several children and surrounded with many potential dangers to them will be well aware which one is the adventurous and which one is the cautious. She will know whom she can reason with, which child she would need only to threaten and which one she would have to smack. Wilfulness comes in all sizes, and siblings all differ.

I was probably a horrid little bratling who would regularly require a deserved reminder. Nature causes a pain in the tummy if the wrong food has been eaten or the right food is eaten the wrong way. The pain is soon forgotten when it is no longer there but the knowledge you must be careful what you eat and how it is eaten remains for the rest of your days.

Talking about body language (the more delicate of my readers may choose not to read this paragraph) I seem to recall on several occasions and in various abodes when a new baby was being blatantly exploited. It was not uncommon for a grandmother leaning over a freshly powdered infant to say in a sing-song voice. 'Smack-a-botty, smack-a-botty, one, two and three,' and at the same time giving gentle taps on the child's bottom. Then – here it comes, as often as not overcome by the desire to attack, she would bend down and kiss the powdered area – yuk.

I can remember quite clearly the times when any one of my sisters managed to get on the wrong side of Mother, which was very difficult. At such times it was quite sufficient for her to threaten the culprit about what would happen when Father came home and heard all about the misconduct. This usually meant the errant daughter going to bed early and pretending to be fast asleep when Father looked in on his slumbering dear child. I do not think he was fooled for one moment by any of his daughters' hibernating acts. If they did not fool their younger brothers, what chance did they have with Father?

Looking back I think fathers in general can be excused a lot for their strictness and irritability, especially if things did not go too well under the strict and demanding type of working regime of that era.

About eighteen months before the war started I had a perforated eardrum following an operation on my leg. It was thought by some members of the family at a later time that perhaps I had suffered earlier ear damage through a slap from Father with had accelerated the ear trouble after my leg operation, but I am certain this is not so.

My ear infection followed an operation to remove an abscess from my groin, in pre-penicillin days. Our doctor told my parents that the ear problem was almost certainly caused by some of the infection escaping from the abscess into my body. It took me literally a year to get back on my feet again, and the worst I was left with was a slight, disappearing limp, a little deafness in one ear, and losing a whole year at school. Father by this time had long since stopped threatening to cuff either Eric or I, which could have meant that life was becoming less stressful for him, or it may have been that both his sons were over the little monster stage.

Later on I mention a similar ear condition with one of my sisters, following an illness she had, and Father at no time raised a finger against any of his daughters.

From just before the start of the war was probably the time when the threat of forfeiting any pocket money was introduced, when either Eric or I overstepped the mark. In my pre-evacuation days pocket money was index-linked to the price of a seat in the BB Cinerama picture house at Eglington Toll in Glasgow. The cost then was fourpence. Alternatively we might have been given some punishing task to do in the home like tidying up the boys' bedroom (Stalag stuff) or being house message (shopping) boy. Whatever it was it prevented us doing something else; therefore we resented the time wasted on doing it. The honest truth is that I cannot remember any particular task that was given as a punishment from the other run-of-the-mill chores we had to do in any case, which to both of us was one and the same thing. There must have been the added confusion of what I thought Eric would do and he wondering what I thought he would do: which I think you will agree was as good a reason as any for both of us not knowing the why, which and wherefore or what was done by whom. Anyone from a large family will know exactly what I mean.

Before the war I can recall standing in line with other children awaiting a jab in the arm (probably anti-diphtheria). The same needle was used throughout, though wiped with a sterilised piece of lint after each inoculation. If sticking a needle into a child's arm isn't violence what is? Clearly what is sometimes good for a child does not always come naturally without some sort of physical assault taking place.

But back again to seaside Prestwick where I now knew the streets pretty intimately because I had a part-time job working after school hours during the week and also on Saturdays. I delivered fish for Hogg's the fishmonger who owned a shop on the main street. I enjoyed roaming around on the heavy message-boy bike with the heavy wicker basket at the front. One of the perks that went with the job was the parcel of fish I was given on Saturday night when the unsold (no bad pun intended) remainder of the fish stock was divided up amongst the staff after closing time, and which was gratefully received at home.

Let me tell you about the five May children and where they were at this particular time and also mention that there were roughly eighteen months to two years between each of the five children. The eldest was Clara who was married in Troon (the next seaside resort north of Prestwick) a few months prior to the war in 1939, and was now called Mrs Charles McGibbon. She stayed in Giffnock which is a southern district of Glasgow.

Sybil, the second eldest, was living at home and worked at the airport. Eric and I were still at school with me being the baby of the family and fifteen months younger than my brother. Joey (short for Georgina) being the third eldest, was away from home and nursing in an isolation or fever hospital outside Kilmarnock which lies about ten miles on the road towards Glasgow. Joey managed home when she could for a weekend or a couple of days during the week when she had time off duty.

We were neither a noisy nor demonstrative family, but were always a close family, sharing the same sense of humour. I cannot remember any fearsome volatile incident where voices were raised in extreme anger and there was no-one in the family whom I could say was fiery-tempered. There were the odd very theatrical and over-acted dramas played out amongst my sisters – Clara in particular – but we all knew it was another Bette Davis trauma that would finish in a dramatic exit. There were bound to be some serious quarrels under our roof but they must have been kept pretty well under control. I'm sure the whole family would agree that we had our mother to thank for the peace and quietness of the home that I remember. There was a strict code of behaviour for the children in that parents had to be obeyed and your elders had to be given the courtesy of being listened to.

Parents in general at that time tended to down-rate their own children with expressions like 'Having too many brains than are good for you', yet speaking of the good qualities in others, which might well have been a Scots trait amongst parents to prevent their child getting a 'swollen head', as well as preparing them to handle the disappointments that might be lying in the future.

The closest thing to show of affection would be to receive a kiss on the cheek and a hug from Mother or a close aunt, but outside the immediate close family it would mostly be a touching cheek to cheek ceremony, if that would suffice the occasion. My brother and I would have to be given a push from behind on a sister's birthday to deliver a brotherly kiss.

Eric and I were pupils at Prestwick High School, where as secondary scholars we scored high in attendance, but average in all things academic.

During this youthful and naive time, the two May boys still thought the war was something happening somewhere else, and didn't honestly give much attention to it. We merely assumed that if the war was not over by the time we were called-up then we would get our chance to fight for our country. There was no doubt in our minds who would win the war. It was merely a matter of when.

Eric always had a hankering to go to sea and one day to become a ship's captain. It was no surprise to anyone when he joined the Sea Cadets, which meant him travelling through to Ayr where their meetings were held, whereas I joined the Army Cadets through the school. Ayr Academy was the headquarters, though the platoon that I became a member of held its meetings at Prestwick High and consisted of its volunteer male pupils from the secondary classes. The O/C was Mr McBean, who was one of my teachers and who later became Captain McBean. I rose to the giddy heights of Quarter Master Sergeant and displayed on my left uniform arm a small red diamond cloth insignia. This meant that I had been successful in an examination set and sat at Ayr Army Barracks for possible officer training material when I reached the age for military call-up. Perhaps being a founder member of the Prestwick Platoon was taken into consideration when my assessment was made for I do not recall anyone not passing his Part 'A', as it was called. Our platoon made several visits to the barracks for military lectures and unarmed combat. What we were taught to do in matters concerning the latter should have produced a generation of young thugs, but for some reason it didn't.

20, Bellrock Ave.
Prestwick.
4th July 1942

Dear Ian,

Thank you very much for your nice note, we were both so pleased to receive it. I sent a few things for you to eat with mother. I hope you enjoy them. It took me all my time to pack the two bars of chocolate as you can well imagine, but I heard you were rather hungry so I resisted the temptation. I expect you to come back with your chest covered with big strong black curly hairs and rippling muscles on your arms, and if you don't, I'll want to know the reason why

Letter received at Army Cadet Camp, 1942.

2

my lad. Probably too much ice-
cream, lemonade and cream cakes
~~in~~ by the dozens, maybe you've had
lots of strawberries my pet with
nice thick cream — oh sucks — am
I making your teeth water love?
No kidding I am if I were you
I would take advantage of the
lovely fresh air. Sleep with less
blankets on you at night and if
possible outside; I mean right out-
side the tent, don't be a sissy and
get soft. If they get you up at seven
you get up at six or earlier if you
wish; go for a good five mile hike
then come back to find the last piece
of bacon has gone and there is
nothing left for you (sucess), but
don't let that get you down what
do you care if you miss break-

3

fast the walk was well worth it, or was it? now if you should feel tired after this long hike and having had no breakfast just go back to bed dear and have a good sleep till dinner-time. Try and arrange to get your dinner served in your tent maybe one of the officers would oblige. By the way Ian how many stripes have you managed to pinch, don't wear too many or they may get suspicious.

Don't take everything I say too serious dear or you may find yourself in trouble, but I do hope you are enjoying yourself and remember you are a soldier and therefore you have to take orders even though

4

you don't like it. If you are a good soldier you will get on dear and who knows maybe some day you will be an officer. So when your tired and fed up just remember that.

You haven't so very long now to go till you will be back home again. Take care of yourself dear and remember you are the only boy now in the family. make them proud of you by being a fine fellow not only in your uniform but in everything you do, so be good darling and God Bless you.

Lots of love,

From,

Frank and

Sybil.

~~5th~~ 1 McNeill Avenue
Prestwick.
5th July 1942.

My Dear Dan,

I arrived safe after an exciting journey – you see when we arrived at the station in Girvan – a train was ready to start so we asked if it was a Glasgow train – yes. so in we went. Allan had gone to make himself comfortable & the train started to move out of the station. Mr Howie & Mrs Anderson got out by the time my turn came the train was gaining speed so I said no I'll remain where I am. Off I went not knowing where I might land as I discovered the real train did not leave for another 15 Min. To my great joy we went right through to Prestwick – what joy to find I had arrived right after all.

The others came with the later train.
I can see you laughing Dan – that's rude.

We all enjoyed our day at Girvan & hope you boys enjoyed yourselves too.

Did you enjoy the good things?

Your small niece was here today with her mother & father & was very good. At Troon the pram & baby were put in the van & dumped at Prestwick, she slept through it all.

You will see her next Sunday, all being well. Well dear I am looking forward to having you beside me again, so cheerio till Thursday. Father & Jenny join me in sending love to you.

Mother.

A camp follower reports back, 1942.

I enjoyed the time spent in the Cadet Force which included an annual camp at Turnberry which lies about fifteen miles south of Prestwick along the coastline south of Ayr. It is known for its championship golf course. It had a lighthouse that was not in use at the time and the scant remains of a castle. In our platoon everyone knew everyone else with all of us attending the same school that taught up to the Third Year Leaving Certificate standard of Scottish education. After this was completed it meant either continuing with one's higher studies at Ayr Academy, if such was desired, or starting to work. Mr Bean was a popular teacher who knew how to handle boys in the classroom as well as on the sports field and parade ground. I can remember a number of these boys along with their names, but unfortunately with others it is only their faces I can only now recall.

The group of friends I was in amongst all joined the Cadet Force. I can remember that Peter Anderson, Ronald Neill, Allan Baker, little Johnny Buxton, Tom Marks (who won the first .22 shooting competition), Ian McEwan, Jim Howie and the Allen Twins were some of the original members of the school platoon.

The Cadets were to be used as runners for the Home Guard in the event of a German invasion and whenever the Home Guard were holding outdoor exercises then we were out with them, but that was after having gone round knocking on the doors of those warriors who had slept in, for these military manoeuvres always took place on a Sunday morning.

It wasn't all outdoor stuff. I can remember an indoor display held in the Town Hall before an invited audience when the Home Guard did their best to instil confidence into the gude people of Prestwick, (a hard job), on just how fit they were to tackle the might of the German Army. This was followed by the Cadets giving a few pieces of crowning examples about gun totin' expertise along with a reassuring demonstration of how we would and could help in the event of the expected invasion. The evening ended in our platoon acting through a thumbnail sketch of *Robinson Crusoe* that was so nonsensical it had to be seen to be believed, but it went down well with the audience. It had been scripted by our Second Lieutenant who had not been with us very long.

I must have been growing up or entering a slightly more mature phase in my life for I no longer climbed fences or searched for gaps along them that I could squeeze through, but now preferred to look for a gate. It was a strange twist of fate that part of the Cadet training exercise was to instruct on how to climb fences or look for gaps in them to squeeze through. Strangely enough many of the Cadets were exceeding good in this particular practice.

The Home Guard were issued with American rifles which I think were called P17s. They were identified by a red band painted around the barrel to ensure that they were only loaded with their own type of ammunition and not the kind used by the standard British Lee Enfield rifle. Word had it that there was great difficulty in obtaining the British size (0.303). It seems they had an adequate supply of rifles and plenty of ammunition but neither fitted nor could be adapted for use with each other. This had all the hallmarks of a victorious British disaster that somehow finished up in achieving something great. Was this yet another wartime secret that was kept from the German High Commands? I have no doubt that at the right time either the proper ammo arrived for the P17s or a supply of Lee Enfield rifles arrived for use of the 0.303 size bullets, and that it happened long before the Home Guard was disbanded.

Obtaining anything at all during the war was quite an achievement and to put on any sort of a show that had the slightest splash of scenery in it usually meant a lot of people being involved, with each donating their services or playing their respective part. There were, of course, no new gadgets, only well-used ones. There was no such thing as someone coming in and saying, ‘Look what I’ve just bought. It’s the latest thing.’

Cameras were a typical example of this and the box Brownie was still a family favourite in the home. Focusing or finding the group to be photographed was usually carried out by the operator asking someone in the group to keep raising or lowering an arm or merely wave it about until the photographer first finds the group and focuses on to it. After that the arm owner would be asked to drop his or her limb and everyone would be asked to smile, then all waited for the CLICK. A lot of those films came out remarkably well.

Prestwick Airport had grown considerably since the pre-war days when I first saw it. In those days there was only a wind sock, a cluster of wooden huts and a sprinkling of Tiger Moth planes. The only proper building in the vicinity was the Orange Field Hotel that had long since gone. Amy Johnson's and Jim Mollison's names had been bandied around as having been regular visitors at one time, and it must have stirred a few memories in the minds of many local people on hearing of Amy being killed when her plane crashed into the Thames Estuary. Even at the time of writing there are still a lot of people who doubt that such an experienced flyer would run out of fuel as the official report stated. During the war she was one of an all-women team who delivered aircraft from the factories to the various RAF Squadron airfields throughout the country.

One other pre-war memory that comes to mind was of the Irish tattie hawkers (potato pickers) arriving in the area surrounding Prestwick for the gathering in of the Ayrshire potato crop. They were mostly transported on the back of open-aired lorries and well above the numbers that safety levels should have allowed. They could usually be heard a long was off singing some Irish song at the top of their voices on their way to or from a farm.

It was probably because of the wartime security risk and travelling difficulties that the traditional potato lifting force was discontinued, and after the war mechanisation on the farm saw to it that an imported labour force would never again be required.

During the war both the planting and lifting of the potato crop was done mostly by schoolchildren. Digging for Victory went on in every school that had access to an allotment and Prestwick High played its part in growing and producing fresh vegetables. The maths teacher, Mr Gunn, was the leading light in this field, and it was he who organised the secondary classes to do a couple of hours at the school allotment each week, and more than that when the summer final examinations were finished. There could have been no greater love of one's country than to give up one's time at school, as was clearly demonstrated by the girls and boys of Prestwick High by digging, weeding or simply gathering vegetables which had been grown in the school allotment, depending on what time of the year it was.

Gas masks had to be carried to school and put on and worn during the frequent air raid test-alerts. At the same time we had to 'take cover' beneath our desks. Many homes had their own stirrup pump for fire-fighting. This was a portable pump that was operated by hand and consisted of a plunger operating inside a barrel that had a bracket attached to it which had a landing on the ground that the user put his or her foot on to steady or anchor it. A hose from the barrel suction line was put into a bucket of water, and the hand pumping action was sufficient to give an adequate jet of water from the hose nozzle. We had all been warned about how the first wave of enemy aircraft would drop incendiary devices that would mark the target area for the heavy bombers that would follow. Fortunately our stirrup pump was never used for the purpose it was bought for and was relegated to watering the vegetables surviving in the garden.

House windows had sticky strips of paper running vertically and horizontally over the glass to give a measure of protection against blast, and for the same reason brick walls or sand bags were put in front of all main entrances to public places. The schools in Prestwick were one-storeyed buildings and brick walls were built in front of each window to about three quarters the height of the window, which also had the anti-blast strips of paper on it.

Our school teachers donated a lot of their spare time to supervise pupils as well as taking on their extra wartime roles. Mr McBean was the O/C, the School Cadet Force, Mr Gunn was O/C, the Green Brigade and Mr Leach was the O/C, the Prestwick Home Guard. The French Teacher, Miss Sadler, was an auxiliary nurse at the Ayr General Hospital. I'm not sure about the others, but I would not be surprised if Miss Hamilton, who taught science, had something most sinister to offer the Nazis and which still remains 'hush hush' to this day. Mr Murdoch taught English, and would, I am sure, have had something up his sleeve that would have left the Germans trembling in their boots. The headmaster, Mr Scott, somehow or another managed to keep all this patriotic war effort under control, yet still ensured that his pupils received an education that would help them to exist in a topsy-turvy world.

One day brother Eric was down on the beach with some of his friends when they came across some boxes which had been washed in by the tide. The boxes contained packets of tea and dried eggs along with some small handy tins of sweets. The boys divided up the find and carried away their share.

After the initial trauma of bringing home some food which did not belong to him had died down, and after it had been established that the covering of the packages were clearly marked 'Ship's Stores', it was left to our imagination as to what had taken place, causing the boxes to be washed up on the beach. The tea and powered egg were sealed with paper foil and Mother told Eric that he must take the lot, including the sweets, down to the police station and explain how he got them, which Eric said he would do, and I knew he wouldn't. He said with a great air of innocence that before he took anything away he would first check to find out if any of the packets were damaged, and believe it or not, he discovered that the foil covering the packets of tea had been very recently torn. He reckoned that it would just be a waste of time bothering to hand in impaired tea to the police, who must have much greater things to worry about. Mother finally agreed with him over the tea, and relented in the case of the sweets, but the egg powder had to be returned. She said how difficult it must be for the sailors not getting fresh eggs when they were away from home.

Once outside the home Eric produced some packets of tea from his pocket, then carefully unrolled the foil where the two edges were joined, and removed the top layer of the packets of egg powder, replacing them with packets of tea, and to make a professional job of it, slightly tore the tin foil.

Our neighbour was a retired policeman. He kept chickens in his back garden and his hens produced eggs no-one we heard of ever tasted. However, the brothers were certain about two things. We knew about the hens because we heard them and we knew they laid eggs because their owner told us they laid eggs.

When we finally saw him that late afternoon Eric called out to him, 'Good afternoon sir, do you think the police station will be open at this time?'

'The police station is open all the time,' replied the neighbour, 'and what would you be wanting there at this time of day?'

Eric told him what he had found on the beach and that his mother had insisted he took it down to the police station as they would know best what to do with it.

He seemed just a little bit interested, replying that mothers knew best, then asked what it was that had been found.

The question had been anticipated by the older brother. 'I can just see the top, and I think it's tea. There might have been a wee drop of sea water got in but it looks fairly dry to me. Would you like to take a look in it yourself?'

The retired policeman gave a close inspection and agreed that it could well be packets of tea, and fairly dry as well. He then suggested that he would take the parcel down to the police station as he was familiar with these procedures.

We both looked most reluctant.

He continued by saying that as we had been so very honest, he would give each of us a couple of fresh eggs to take home.

We still looked reluctant.

He raised his offer by telling us that he was sure Mother would like a half dozen fresh eggs.

Eric pushed his luck and repeated that Mother had told him to take it down to the police station himself, and added, otherwise we would be breaking the law, and I agreed vigorously.

'Oh,' said Mr McCafferty, 'there's no fear of that. I've known your aunty a long time and we have been good neighbours to each other. Just you tell her you met me and I said I would take care of everything no matter what happens. Now I'll just go into the back of the house and bring you out six wee eggs. Not that I'd want to stretch it to a dozen.'

Both of us knew the size he mentioned was the most truthful thing he would say that day. He soon re-appeared with a bag of wee eggs. 'There you are, boys,' he beamed, 'you just take these eggs straight home, and I'll take care of the package for you, and I promise neither of you will hear any more about it.'

Eric carried the eggs home, and we both wondered if Mr McCafferty would like the taste of powdered egg.

In hindsight I'm sure the gentleman had been an excellent neighbour to my aunt. He might well have been leading Eric and I on and had a good laugh at the consequences.

*

It was a sad day when Italy entered the war on the side of Germany in June 1940, laying to one side the international turmoil there must have been from such a new development. Let me tell of how it affected me in my small world. A large number of Italian immigrants had settled in Scotland. Even before I was born they were certainly part and parcel of Scotland. It seemed so unfair that these Scots of Italian descent were affected by this latest spread of warfare with the backlash they suffered because of it. I saw the damage done to the Italian-owned shops when their windows were smashed and derogatory slogans were daubed on their property. I had always assumed our society could not produce that sort of frenzied outburst against a minority group.

My early memories of a typical 'tali's café' was that of the original and now elderly immigrants sitting beside the shop till, chatting away to each other in their mother tongue. One or some of their children, now married, are serving the customers and speaking with a Scots accent. The following generation are either helping in the shop or conversing with their grandparents. It seemed to me that Italian was usually spoken by the family when addressing the grandparents. The Italian cafés were always clean with courteous service, which in itself would explain their popularity. They were naturalised British subjects and hardly a threat to our society.

The violent behaviour and out-pouring of abuse directed against those of Italian descent when Mussolini entered the war must have left many people with more than a trace of unease since that time about a malady that could be lurking just underneath the surface of our own society and ready to attack some toothless threat. Up till that time in 1940 I had been told that such behaviour could only happen in Germany or some other such-like country.

We can take a break now and I will leave you to peruse the following pages which I hope might trigger off some memories or thoughts of your own about the times they tell about.

WAR CERTIFICATE "A"

This is to Certify that

Cadet Ian James May C.Q.M.S. D Coy.

of the No. 3 Cadet Bn:, The Royal Scots Fusiliers

passed the examination for

War Certificate "A"

held on 4 Jun. 1943 *at* A Y R .

[illegible signature], Lt/Col.

Officer Commanding,

No. 3 Cadet Bn:, R.S.F.

The War Office,
London, S.W.1.

[illegible] 19__

[illegible signature], Col.

for *Major-General,*
Director of Military Training.

Perish the thought, we all passed.

"In the examination for War Certificate "A" the cadet named in this Certificate showed a satisfactory standard of proficiency in :—

Drill.

Weapon Training. Rifle (including T.E.T.s)

* BREN (including T.E.T.s if any).

Map Reading.

Field Intelligence and Section Leading.

Before taking the examination, the cadet reached the required Physical Efficiency Standard by passing, according to the requirements of his age group, the Tests shown below and numbered ________ †

Agility
1. 100 yards sprint.
2. Standing Long Jump.
3. Running High Jump and Vaulting.

Endurance
4. 1 Mile Run.
5. 5 Mile Walk.

Strength
6. Rope Climbing (15 feet).
7. Heaving and Abdominal.
8. Swimming.

Officer Commanding

Major David MacBean

After passing the examination, the cadet received instruction in the following additional subjects.

The cadet has attended the following courses :—

‡ Place.	Subject.	From.	To.	Result.
/	/	/	/	/

Officer Commanding

....

* Insert particulars of automatic weapon or delete.

† Insert numbers of Tests passed.

‡ Insert particulars.

P.T.O.

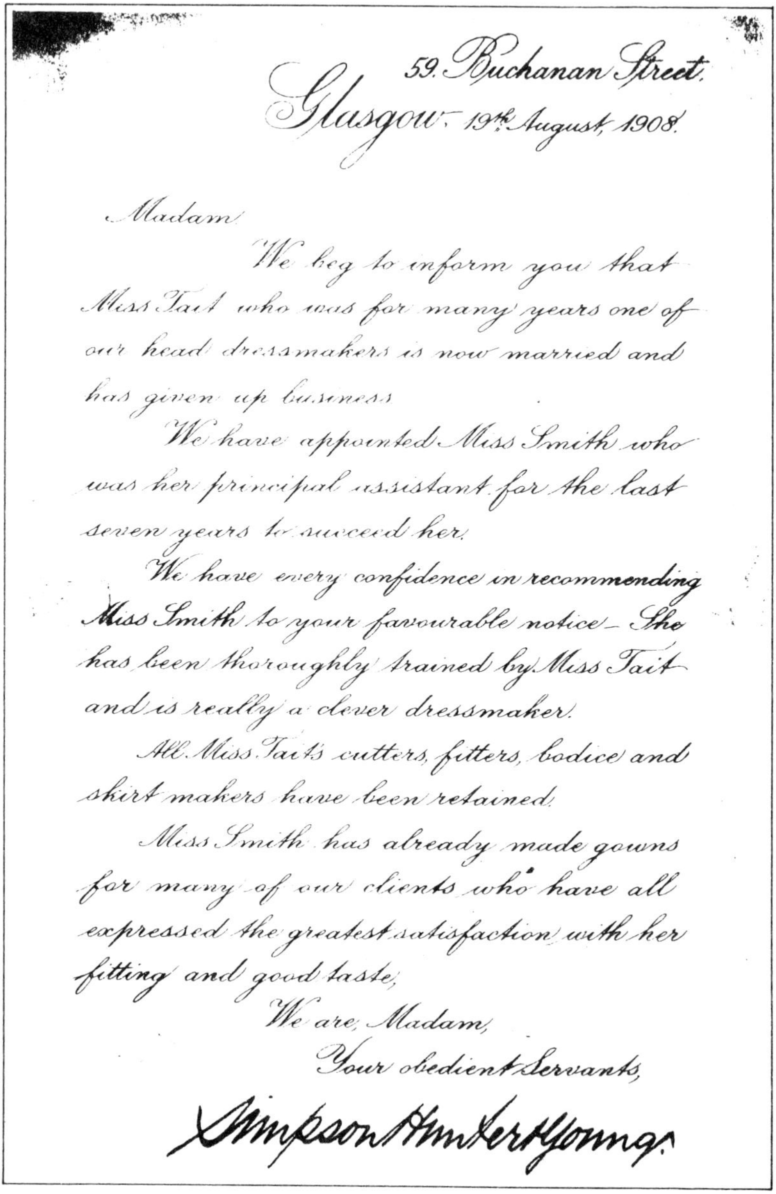

59. Buchanan Street.
Glasgow. 19th August, 1908.

Madam

We beg to inform you that Miss Tait who was for many years one of our head dressmakers is now married and has given up business

We have appointed Miss Smith who was her principal assistant for the last seven years to succeed her.

We have every confidence in recommending Miss Smith to your favourable notice – She has been thoroughly trained by Miss Tait and is really a clever dressmaker.

All Miss Tait's cutters, fitters, bodice and skirt makers have been retained.

Miss Smith has already made gowns for many of our clients who have all expressed the greatest satisfaction with her fitting and good taste,

We are, Madam,
Your obedient Servants,
Simpson Hunter Young.

Mother's appointment as head dressmaker, 1908.

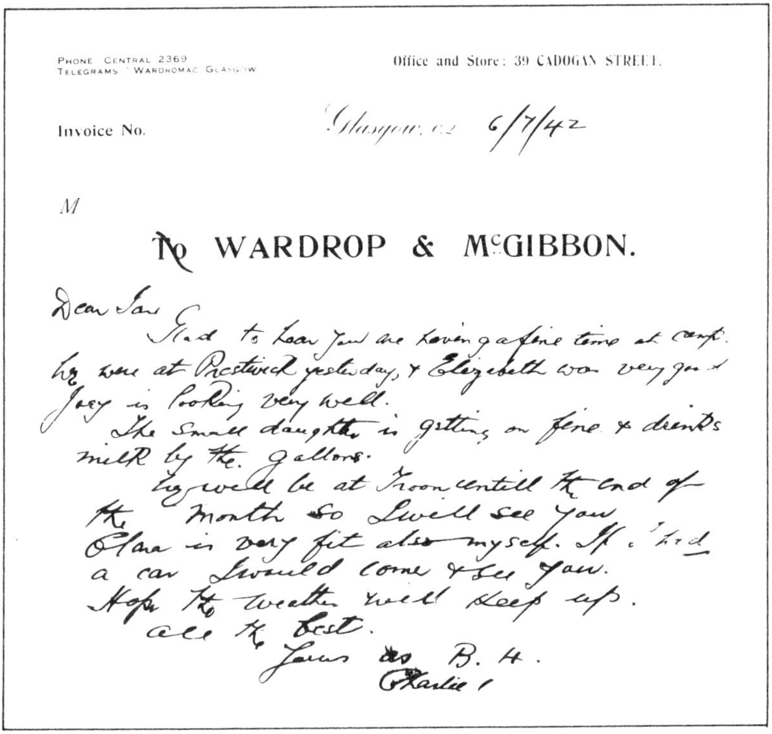
PHONE CENTRAL 2369
TELEGRAMS "WARDROMAC GLASGOW"

Office and Store: 39 CADOGAN STREET.

Invoice No. Glasgow, C.2 6/7/42

M

To WARDROP & McGIBBON.

Dear Ian

Glad to hear you are having a fine time at camp.
We were at Prestwick yesterday, & Elizabeth was very good
Joey is looking very well.
The small daughter is getting on fine & drinks
milk by the gallons.
We will be at Troon untill the end of
the month so I will see you
Clara is very fit also myself. If I had
a car I would come & see you.
Hope the weather will keep up.
All the best.
Yours as B. H.
Charlie!

Above: Amongst other things, being kept upto date on my niece's drinking habits, 1942.

Left: I had great trouble spotting the difference. There must have been better things to do with the coupons, 1942.

1 McNeill Avenue
Prestwick
4th July 1942

My Dear Ian,

I do trust you are all enjoying yourselves, only another day & camp will be over. It's been a great experience for you boys & something you will always remember

Joey's birthday is on the 10th so I have enclosed this card. post it as soon as you can on the 9th so that it will arrive Friday morning 10th

Syb. & Frank are coming here for tea tomorrow. They expect to leave for Belfast on Friday.

Frank left his bike here & believe me Ian, I have been having the time of my life.

Quietly speaking I think I've ruined it but thats nothing look at the fun I've had — Oh boy. oh boy.

Cheerio darling boy

from
Your Affectionate Mother
Annie May.

P.S. Have enclosed Joey's address.

A mother ensuring a brother's duty to his sister is carried out, 1942.

3

During those early war years I never gave it a thought that the youth of my age group might have missed out on sport. The generation before us were not around to generate any enthusiasm or give advice, as they, along with all the professionals, were away at the war. No-one was looking for, or encouraging future sportsmen let alone Olympic material. All that was wanted was the stuff that turned young boys into good fighting machines.

At school there was an excellent female gym teacher but whether this bore any wartime significance, I do not know.

The first experience in my sporting world was when I was eight or nine years and somehow managed to get myself lost at Ibrox Park during some pre-war football match. Father had taken his two male offsprings to the game, but all I can remember of the afternoon was being passed overhead from person to person until I finally reached a policeman who sat me down on a concrete block on the sideline. Sometime later Eric came and claimed me. I had a wonderful view of the play but I do not think I have been to a proper football match since.

Long before that occasion, so I have been told, there was a women child-minder who was supposed to take me out in my pram but stopped at the first pub until all her money was spent. She was alleged to have wrapped me up as a parcel and carried me inside with her in case I came to harm. It wasn't every pub who welcomed women but it was illegal to allow any sort of minor in. It seems I was destined to find myself in strange places.

But back (or is it forward?) to Prestwick once again, where I remember one Saturday afternoon being one of a bunch of schoolboys playing 'footer' (football) in the school field. When the game was over Ronald Neill and myself agreed to walk with little Johnny Buxton to his home in Monkton which was just a short distance past the airport. Somewhere along the route we met up with John's sister and a friend of hers who were also heading towards Monkton, and we all finished up at the Buxton home where we were introduced to his pet white rabbits that had been multiplying. When we left it was with a strong show of character that the visitors were not each clutching a rabbit as a new-found pet. It may well be that John and sister were inviting their friends around in the hope of finding homes for their growing number of pets. I should add at this point that I did get a rabbit from John some time later. Pet owners during the war had to be careful that they did not give one away that would soon end up in the pot.

Along one stretch of the return route there was a large hedge where Ronald and I found a blackbird hopping around on the ground with an apparently damaged wing. We tried to catch it in order to help it if we possibly could. However, an elderly lady came along and objected strongly to our efforts in trying to capture the creature. She obviously had not the slightest confidence in our combined endeavours to catch it or our motives for doing so, and insisted we leave it alone and move away immediately.

Both of us returned to my house where I found a cardboard box; then the pair of us returned, determined to find out if the bird was still where we had left it, but there was no sign of it. We returned home with an empty box. I would like to believe that the lady with her box had managed to get there first.

Both Eric and I had a season ticket for the open-air Prestwick Swimming Pool. The May sons and their respective groups of friends must have been extremely hardy and bubbling with good health for they spent a lot of what the landladies called the 'summer months' down at the pool. Thinking back, the weather must have been self-made in our minds for each of us managing to endure the hours we spent in the water. I'm afraid it must have been a skill I have long since forgotten.

Ah yes, at least the swimming pool made me notice the curves and rounded shapes on the girls' bodies that somehow or another I failed to notice before. I don't remember any of the girls whom I knew personally using the pool, although they must have. The girls who did use it could well have been visitors who were slyly admired by boys ogling them in their one-piece bathing costumes, some of them designed with a little fringe affair around their hips more like a curtain pelmet.

I honestly don't know what most of the local girls of my age group did outside school hours. There was very little contact between them and the boys (at least I think so). As far as I am concerned they must have held secret rallies somewhere amongst themselves. Perhaps that's not quite fair because probably the boys were busy doing what boys did and the girls were beavering away at their own pursuits. Maybe, and I just say maybe, there might well have been some of my gender and age spending too much time eyeing the one-piece bathing costumes and trying to figure something out that they didn't want to ask about.

Describing the swimming pool as being open-air is merely another name for calling it windswept and chilly. Prestwick, like most seaside resorts, had a powerful landlady lobby that vetted certain weather-portrayal words. An example was the translation of 'damn cold' into 'bracing', or the weather being 'nice and fresh' meaning 'blowing a gale'. 'Braw morning' means 'it's all right providing you keep moving'. A last line of defence is to give a slight shrug of the shoulders and smile, then very quietly say, 'It could be worse.' And this is said when its silent standard reply is well known to them. 'Aye! But you could say the same to me if I was a guy near dead.'

North of the Glasgow/Edinburgh line they have the same type of taboos. No-one, for instance, mentions certain words in public like 'midges' or 'clegs'. People visiting from the South (England), must find such things out from personal experience. I'm sure it must have been a Scottish landlady who first coined the phrase, 'Och, it's grand tae get the cobwebs all blawn awa'. It does a body a power o' guid.'

My sister Sybil made a pair of swimming trunks for me when I was thirteen, and on trying them on at home, I thought they were a bit skimpy and slack, but nevertheless I decided to wear them the following day. After my first dive found myself frantically clutching on to them at ankle level, and swearing to myself that it would be the last time I would wear anything home-made if I were to dive into water wearing it. As it turned out, Sybil altered the swimming trunks, and I did use them again before a disappointed audience of so-called pals, but only after I had been told the bare facts regarding clothing coupons. I thought it rather ironical, under the circumstances, to be lectured by someone else about bare facts.

At that age I was not exactly an Apollo, with or without my swimming trunks, and perhaps you can best draw your own conclusions on my body structure from my family's unbiased description of me as being tall and skinny, with shoulder blades giving the impression I was sprouting a pair of wings.

Sexual awakening and physical maturity seemed to creep up on me, as I suspect it did with my friends, and discussions about it were contained to a very small part of our lives, probably because it was easier to ignore it completely than it was to talk about it, especially if you didn't know how. Sex was not talked about very often but when it was it would only be with one or two of one's intimate friends and never in a large group. Physical changes were so slow that they went un-noticed until some body chemistry gave your mind and body a new dimension. The girls I knew, meaning the girls in my class, all seemed to dress so as not to show, or at least not to accentuate any growing-up change.

To talk about sex with an adult was always discouraged, at least in the case of boys, and the equivalent of an open discussion would be a book discreetly left in your bedroom, which I vaguely remember partly reading. I never read it right through because I found it hard going, being constantly reminded of the serious and responsible nature of the subject, and in any case I think it was written in all probability for medical students in their final year.

I remember in those younger years using my father's razor after applying a soapy frothy mass on my boyish face with his shaving brush, but that was in the early days when a puff of wind would probably have had the same effect on my facial fluff as Dad's razor and not nearly as dangerous. It was strange how boys were never taught how to shave and just had to experiment casually with something as sharp as a razor.

Life in some ways then seemed more natural in that it was not uncommon for a young mother to remain by the fireside and suckle her baby at her breast when the rest of the company took their places at the table for a meal. Nobody paid any attention to a mother feeding her infant. Nature's feeding system was well-known to most young people, starting from basic knowledge of farm animals to the tabby cat feeding her kittens.

The usual meeting between the sexes was casual and pleasant as both of each gender were on their best behaviour with easy smiles and stilted conversation. Outside of a story book there was no such thing as a sulky or ill-tempered girl. Hollywood films and twopenny novels told us that all marriages were happy and made in Heaven. As for the birth of a child, all that was required was a kindly doctor who washed his hands and asked for a copious supply of hot water before quietly telling the father-to-be that it was time for him to leave the room.

Pregnancy and birth were very much a female affair with men more or less discouraged from enquiring about a mother-to-be. I don't think we were supposed to have noticed that anything was happening. In the adolescent (the word teenager had not yet been invented) world when being told about a new arrival a young male would be expected to receive the news without comment, whereas a girl would ask the weight of the child and how the mother was. Males were not expected to be too interested in actual birth matters and new fathers never even seemed to get a mention other than when he would 'wet' the baby's head with his relations and friends.

I had reached the age now when King Sex was ordering his hormones into action throughout my body, causing me to sprout upwards and develop a lot more muscle power. It was hardly to be unexpected that his gude Lady Sexina had already started a similar process on the girls of my age a few years earlier, but with different results. My centre of gravity seemed to remain pretty much in the same place after the process, whereas at a guess I would say the girls' shifted a little bit forward and down.

Probably if we had known the control that Rex Sex and Regina Sexina were capable of wielding over their subjects by causing a silly spring season in most, a fevered summer heat in some, a nostalgic autumn in others and a depraved wintertime in a few we would have been scared out of our wits at the age of fourteen or fifteen. Perhaps God had a prissy old aunt who thought her nephew had made things too easy for human beings and had added a few ingredients of her own into the recipe of our bodies that He hadn't been aware of. It was all so very confusing.

I had no doubt in my mind and have had none since that there is one Creator who is the controller of Time, Matter and Being, whence all Things came. It was therefore in His design that I should be born into a very nice family where dire want was unknown and for that alone I will be eternally grateful to Him. However, since those innocent days of long, long ago I have one criticism to offer, not of Him, but His Parents for allowing any Child of Theirs to programme in some of the more esoteric complexities of human sexual behaviour I was later to learn about. That part of human nature would never have been conceived if His Parents had been a respectable Scottish couple.

Very often during the school summer holidays boys would cycle out to the surrounding farms or market gardens and pick up casual work, albeit a few hours a week. It was by doing this that I found out how over-economical farmers were with their money. I travelled at first by borrowing Frank's (Sybil's fiancé) bike, until finally, through my continual and very audibly expressed hope, I did manage to get one of my own. A few days prior to my fourteenth birthday Mother acquired a bicycle at an auction room in Ayr and from then on I found I could do twice as much in half the time on the quiet wartime roads with so little traffic on them.

I would like to think that as a cyclist I never caused an accident to someone else without knowing it. I would also like to think that I only had one collision, but I doubt it. The one I do remember was on Frank's bike, and left me with a permanent reminder on my inner right wrist in the form of a scar. I had learnt over a period of time that Frank's front wheel had several repaired punctures in it and I had somehow or another managed to find an inner tube of the same size of wheel. I borrowed his bike on some pretence and fitted the new inner tube on the wheel. As it happened, when I was returning the bicycle I had an encounter with a butcher boy's heavy delivery bike and Frank's front wheel was badly buckled. Managing to get an inner tube when there was a shortage of everything was hard enough but a brand new wheel for a particular model was something else. However, a local garage managed to straighten out the buckle, which was lucky for me. What was supposed to have been a pleasant surprise for someone turned out to be an absolute disaster, but such was part of life for a fourteen-year-old. Frank wasn't upset in the slightest but with Mum and Dad one would have thought it was their bike. I mention this episode to remind the Reader that during the war damaging a bike was not far removed from damaging a car. It was also a very popular and important form of transport on the empty roads because of the wartime ration restrictions on petrol for the few who owned cars and had the coupons to use them.

During the potato sowing and lifting (tattie houkin') season the local farms would send a horse and cart to pick up the schoolboys, (I can't remember any girls going) from a central point. At such times the schools were closed for a week and the arrangements about which farm one worked on must have been made at the school before it closed. I used to be in the group that went to Shaw Farm.

One sad memory was the sudden death of the Cadets' Second Lieutenant. He was the one who wrote the *Robinson Crusoe* script played out by the Cadets during the Home Guard open evening. He had been introduced to the platoon by Captain McBean and I seem to recall being told he had been a student at Glasgow University. What had happened to his leg I don't know but he had a pronounced limp and walked with the aid of a stick. He was very popular and had an easy smile. His death coming only after a matter of months with the platoon came as a shock to us all. Probably for most of our group it was their first experience of a young person personally known unexpectedly dying. The Cadets from Prestwick High School marched behind the hearse to the little graveyard in Glenburn where he was given a military farewell by the Home Guard.

Prestwick was never bombed during the war although it did

have its share of air raid warnings during 1941/42, and having a prime target in its midst made it a sensitive area. The nearest I managed to seeing anything vaguely resembling defence-activated searchlights in the sky over my home was sighting the darting colourful Northern Lights or Aurora Borealis. The closest thing to the bursting of anti-aircraft shells in the heavens was the fascinated watching of shooting stars burning themselves out, with me making a long forgotten wish with each one I witnessed.

The punishing air raids that other places suffered did not come to Prestwick and mercifully it was spared such carnage with its loss of life and terrible injuries. That was something in itself to give thanks for, but to say there was never a nasty incident would be wrong. The largest fire I had ever seen was the main building of the airport well and truly ablaze. Teachers and pupils alike had an excellent view of the blaze the day the airport burnt. Arson, accident or incident I don't know, but a lot of damage was done and the emergency resources were tested from far and near.

Looking across from the school field in the direction of the airport that lay across the single train track line and the unseen Pow Burn it seemed no great distance to the airfield. The planes that were parked or dispersed could be seen quite clearly. There were no buildings between the grounded planes and the school, only a scattering of trees and bushes.

The school's side and rear walls faced out onto what was called the School Field. At the bottom of the field and more or less in the same line with the back wall of the school and the airfield ran the afore-mentioned railway line that serviced the colliery at nearby Glenburn.

I have already mentioned Glenburn in connection with a sad occasion and I would like to briefly mention that it was a very small coal mining community consisting of a short row of miners' houses which were built fairly close to the nearby Glenburn Pit, that stood a respectable distance from the well-kept Glenburn Cemetery.

There was also a 'steamy' there for the respective household washings along with public baths used by the mining community. The Pow Burn flows past nearby, and there was a pleasant walk along a tree-lined path on its southern bank where the branches waved their reflections on its surface as it flowed on through the golf course and into the Firth of Clyde between Prestwick and Troon.

My school (and probably other schools) did, on at least one occasion that I remember, shelter refugees from Glasgow following a bombing raid and, for want of a better word, it meant a holiday for all the pupils. I cannot remember exactly how long they stayed or where they later dispersed to, but their stay in the school register in my memory as usually lasting a few days. Here was another level of civilian movement – and this time done out of necessity – but for some reason I never got to know, or even speak to, any of them. There had been the voluntary official evacuation scheme that I had been involved with and there were many other children sent independently by their parents to live with relatives, as, taken at random, a Mr and Mrs Baker in London had done when they had arranged for their son, Allan, and his sister to stay with an aunt and uncle; and as a Mr and Mrs Reid in Glasgow had likewise done with their daughter, Anna, when they sent her to live with her grandmother.

During the time when our cities were being heavily bombed by the Luftwaffe I was too young and indifferent to seriously think of the consequences or the effect it must have had on evacuees hearing about these raids on their respective homes. One of my school friends, Allan Baker, and his younger sister had been sent by their parents in London to stay with their aunt and uncle in Boydfield Avenue, not far from where we lived. Allan's father worked on London Transport, and Allan was the first Cockney I had ever met. Both he and his sister must have had some terrible nights thinking of London at the height of the Blitz. They returned home when the skies over London had been made much safer to live under and that was shortly after I had left Prestwick.

Jim Howie was another friend who was also in my class. Somehow or another Jim had dual British/American nationality. I must have been told at least one hundred times how this came about but in all honesty I cannot recall who married who or where or when but America must have come into it somehow. The last I heard about Jim was of his intention to join the American Forces when he reached the call-up age.

Prestwick had two picture houses which were well frequented by the local populace. There was the Broadway in the main street, and round the corner in Kyle Street there was the Bug-Hut, where at one time it was possible to obtain a ticket of admission with the payment of four clean jam jars. The Broadway was far too up-market to even consider such a form of barter for one minute, and even a German paratrooper would have had to pay in the proper currency to gain admission.

At certain times of the year there used to be an Any Questions public programme held on Sunday afternoons in the Broadway which was very popular and well attended. Mr McBean played still another part as a member of the panel who expressed their thoughts and gave their opinions in reply to topical wartime questions. A lot of young people showed a keen interest in these public discussions.

Between the two cinemas in Kyle Street was Dumpers, the billiard hall and probably the wickedest thing any fourteen-year-old boy could do during these days was to frequent a billiard hall. Our group descended on it when we could at one stage of our growing-up period and committed the cardinal sin of 'playing for the table'. I pleasantly enjoyed discovering that the road to hell was paved with amongst other things, billiard tables.

Now and again there would be mock air raids as a practice for the various civil services, and the school pupils, along with other volunteers, were used as pseudo casualties. Each person was given a card at the commencement of the operation, (no pun intended) giving the details of the injuries they had sustained. Each quasi casualty was then asked to lie down either on the road or pavement inside an area which had been cordoned off for the demonstration.

I enjoyed the ride in the back of a makeshift ambulance that was a converted van designated for that purpose. On one occasion it was Miss Sadler, my French teacher, who was at hand to attend to my broken pelvis injury, (as my card stated), and remove the mark from my forehead that indicated how much morphine had been administered to me.

A lot of people felt sorry for the Home Guard whenever there was a mock commando attack on the Airport, as they were expected to assist the military personnel defending it. Unfortunately for the local gentry the commandos always seemed the fitter of the two, which was proved by the number of bruises left behind as a memento of the exercise. The Army Cadets were used as runners for the Home Guard on these occasions, and, thank goodness, non-combatant. The nearest thing we got to active service was the making of range cards which the Home Guard might ultimately have to use. It entailed finding a strategic position that could be used by a sniper or by a defending force either along the beach-front or on the golf course, and from that point make an accurate card showing any part of the landscape which would afford cover for the enemy, giving the range in yards and its compass bearing along with a brief description, i.e. bunker, tree, sand-dune, etc, and how many people each could conceal.

Probably the most horrific time of the year was the preparation for the Annual School Dance. In Scottish state schools there has always been the system of mixed sexes in the classroom but not during time spent in the gym hall, where it was either boys or the girls. The exception to this was during the few weeks' lead-up to the school dance when the rudiments of the waltz and quick-step were painfully taught to the budding dancers. Country dancing came a lot more naturally and for some reason we could all do that type of dancing much better than the modern dances; perhaps the former was at times practised as exercises during gym periods. The traditional dances were good fun whereas the modern dances didn't go down too well, with both sexes tending to keep a distance of at least six inches apart, and when any actual body contact caused confusion and blushing from both partners. Such was the agony of 'growing up'.

Talking about girls, I should say that the ones I knew and could call friends in the strictest sense of the word were either in the same class at school or lived nearby or a combination of both, which meant that the respective parents or guardians knew, or at least were aware of each other through no other reason than living in the same vicinity. One of these girls was Beatrice Wilson, who stayed in Weir Avenue, and just a few doors from my friend Ronald. I had been to a few parties Beatrice's mum had organised for her and I recall how her dad managed to get things started by playing his ukulele which he was good at, and getting the young revellers to join in singing the well-known or well-worn songs of the day.

At all house parties held for young people, the songs, games and quizzes were always supervised in such a way that if any parent wasn't in the room where the party was being held, then he or she would enter it at any time they chose. Knowing that great and mighty virtue was just a door away damped down any ideas of high-jinks. Looking back I do not think it detracted from the enjoyment in any way.

Miss Sadler must have had a suspicion that I might have a slight hearing problem or was tone deaf because she asked Eric about it, and he revealed all. After that she placed me in the centre of the classroom about three rows from the front, briefly explaining to the class the importance of hearing everything that was said by anyone at school. She did it so well I do not think any of the class would remember the incident. I had a feeling from then on that all the staff knew about me. Looking back I realise how fortunate I was to have had such good teachers.

Another schoolgirl, Sandra, lived nearby, and like Beatrice was a genuine Prestwickonian. I did not really know many girls, only the ones that lived nearby; therefore at both the school or Cadet dances, being so basically shy at that age, I had a very limited scope in what girl I could or would dance with. I have a feeling it wasn't a problem that solely affected me.

Each rule has its exceptions, but taken in a general sense, the average thirteen/fourteen/fifteen-year-old did not have the intense relationships that were to become so commonplace a generation later. There were plenty of crushes, blushes and heartbreaks which never succeeded in destroying the underlying romantic fantasy contained in both sexes, but any mild flirtation was regarded by their elders as something to keep their eye on. In those days a boy could earn himself the label of being called a 'Jessie' if he were suspected of making too great an effort to appear attractive or distinct, and of a girl doing too much of the same thing, it would be said by her watchful female adults, much to the confusion of anyone learning English 'That one will bear well worth watching.'

The guiltless years where childish wrongs were so predictable, and yet so well tolerated and where simple anatomy may have at times briefly flitted through a young mind, provoking a mere passing interest, were now in the past. A new interest was starting to appear; noticing points of physical attractiveness in the opposite sex, and the seeking of bashful opportunities to share their company. This also coincided with the developing of a new-found ability to hear out long-winded and poorly delivered sex-flavoured jokes amongst schoolfriends. At this time and age I began entering another phase in the chemistry of my body, and left behind the innocent years.

Probably the first worry I had about girlfriends, and a problem no doubt common to most boys, was how to get one. The second worry would be the distressful thought of how not to have her when it so suited. This meant not interfering with any sporting activity or any other manly pursuit. At this age the notion of someone of the opposite gender always with me wherever I went was somewhat suffocating. It was a relief to find out that there was a time and place for girls. For me it could not be otherwise.

Whenever one of my pals came round to my home and I did not or could not go out with him it was a very easy matter to say 'No!' I could as easily quarrel amongst my group of friends or even fight with one or two of them, but that did not stop us being together the following week. Young males seemed to have the knack of keeping life as disentangled as possible and carrying on in their own brand of simple normality.

When sister Clara was expecting her first child, Elizabeth, I used to visit her quite regularly at weekends by bus. It was probably when her husband Charlie was on fire-watching duty, or maybe Mother had some bits and pieces in the way of food and clothes which she wanted Clara to have at that time. During one of these stays in Giffnock the Luftwaffe made an unwelcome visit over Glasgow, and so it was that Clara, along with an air raid warden and myself, spent the best, (if I may use that word), part of the night in the Anderson air raid shelter. My greatest worry during the raid was whether Elizabeth would wait until her proper time, but as it turned out, all was well when came the 'All Clear', and thankful, long-awaited dawn. Elizabeth had played it smart by apparently not thinking much of the outside world on that occasion.

The nearest building to receive a direct hit that night was in a residential street in the Shawlands Cross area that was not very far from where I was, but a long way from the city centre and far from any industry. The following day I saw the damage done and I was amazed how the typical three storey stone tenement had withstood the explosion. The roof and upper flats had been demolished but the centre and lower flats still remained standing, although badly damaged. This was my first personal sighting of war damage, though not my last, because for many years to come I was to become quite accustomed to passing bomb-damaged buildings and sites in cities throughout the country, in war and peace.

During the air raid of that previous night I left the shelter to slip into the house to make some tea while there seemed to be some sort of a lull in the attack. Finding cups and filling the kettle with no lights on didn't take me too long, and I don't think the kettle had finished boiling when the 'bangs' started up again. I could not say whether the noise was ours or the raider's in origin. I made the tea and, on my way back, knowing the searchlights were on our side, I had the feeling at times that they seemed determined to expose me as a target to the Germans. It must have been about that time when the building in Shawlands was hit. I heard much later that the ice rink there had been used as a temporary mortuary for many of the city's victims during the spate of air raids it suffered.

Father was fire-watching that same night in his company's office in Bothwell Street which lies near to the centre of Glasgow, and he, along with all the other watchers, must have been kept on their toes all night in case they were needed. As it turned out Bothwell Street, and No. 53 in particular, survived without incident.

This, for some reason, reminds me about Dad, who very rarely talked about himself, telling me of a time just prior to the outbreak of war when he made a company purchase for an excessive amount of timber from somewhere in the Baltic region that was to be used in the shale mines as pit props. (The northern variety of tree contains a harder type of wood and 'creaks' a lot when it distorts under pressure.) He had thought it quite probable at the time that this source of timber might be cut off in the event of an outbreak of hostilities with Germany. What he had done on that occasion must have later pleased him no end before he would have mentioned it to his family. Perhaps the memory of it gave him that little bit of 'well being' and consolation during the many nights he carried out his fire-watching duties.

Looking back to that time I must say that I still remain impressed by how the civilian, auxiliary and professional services were all organised for each one to play their part. I might very well be getting my test-raids and actual raids mixed up and what I remember from each. Quite honestly no-one seemed to make a big thing of anything that happened. The morale amongst everyone whom I came in contact with must have been high because I do not remember it being a great topic of conversation. People just got on with what they were doing. The Glasgow air raid I have just mentioned must have led to another evacuation from the city which I know nothing about, but like everything else it was another planned piece that had fitted exactly into the over-all contingency plan and picture of what was to be done when the city was under attack.

My brother Eric finally satisfied his boyhood ambition when he started on his chosen career as a deck apprentice in the Merchant Navy. After his basic study time his first voyage took him across the North Atlantic to New York which we heard all about on his return home. During wartime no-one knew the why, where and how of any ship movement, and the public were constantly being reminded by posters showing a British ship sinking or just a plain lifebelt floating in the water with such words as, 'Careless Talk Costs Lives', splashed across it. Eric told me the only thing he had lost was his cap during a storm in the Atlantic. He had joined the *Empire Spring* at Greenock on the Firth of Clyde and then sailed over to the ice-free port of Halifax where her cargo was loaded. The ship returned to Manchester where Eric was given about ten days' leave. It did not seem very long before his recall from the owner's office in Liverpool arrived, instructing him to rejoin the *Empire Spring* in the Manchester Docks.

The last sight the family had of Eric, and that included his girlfriend, Rhona, was of him leaning out of his carriage window waving us good-bye as the train puffed its way out of Prestwick Station in the direction of Glasgow.

Several months later Father received the dreaded cable telling him that the *Empire Spring* on which his son Eric Watt Smith May was serving, was long overdue and must be presumed lost through enemy action. It took a U-boat attack on a merchant ship somewhere in the cold waters of the North Atlantic for the long colourless tainted arm of war to finally reach into the May family and touch us all with its wintry un-feeling fingers. Eric was seventeen years old when he was lost at sea.

I never really discovered how the loss of her eldest son affected Mum as she never spoke of it, or outwardly showed any obvious grief. She remained unchanged from what she had always been to me; although she must have lost some of her sparkle I did not detect it at the time. I have already mentioned she was a deeply religious woman who was always ready to support others when her presence was required and nothing appeared too much for her to do. I think her inner strength came from her unshakable belief that as a mother others depended on her. Her God was not the kind to be kept in some locked box hidden away somewhere and produced when convenient or on demand, but was very much a part of her being. I do not think that anything in this world could possibly have changed her attitude towards morality or religion.

My sisters often said over the following years that they thought Mother had never fully recovered from Eric's loss and silently grieved for a son who had died at some unmarked spot somewhere in the grey waters of the Atlantic Ocean. She would have wished that end only on herself if she had been given the choice. She went through what so many other mothers had to endure as a result of war.

And when it ends, its tarnished ghost eternal haunts,
Through war-won stains, from each unmeasured thorn.
As yet no army known, can better cease its taunts,
Than yester's stolen smile, remembered each new morn.

Father never competed with Mother to give or receive affection from his family and I have no idea how much support he managed to give her at that time. He was not an emotional man, but I cannot recall any father or grown man who was. It would be harsh of me to say that he was a cold-natured type of person as there was not even a hard or cruel streak in him, and, yes, by all means strict but no more. He had always supplied the financial means to support his family, and did it without feelings. He supplemented the home and maintained the reliable father figure. If his family received a common inheritance from him that was to last their lifetime, it would have been to read and listen to informed opinions on any subject that interested them, then make up their own minds.

I was a mere boy when the war started and a young man when it ended. Like most young males I thought it was an exciting time to be living in, where one wartime adventure led to another. Youth was neither forgotten nor ignored. There was inconvenience for grown-ups who were out working and frustration for those preparing meals but there was no real hardships for the young through wartime shortages. After all; what young man in his right senses living under such circumstances would dream of complaining about the style of his clothes or not having enough bath water?

Looking back I had no idea – how could I? – of how truly terrible it must have been for middle-aged people both at home and away fighting. The wartime partings for them must have caused a great hurt on every occasion for unlike those younger than they, they must have known only too well the dirtier side of war. These were the ones who had heard from their fathers and uncles how futile and cruel wars were. They would also have read for themselves the terrible accounts of the fighting in the war to end wars that was fought just a quarter of a century before and against the same foe. Many of them would have been the same age at the end of the 1914–18 as I was at the start of the Hitler conflict. Wars are much simpler to the young and trusting.

THE PRICE (1942)

I wont forget, this special time standing quite still,
A listening ship sinks slowly down, the end of an eager kill.
Debris afloat midst grasping arms, marks the place of the unseen attack,
And the hunter mute-blind to human hurt, glides back to the U-boat pack.
What garden grows cruel winter crop, where spring sperms warring spawn?
That marshal freedom's autumn chill, to granite-guard its summer's dawn.
Yet still one wisp remains, to haunt this kinsman's will:
I won't forget, this special time stands quite still.

Proud cargo ship the *Empire Spring*, staunch sailed with groan and sigh,
Till she showed her finest warrior look, to the lens of a periscope's eye,
Now sadly sleeps deep on the sea's dark floor, amid sunk sisters long at rest,
Far moved from time when stoutly crewed, by mere men who gave their best.
At fresh sixteen years one chose the sea, but too young to pick the ship,
Grim wartime's choice was never his, chance-choosing his fate-final trip.
When iron hull burst open, and wound filled with ocean's chill:
I won't forget, this special time stands quite still.

Penned pious clear or pirate bold, all had 'signed on' ship article laws,
To sail under its red coloured ensign, with their mix of merit and flaws.
Though whether in gold-marked uniform, or shiver-soaked in lesser attire,
When alone and adrift each were equal, afore sucked down in an oily mire.

None died for praise nor medals, just siege-freeing a lone castaway isle,
By doing their jobs against fearful odds, in true typical sea-faring style.
He died three years short of twenty, a war legacy's odious pill:
I won't forget, this special time stands quite still.

War widows once were waiting wives, the change-chance was no-one's choice
Each casualty cost one lit lantern lost, and peace-price a vanished voice.
And what of sweethearts like Rhona? Innocent caught in a hard callous net,
Her rover's romance savage-sudden ended, and too young to learn to forget.
What live last thought was within him? what final scene glimpsed the crew.
Whose face appeared? whose voice was heard? only each drowned seaman knew.
At the close of a tragic sea-scene, heavy etched by memory's quill:
I won't forget, this special time stands quite still.

Proud Father's smile spoke fond farewell, to son's laughing fearless face,
A Mother's tears spliced sister's kiss, then a young brother's last embrace.
Unheard by him was time's cheerless call, mute-beckoning him quietly away,
And giving not the mere-briefest hint, of a family's last full circle day.
For he died amongst sound seamen, silent shrouded beneath wallowing waves,
Where wild winds wafts vague voices, from remote restless unmarked graves.
Our parting lasting scene still helps, no longer bodes of ill:
I won't forget, this special time stands quite still.

For all souls lost in water's-warred, sea's great bastion bells
will ring,
Each one was a special shaped droplet, from life's richest
flowing spring.
Though war's worst dread engulfed Eric, his memory will
constantly remain,
Just as always he was and had wanted, steaming sure in a
safe convoy lane.
I still sense his easy presence speak, that is there with his
each recall,
And a brother's friendly home welcome, into great gang-
way's hatchway hall,
When we meet once again together, atop my last hurdle hill:
No! I won't forget, this special time stands quite still.

Sisters Sybil and Joey were not far away from home at this time. Sybil was now married to Frank and staying in Bellrock Avenue at the other end of Prestwick to where our house was. Joey had already left Kirklandside Hospital where she had been a student nurse. Her leaving there was due to having contracted an infection which had left her with a permanent hearing loss in one ear. A few months after her illness she finally left the nursing profession on medical advice and soon afterwards joined the Woman's Land Army in October 1941 where she remained until the end of the war.

Sybil was to meet her future husband when both of them were working at the airport during the early part of 1941. Frank was a native of Northern Ireland and working in the Aeronautical Inspection Department, (AID), where Sybil was doing secretarial work. She became Mrs Frank Tilson when they were wedded in St Ninian's Church in April 1942. Their wedding reception was held in a small hotel in the main street and after a short honeymoon (I can't remember where), they both returned to continue working at the airport until Frank was moved to the Largs branch the following year. The highlight of the wedding was when the minister was forgotten after the service. The poor chap had gone to remove his cassock and surplice and when he returned everyone had gone. Mother realised at the hotel what must have happened and found a

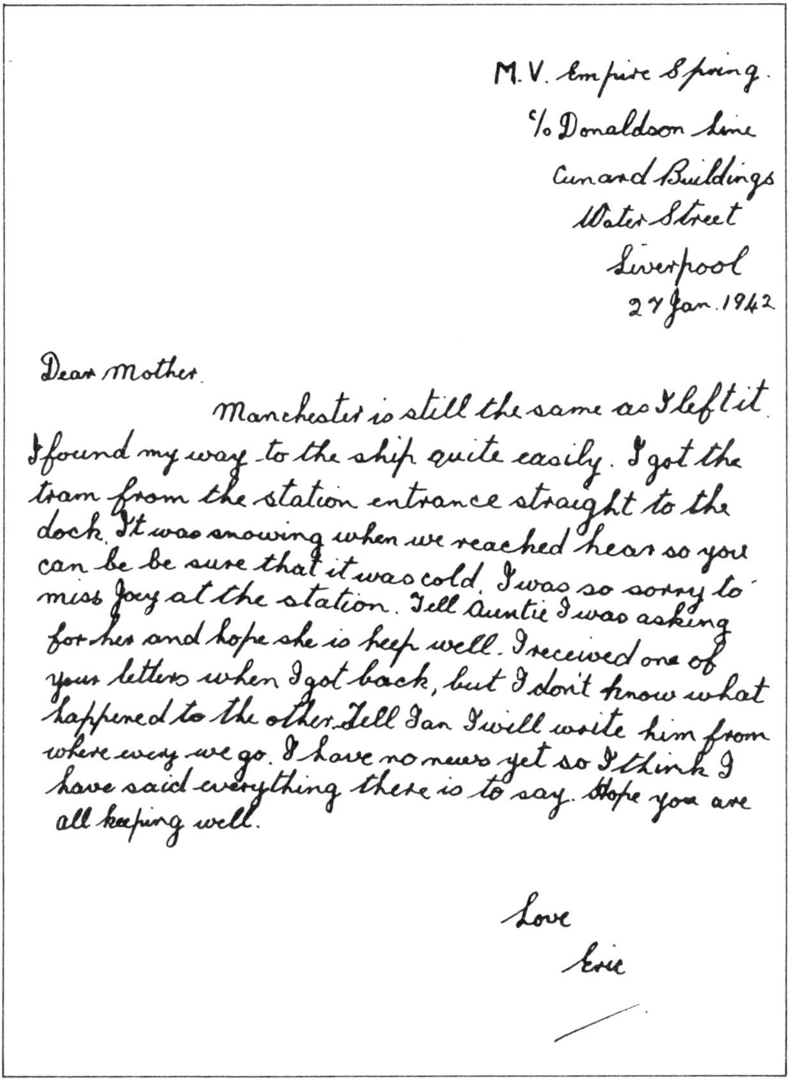

M.V. Empire Spring.
C/o Donaldson Line
Cunard Buildings
Water Street
Liverpool
27 Jan. 1942

Dear Mother.

Manchester is still the same as I left it. I found my way to the ship quite easily. I got the tram from the station entrance straight to the dock. It was snowing when we reached hear so you can be be sure that it was cold. I was so sorry to miss Joey at the station. Tell Auntie I was asking for her and hope she is keep well. I received one of your letters when I got back, but I don't know what happened to the other. Tell Ian I will write him from where every we go. I have no news yet so I think I have said everything there is to say. Hope you are all keeping well.

Love
Eric

I suspect there were three letters written on 27 January, of which two were sent to his own address. 'Frenchie' was Miss Sadler, our French teacher, and Eric jokingly regarded me as one of her pets. I cannot remember getting the sixpence but I still intend to take the matter up with Sybil who is now 72.

M.V. Empire Spring.
% Donaldson Line
Cunard Buildi-
Water Street,
Liverpool.
27-1-1942.

Dear Ian,

If I have enough money I'll get you
the lighter I promised you. I hope you enjoy being
back at school. Is F[illegible]ckie still as soft as usu-
ally. My journey [illegible] to Manchester was
reasonably comf[illegible] except for the stiffness
~~[illegible]~~
please try to get the 11 [illegible] alright. Would you
asked Sybil to give [illegible] dance with Rhona. I have
bag to the station. Tell Jimmy sixpence for carring my
him and hope his foot is alright now. I was asking for
I was asking for her and hope she is still. Tell Joey
keeping well. job with the cows. Hoping you are all

Love
Eric.

No. 24 F.1.

ACCOUNT OF WAGES.

(Sec. 132 M.S.A. 1894).

ISSUED BY THE MINISTRY OF WAR TRANSPORT.

EMPIRE SPRING
NETT TON. 4147
OFF. NO. 167002
REG. GREENOCK

Name of Ship and Official No.

Name of Seaman.	Ref. No. in Agreement.
Eric W. May	59.

Date Wages began.	Date Wages ceased.	Total Period of Employment. Months.	Days.
8.12.41	19 JAN 1942	1	12

EARNINGS.

	£	s.	d.
1 Months at £16/8 per month		16	8
12 Days at .... per day		6	8
Increase of wages, on promotion by £2 per day for .... months......... days*	1	1	6
	1	7	3
Overtime .... Hours at			
Extras War Bonus & D.S.	9	16	
TOTAL EARNINGS .... (A)	13	8	1

DEDUCTIONS EXCLUDING ALLOTMENTS.

Date.	Particulars.	£	s.	d.
	Reduction of wages, on dis-rating by £......... per month for .... months .... days*			
	Advance on joining	–	–	–
	Fines			
	Other Cash Advances, Stores, &c., supplied (*in order of date*) :—			
	Tobacco			
	s/c		16	
Dec 29	Cash	4	10	4
	Health and Pensions Insur. Contributions for 7 wks.		6	8
	Unemployment Insurance Contributions for 7 wks.		2	11
	TOTAL	5	15	11
	Cash on leaving Ship			
	TOTAL DEDUCTIONS, exclusive of Allotments .... (B) £			

	£	s.	d.
Balance without deducting Allotments—Deduct (B) from (A)	13	8	1
	5	15	11
	7	12	2
Allotments			
FINAL BALANCE .... £	7	12	2

The above Account of Earnings and of Deductions exclusive of Allotments is correct.

Signature of Master ....

Signature of Seaman ....

Port .... Date 19 JAN 1942

CLOTHING X COUPON	CLOTHING X COUPON	CLOTHING X COUPON	CLOTHING X COUPON
CLOTHING X COUPON	CLOTHING X COUPON	CLOTHING X COUPON	CLOTHING X COUPON
CLOTHING X COUPON	CLOTHING X COUPON	CLOTHING X COUPON	CLOTHING X COUPON
CLOTHING X COUPON	CLOTHING X COUPON	CLOTHING X COUPON	CLOTHING X COUPON
CLOTHING X COUPON	CLOTHING X COUPON	CLOTHING X COUPON	CLOTHING X COUPON

(FOLD HERE)

PRESTWICK AYRSHIRE

Date Stamp

This Card may only be used by or on behalf of the person named below

CLOTHING CARD

Ration Period to 31 May, 1942

Serial Number AB 342455

For official use only

Name Eric May

Address 1 M^c [illegible] Ave

Prestwick

Ayrshire

National Registration Number SGCB3/5

Left: front.

Below: back.

Everybody had one.

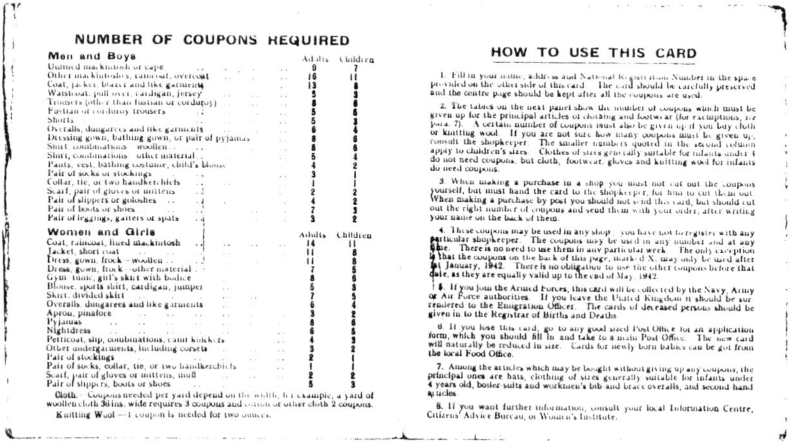

NUMBER OF COUPONS REQUIRED

Men and Boys	Adults	Children
Unlined mackintosh or cape	9	7
Other mackintoshes, raincoat, overcoat	16	11
Coat, jacket, blazer and like garments	13	8
Waistcoat, pull over, cardigan, jersey	5	3
Trousers (other than fustian or corduroy)	8	6
Fustian or corduroy trousers	5	5
Shorts	5	3
Overalls, dungarees and like garments	6	4
Dressing gown, bathing gown, or pair of pyjamas	8	6
Shirt, combinations—woollen	8	6
Shirt, combinations—other material	5	4
Pants, vest, bathing costume, child's blouse	4	2
Pair of socks or stockings	3	1
Collar, tie, or two handkerchiefs	1	1
Scarf, pair of gloves or mittens	2	2
Pair of slippers or goloshes	4	2
Pair of boots or shoes	7	3
Pair of leggings, gaiters or spats	3	2

Women and Girls	Adults	Children
Coat, raincoat, lined mackintosh	14	11
Jacket, short coat	11	8
Dress, gown, frock—woollen	11	8
Dress, gown, frock—other material	7	5
Gym tunic, girl's skirt with bodice	8	6
Blouse, sports shirt, cardigan, jumper	5	3
Skirt, divided skirt	7	5
Overalls, dungarees and like garments	6	4
Apron, pinafore	3	2
Pyjamas	8	6
Nightdress	6	5
Petticoat, slip, combinations, cami knickers	4	3
Other undergarments, including corsets	3	2
Pair of stockings	2	1
Pair of socks, collar, tie, or two handkerchiefs	1	1
Scarf, pair of gloves or mittens, muff	2	2
Pair of slippers, boots or shoes	5	3

Cloth.—Coupons needed per yard depend on the width, for example, a yard of woollen cloth 36 ins. wide requires 3 coupons and cotton or other cloth 2 coupons.

Knitting Wool—1 coupon is needed for two ounces.

HOW TO USE THIS CARD

1. Fill in your name, address and National Registration Number in the space provided on the other side of this card. The card should be carefully preserved and the centre page should be kept after all the coupons are used.

2. The tables on the next panel show the number of coupons which must be given up for the principal articles of clothing and footwear (for exemptions, see para. 7). A certain number of coupons must also be given up if you buy cloth or knitting wool. If you are not sure how many coupons must be given up, consult the shopkeeper. The smaller numbers quoted in the second column apply to children's sizes. Clothes of sizes generally suitable for infants under 4 do not need coupons, but cloth, footwear, gloves and knitting wool for infants do need coupons.

3. When making a purchase in a shop you must not cut out the coupons yourself, but must hand the card to the shopkeeper, for him to cut them out. When making a purchase by post you should not send this card, but should cut out the right number of coupons and send them with your order, after writing your name on the back of them.

4. These coupons may be used in any shop; you have not to register with any particular shopkeeper. The coupons may be used in any number and at any time. There is no need to use them in any particular week. The only exception is that the coupons on the back of this page, marked X, may only be used after 1st January, 1942. There is no obligation to use the other coupons before that date, as they are equally valid up to the end of May, 1942.

5. If you join the Armed Forces, this card will be collected by the Navy, Army or Air Force authorities. If you leave the United Kingdom it should be surrendered to the Emigration Officer. The cards of deceased persons should be given in to the Registrar of Births and Deaths.

6. If you lose this card, go to any good sized Post Office for an application form, which you should fill in and take to a main Post Office. The new card will naturally be reduced in size. Cards for newly born babies can be got from the local Food Office.

7. Among the articles which may be bought without giving up any coupons, the principal ones are hats, clothing of sizes generally suitable for infants under 4 years old, boiler-suits and workmen's bib and brace overalls, and second hand articles.

8. If you want further information, consult your local Information Centre, Citizens' Advice Bureau, or Women's Institute.

car with sufficient petrol to return to the church and bring him to the reception. There was one thing that wartime brides had to do without, and that was the ringing of wedding bells as that sound was now the warning signal to the populace that the expected German invasion had begun. The newly-weds in those days had, amongst other things, to swap the pealing of church bells for the joys of sharing clothing coupons and ration books.

The Glasgow air raids had no ill effect on expectant sister Clara, nor apparently on daughter Elizabeth who decided after all to arrive on schedule on 21st May 1942. The same year Clara lost her brother our parents gained their first grandchild.

Old Aunt Bell and my father were the last remaining children of a family of thirteen, she being the oldest and he the youngest. When Elizabeth was born my aunt was seventy-six years old and had been complaining of this and that since whenever I could remember. Mother had been in every sense her handmaiden, taking care of all her wants and serving three meals on a tray each day in her room. I cannot remember her ever leaving the house to go anywhere. She made a profession of being one of the older generation and was by nature a born survivor. Aunt Bell would never admit to reading either the *Ayrshire Post* or *People's Friend* from cover to cover as she constantly complained of becoming too tired whenever she made the (brave?) attempt to read anything, but just try forgetting to purchase these publications and she would soon remind you about it. I do not remember any friends calling on her or Mother telling of any but perhaps they had all pre-deceased her. On the other hand maybe she never had any.

As children Aunt Bell and Father had been brought up in Dunfermline (the Kingdom of Fife) and later in Leith. My grandfather had been a pattern maker who designed iron castings of which many were used in the building of railway bridges, which included the Forth Bridge. It was around the time that railway companies were expanding and having bridges built for them across rivers and canals, which apparently kept Grandfather very busy for it appears he was very good at his job. My Aunt Bell was the eldest of the family. A tragedy occurred when most of the children died as a result of drinking affected milk from a diseased cow. (It was a normal practice for many families to either share or have their own cow.) From then on Aunt Bell ran the household and assumed the caring role over her younger sister, Nellie, and brother Jack (Father).

Later on, after the death of her parents, she moved with her sister to live over in Glasgow to be closer to her brother Jack who was now working there. Both the sisters ran a sweetie/tobacconist-type shop, and I can very well imagine the trepidation of any youngster entering the shop with either of those fierce aunts of mine behind the counter. Mercifully, not surprisingly, they both remained spinsters for the whole of their lives.

Joey told me many years later about a visit she once made to the shop with Clara and Sybil as young girls. A man in working clothes came in and made a purchase, but the looks both aunts gave the unfortunate fellow was such that they did not encourage common people as customers. Such was their attitude, but they would take money from anybody. To say they were mean was an understatement as each of my sisters received just one sweet before they left for home.

At the time of writing, such fearsome ladies of yesteryear, and there were quite a number of them, would be made to wear a ball and chain to protect the general public or a mandatory warning notice would have to be displayed outside their premises cautioning the reader that entry could damage your wealth as well as make you very ill.

I think the end of the war started to see the last of these ferocious and woefully independent ladies who ran shops apparently only for their own convenience. Scottish towns and villages seem to have had their fair share of them of what I can remember being told about them, and of course the same species could also be found running boarding houses. Placing aside for the moment the hardships encountered and heartbreaks suffered in the normal process of living, I cannot help but consider the heavy losses amongst the young men during the First World War must have left its effect on at least a generation of young ladies. On reflection I do not think I have been very fair on the many pleasant and homely landladies that there were as well.

During the latter part of 1942 both Mum and Dad came to the

agreement that they should return to live in Glasgow. Father's health was not too good then, and it was thought that cutting out the daily return journey to the city would be the wisest move to make. I don't think Mother objected too much at leaving a house with such a recent bitter memory.

My schooldays at Prestwick were a happy period in my life, and I hold pleasant memories of it. It was a reddish stone chalet-manor house building that was set back from the road just the correct distance to make it aloof and distinctive. It was part surrounded by a high wall guarding its flanks and rear. The two gateways into the playground left no-one in any doubt that they were entering or leaving the precincts of a seat of learning and added a flavouring of respectability upon the chattering hordes of spontaneous youth that entered through them. The building seemed to produce the correct degree of smugness and gave the impression that the field it had been built in was its own personal estate. It echoed through the years a stability that one could easily associate with a church.

I consider myself fortunate in having retained such an image as later generations elsewhere, when asked about their schools, may very well recall some glass or concrete monument to some woeful economy and political remissness.

I am absolutely sure that as a pupil I never gazed intently at any part of the school building with the intention of remembering it for later years. Education and preparation for the future for each pupil, in whatever field it may lie, is the paramount business of any school. I can only assume, therefore, that the school image I conjured up was the single representation of all I had absorbed inside its walls. This leaves me with the thought that even ordinary pupils from secondary schooling might well unconsciously carry the building as a security anchor that remains an identity attachment every bit as strong as the claim of others that only fee-paying schools can do.

To wear your past schooling with pride is one thing, but to sport it only to open doors barred to others is another. Thankfully for me such a habit was never taught nor expected, but personal endeavour was. I was given an honest education with no shortcuts or bargains. It taught me to be philosophical over disappointments

– not quite true. It taught me to tell others to be philosophical.

Would it surprise you if I wrote that I cannot remember any bullying taking place at school? Such a thing could only have occurred amongst the boys who were at the age where they had to rid themselves of some measure of aggression somehow or another; therefore there must have been some rough and tumble horseplay amongst us. There were no special victims singled out for intimidation. It certainly could not be that we were all 'goodie' clean-cut boys. (What a thought!) The general tolerant pupil behaviour could possibly have been due to the school not having the number of pupils that a senior secondary school would have had and our teachers could therefore have more easily spotted something wrong. On the other hand, where there were siblings and cousins attending the some school word of any bullying, (or any other misbehaviour) would soon have sifted up to the teacher/parent level. If that were the case then the answer to the classroom bully is for as many children as possible to speak about it to their teacher and parents. There is no code that protects someone 'not quite right in the head' who uses an alien streak of nature that others do not quite know how to react to. In my case it was more likely that there were strenuous activities outside the school sphere where excess energy was worked off. Some of the boys could virtually run up the school wall, which I seem to recall to be about eight feet high, and casually go over the top, then 'dreep' down the other side into the field. This showed the degree of fitness there was amongst us. Like most I could only get the top of the wall under my armpit, then slithered back down again on the same side as I started on. The champion was Bob Gemmel whom I remember succeeding several times with apparent ease. At the same time, looking back I must admit there were an awful lot of sprained ankles and wrists or kinks in the neck and hurt knees.

But wait a moment. Perhaps, if we did not bully amongst ourselves it was because we chose another kind of victim. It was quite probable that we were little snobs, tending to think ourselves better than others outside the school. We may have talked and even sneered at other boys not considered to be quite as good as we were. But it's more likely that hearing about the effects of tyranny from each adult source we came in contact with as well as from the wireless, cinema and reading material, had expunged a lot of would-be bullying from our minds.

Another consideration is that we had been moved about en masse from our homes in a manner that no previous generation had done. We were aware what could happen to those who did not match up to the standards of the tyrant, or, in other words, were easy targets for the bully because of their race, religion, lifestyle or state of health. We knew what tyranny was. If any young generation knew what lay behind the unfairness of the bully it was mine for we were brought up to despise the brutish cowards and their cohorts who contrived it. That might sound terribly pious but it was something that stretched from the wagons crossing the American prairie to the school playground and out beyond the hours of lessons and further out again across the seas to the battlefields beyond. There was a behavioural boundary placed around us that, if crossed, simply meant you were in the wrong and therefore could expect no sympathy. In those days excuses were ten a penny and none of them of any use.

The restrictions were in no way a harness for they allowed room for plenty of personal freedom and scope for self-expression within it. A little fighting and a fair share of horseplay amongst male adolescents were both expected and to a degree tolerated but never condoned. A bruise or bandage or leaking blood was not considered of much importance on growing boys/young adults who mostly lived in a world where at times justice and law lay poles apart. If one was involved in a fight with an opponent who had crossed limit bounds of behaviour and you were unfortunate to be brought to book in the matter by parent or teacher, then that reason alone would help your case considerably in judgement over the affair.

I will now mention a school fight which I was involved in. It only concerned myself and an evacuee from Glasgow whom I remember was called Allan and whose surname I have forgotten. It was not a bloody affair or vendetta but merely a boyish thing. It all started (I least I think it did) with Allan somehow or another turning the neck of my shirt back far enough for him to say to others in the vicinity words to the effect that he wondered if the shirt had been bought at Woolworths. The fact that he could do this meant I was not wearing my tie; therefore I assume this happened in the gym changing room. The scene now changes to the playing field outside the school where both of us later became locked in unarmed mortal combat. The outcome was that I won. For a couple of weeks after the fight I was called Gunboat, or was it Tugboat? There was no later animosity between Allan and myself. He chose a target and missed, but what I am trying to say is, had he picked on someone obviously weaker than himself he would have been a bully, but he didn't. Physically we were evenly matched and that day I was lucky.

When one Third Year Class finished its final term in the summer it made way for the next oldest group of pupils and from amongst them would be the faces of the early smokers. Although smoking by pupils was forbidden and cigarettes were rationed it was nevertheless a common and socially accepted habit. Cigs were puffed in the sheds and at the back of the school wall, although not in any great numbers. During my last year of schooling I had a few draws at Woodbines in both those areas. That, as far as I can recall, was the worst that happened at Sin School. I don't think lectures were given at classroom level about the evils of tobacco; in fact there seemed to be little concern over the issue. My parents didn't want me to smoke because of it hindering sporting activities, making breathing more difficult, and there was another underlying reason which probably took precedence over the first reason and that was the warning that no-one had money to burn.

My one criticism of that time was that there was no contact with other schools in the town, which to me, looking back, was a great pity.

One further preparation Mother made before she left Prestwick was to arrange for me to stay on long enough to complete my third year at secondary school level and to find out the results. If my memory serves me right that took about six weeks and I stayed in digs during that time. Before I moved into my new temporary home I was given the usual standard advice meted out to countless sons and daughters before entering anyone's home. It usually took the following form.

'Remember! If you are offered anything say THANK YOU and

DO try to be careful with cups and plates, and for Heaven's sake BE considerate with rationed foods. Try to remember THERE'S STILL A WAR ON.'

I would like to leave this chapter with a true wee story that might help the reader to understand something about the humour of Glaswegians and others living in the vicinity of the Clyde and how they are moulded from young.

Not long before the start of the war Mother had taken Joey into town to do some shopping, during which time the pair of them found themselves in the tearoom of Pettigrew and Stephens. It was evidently a very popular place to have a break between visiting shops.

At a nearby table a young son was complaining about not wanting to finish whatever it was his mother expected him to finish.

'It's been paid for,' she said 'so you will have to eat it.'

'Ah canna,' replied the little boy, 'Ah'm full up.'

'Then you will just have to shake it doon,' said his mother. 'Ca'mon! Staun up and shake yourself.'

The wee soul stood up and shook each leg, one at a time; then he wagged his body about and this was followed by the flunking of his arms. It looked as though the little fellow was dancing some sort of stationary samba, plus a little bit of this and that added for good measure.

It finished when his mother said, 'That's enough. Noo sit doon and finish what's on your plate.'

And a pleased small boy happily finished his food.

THE LAST NIGHT
A STORY

For Molly Hare Saturday night was normally a bit more hectic than others as most of her guests usually left for home the following day, each hopefully refreshed and ready to face another Monday morning. Before they left she was usually preparing for the newcomers. Molly always looked forward to the quiet spell of the evening after the teatime dishes had been cleaned and stored away and the breakfast places had been set out on the table.

Sometimes in the evening she joined the visitors for a little while in the front room. She liked people, the right sort of course, and financially she needed their custom for her widow's pension no longer seemed to go as far as it did a year ago. Molly did not consider herself to be a typical landlady dragon as her sense of humour would not permit it, and in any case she enjoyed running her small B & B with all meals included if required. She had found it much harder to manage a wartime guest house in present times than she had done in times of peace. Dried egg and ration books had not been thought of then, and sliced sausage or vegetables never had to be stretched to their limits, nor be so equally divided.

Her son Ron was serving in the Navy and she had the normal mother's nagging worry and concern about him. It was now just over three weeks since receiving his last letter, or more correctly his scribbled note. She never liked to mention her anxiety over the lack of mail to her friends. That was the way she was.

At the moment she was thinking of the people staying under her roof and trying to place each of them into their correct personality slot. Sometimes she was proved well and truly wrong.

Tom and Jean Wilson had been with her for three nights. Tom was on a ten day leave from the Army and wore corporal's stripes on the arms of his battle tunic. His leave, that was now evaporating away before his eyes, was culminating in a four day second honeymoon in the quiet seaside resort where they both held fond memories from happier times. He was a very fit man who took his good health for granted, and the reason he neither smoked nor bothered about strong drink was simply that having tried both, he was not impressed with either. He was also what one might call a very competent person, which had not gone unnoticed during his short Army career. If he had a fault it was a good one, for he always seemed to do the right thing without it being too obvious. He had had his share of disappointments in his civilian life, mostly by being made aware of the unfairness by others whose names counted more than their capabilities.

Jean was more liberal than her husband, and also knew more about human nature than Tom did, probably because of her working in council offices between the years of her leaving school and getting married. She had dealt with a good cross-section of the general public and had met her fair share of ambitious young councillors before they were each conscripted into one or other of the services. With this latter happening, most of the ladies and gentlemen of the council chamber were secretly relieved by the absence of their younger and more radical counterparts. It also meant a return to discussing the more mundane matters in a manner they found really quite pleasant and reminiscent of halcyon days of yesteryear.

Both Tom and Jean were in their early thirties and had been married for eleven years, during which time they had produced three children. Being a mother of young children, Jean had not been directed into war work, although she did carry out voluntary work for the NAAFI (Navy, Army and Air Force Institute, an organisation which ran canteens and shops for service personnel and their families). This little holiday was something special as it was the first occasion where both of them had been alone with each other since being married, and all thanks to a fussy and worrity grandmother.

Bill Barrons simply could not raise any enthusiasm for golf, ancient, royal or otherwise, and he had no intention whatsoever of playing the wretched game. He had merely travelled with his friend Bob Farrow because both of them had managed to obtain a seven day pass from the Royal Canadian Air Force base where they were stationed. A place that was not only very much isolated but lacked more than just a few home comforts.

Bob, who had been a keen golfer since his teens, thought it a heavensent opportunity to play over a world-famous Scottish course, even though it meant playing with borrowed set of clubs. The arrangement between the two independent friends was that they met up with each other at a hotel in the main street during the late afternoon after having each spent the most part of the day doing as he pleased: playing golf for one; walking and sightseeing for the other. The irreconcilable disparity between them in the field of sport made not the slightest difference to their friendship.

Both the Canadians had arrived in a car that Bob had bought under rather sad circumstances – though not unique for the time. Most of the airfields had a number of private cars owned by RAF personnel. Unfortunately, on a few occasions when an owner did not return from a raid, the family concerned did not want the car and it would be sold very cheaply to someone else in the squadron willing to, and legally capable of buying it. Through this method the two young men had driven to the guest house in an old Bulldog Morris car that had cost its latest owner £12.

Bill had recognised Helen Banks as another one of the guests when she was walking towards the seafront on the second day of his stay and had deliberately caught up with her. They had walked together for nearly half and hour and the young Canadian found her to be very pleasing company. It was when he mentioned her daughter and the likeness between them that she seemed to become more reserved and then remembered she had to do something before going to the school in time for the children coming out. He remembered the next time not to talk about the little girl, and Bill seemed to think that their relationship started to improve from then on.

Both the Canadians were returning to their base the following day.

Helen Banks tended to be reserved and not a good mixer amongst strangers. Her reserve might have been interpreted by some who did not know her as being 'stand-offish' which certainly would not be true. No-one seemed to know much about her except that she was well-spoken, lived in Glasgow and apparently has a daughter called Nancy who had been evacuated into the area and whom she was now visiting. Helen and Nancy were both staying at Molly's as the lady who was caring for the young evacuee was now down in Leeds meeting up with her husband for a few days or perhaps hours. Apparently there had been a whisper that their training period would soon be ending and rumour was rife that an imminent move was due for the Air Force group he was with.

Molly had wanted to be diplomatic as she wasn't sure of Helen's marital position – her ration book gave no indication she was married. It could be that she had recently married a widower with a child whose mother may have died at or through its birth. Sadly such tragedies happen. If that were the case then she must bear in mind that it took a certain length of time to change the wartime documents. Molly found it difficult to put an age to her. At a guess she thought she would be a year or two under thirty. Only in answer to someone's recent direct question had she heard the the child's father had been lost at sea before the war when the child was still a baby and although Helen was given the opportunity to elaborate on the subject, she chose not to do so. Because of this it was assumed that there might be something very much remiss in her relationship with the father, but, of course, nothing was said within her earshot.

Helen was returning to Glasgow the following morning and young Nancy going back to her wartime foster mother.

Tony Spinelli had by coincidence a three day business conference and had arrived with his wife, Sina, on the Monday, like most of the others. It wasn't usual for so many guests to arrive on the same day. Tony's meeting was about scientific matters which he never detailed, and no-one asked him any questions. He had taken the opportunity to bring Sina with him. As their surname implied and their looks belied, they were both of Italian origin. Tony looked around thirty years of age and his wife, who was eight months pregnant, seemed to be about five years younger than he was.

Mrs Bacall was the odd one out. She arrived on the Thursday. Molly's first impression from what she was told by the lady was that she was visiting a friend, and had been left with the feeling that no further explanations were required to be given by the lady. But later on in the day, when her guest returned from wherever she had been, she didn't appear to be any too pleased with herself and told Molly that she would be leaving the following day. By Friday she had changed her mind about leaving and said she would stay until Sunday. Her tone of voice told others that she was used to getting her own way; however, she was pleasant enough in an icy sort of way to those she met under Molly's roof. Mrs Bacall had complained about the train journey she had suffered in order to get away for a short break and how awful it was for a lady to travel anywhere. Even getting a nanny to care for her two children had been difficult and time-consuming. The one she had managed to get was far too old for the post, but younger ones were just impossible to get nowadays. Anyone who could read a face could tell that Mrs Bacall would be a very trying person to live with and even worse to work under.

Although no-one said so in so many words, the general feeling amongst the guests towards her, which included Molly, was decidedly similar, with perhaps one exception. Mrs Bacall really thought she was raising the tone of the guest house by merely being there and that she was admirably putting up with its conditions and people due to certain circumstances that had recently cropped up in her life.

Each weekend Molly had a domestic help from Friday till Monday, who went under the name of Edna. There was no second name attached, or if there was one then nobody had ever heard of it. For some reason Edna's conversation was always a one-sided affair, and this was thought to be accomplished through her perfect sense of timing by always arriving spot on cue to make a comment. By the same illusion as she made her entrance, she contrived her exit.

Mr McGrith was the only permanent guest which, in his eyes, made him the senior resident. He was a widower and had been retired for two years after working at the nearby aerodrome. As a young man he had worked in the south of England with the Southern Railway before joining an aviation company which had later placed him up north where he had remained until his retirement. His wife had died eighteen months before his retirement, and although he had a grown-up married family living in the south, he had decided for the time being that he would rid himself of his house and its unhappy memories of his wife's long illness, yet remain in the area. He tended to be more than a little disparaging in his manner of speaking during any conversation, and left one with the impression he had been talking down to you. For some obscure reason he was a lieutenant in the Home Guard and tonight he was staying at home.

He was slightly confused as to why two Canadians had come to this little town with only one of them claiming to play a round of golf each day. What was the other one up to? Another point that left him pondering was why the so-called golfer had told him that this was his first and only opportunity to visit the UK, yet he had distinctly overheard the same man telling Mrs Hare that he knew nearby Hamilton fairly well. With this Hess business still in his mind he thought it was all very suspicious and he intended to keep his eyes open for anything that appeared the slightest thing out of place or out of keeping with the two so-called Canadians. During such turbulent times one had to be vigilant and be constantly on guard against enemy infiltration or Fifth Column activities. Neither the Government's dire warnings nor his Home Guard training had been in vain.

Apart from the sporting half of the sons of the Maple Leaf, all the residents had moved into the front room lounge more or less immediately following the evening meal. It was a spacious comfortable room with sufficient seats to accommodate all the guests, although it was not exactly what could be called cosy on this darkening September evening. They all hoped that with a little luck Edna would shortly make an appearance with a box of matches and light the already set open coal fire.

Mrs Bacall entered the sitting room, smoking the now familiar cigarette attached to the end of a long holder. She smoked in a quick nervous manner. As was expected, she headed straight for one of the easy chairs and settled herself comfortably into it.

No-one was making any serious effort in conversation, or perhaps it would be more correct to say that all except one were doing their level best not to encourage the permanent boarder to start on his prepared evening topic. By now they had learnt one thing about him and could readily sense he was simply dying to come away with something to say, and was just waiting and looking for the right opportunity.

It was Edna who broke the ice and started the flow of words when she suddenly appeared amongst them, moving quickly to the window, and pausing long enough to say, 'How dull it is,' before drawing the heavy black-out curtains.

Someone replied to the effect that it had been dull all day and then added something about it being a big miss no longer getting a daily weather forecast over the wireless, to which Edna replied, 'It was not the outside climate I was referring to.' She closed the door quietly behind her.

The six o'clock news from the BBC had not been particularly good with heavy Allied shipping losses and continuing air raids bombing cities and towns. There was little doubt that this latest bulletin contributed to the unprogressive atmosphere in the room.

Somehow or another it had been expected by most of the company that Tom and Jean would have gone straight to their room after eating as it had been mentioned during the meal that they might go out to the pictures to see Nelson Eddy and Jeanette McDonald singing in *Rose Marie*. This would have meant having to go into the nearby town by bus. The film had been a source of humorous questions directed at the two Canadians about who gets which man. Someone said it was James Stewart's first acting part in films and no-one contradicted the statement.

Mr McGrith had at last cornered his victim in the form of Helen, and was asking if the child's father was in one of the Services. He spoke as though he knew something the others didn't. Jean moved swiftly in front of Bill, as though to slow down his sudden change of position towards Helen. They each apologized for the near collision. Moments later Bill moved over to stand nearer the chair Helen was occupying while Jean edged herself between them and the last speaker. Jean enquired loudly if anyone had heard how the local shops were faring with so few visitors coming to the resort. But the retired gentleman had no intention of speaking about local topics and steered the conversation away from neighbouring traders by starting to talk about, 'What The Boys In The Armed Forces Were Really Fighting For.' Then he immediately began to answer his own question. 'Which, of course, is to defend the British way of life.' He then continued to talk about family virtues, on which he spent some time, before rounding off about the high standard of Christian morals which every decent man, woman and child should live by. He looked pointedly towards Helen as he finished.

He was obviously disappointed when there was no spontaneous cheer from those listening, but that did not deter him in the slightest way for he threw out the challenge to Tom by asking him directly what he was fighting for and what change, if any, he expected to see happening when the war was over.

It came as a pleasant surprise to each person in the room that someone had been invited by Mr McGrith to say something. Perhaps it might be an interesting evening after all.

Tom had asked himself that very same question at least a thousand times since his call-up and an answer had constantly eluded him. There was always a background of moral confusion over that particular enigma. The BBC question panels always trotted out the proper responses, yet with Tom it seemed that when one vague reason was just about to clear and enlighten him it would suddenly disappear and another uncertain explanation started to take shape but nothing of any substance seemed to endure. This evening was different and somehow rather special for an answer had come to him about one second after the question had been framed. He started speaking as though he had received previous notice of the question.

'My father is a riveter working in Connells Shipyard on the Clyde, and he has been employed there for twenty-five years. He must have met good men, not so good men and probably some very bad men, but it never changed his principal that you shouldn't do anyone a bad turn when you can do them a good one, and he would help anyone who was down on his luck. It was always held by some people that he had a very good reason to do so.'

He paused as though choosing this words carefully and continued, 'I worked in the wages department of the same company and sometimes when I had to go into the yard I would meet up with him. A few weeks before the war started he introduced me to a young man in his mid-twenties who had recently started in the shipyard as a labourer, and who mentioned that it was through Dad knowing one of the foremen that he found his job. I should mention that Connells Shipyard is fairly well known for its employment of non-violent ex-prisoners who are willing and capable of making a fresh start. This arrangement had started within the company some years ago through the interest of a family member sitting on the Prison Parole Board who gave practical assistance in released prisoners' rehabilitation where and how possible. Having said that, I can now tell you that I had a feeling rising at the back of my mind about the young labourer.'

Tom stopped suddenly as though for breath, but the interest showing on the listening faces made him start again.

'At home I asked Dad about the young man and he told me that his father had been killed during the Battle of the Somme in 1916, leaving a widow with four children, the youngest of which was the chap he had introduced me to. Nothing had been made easy for the boy's mother to bring up the children of a non-commissioned soldier killed in action. This particular son, like many others, had to leave school when he was still only twelve years of age and turn his hand to anything that would earn him a few coppers to take home. He had a good singing voice and had even gone around the Glasgow tenement back greens singing tear-jerker type songs for the one or two pennies that were wrapped up in a piece of newspaper and thrown down to him by caring housewives who could ill afford such extravagance.'

As though to brighten up his topic he added the information, 'In Glasgow there's a saying that you will never be short of anything you give to someone who needs it.' He returned to his story.

'My call-up had been deferred because of the work I was involved with and I was well aware that it would only be for a relatively short period. This other young man I heard had failed to pass his physical examination, apparently due to a minor chest complaint and was told he would have to return at some later date for another medical. Following this he tried for garden work in the better-off parts of the city, and that was when he came upon a house where the family were obviously away from home. A neighbour became suspicious and telephoned the police, who found him leaving the premises with two bottles of milk that were a few days old and which had been forgotten and left outside the back door. He was also found to be carrying six carrots, a handful of Brussels sprouts and two small lettuces from the garden. For this theft he was sentenced to three months' imprisonment by the magistrates court, which he served out in Barlinnie Jail. He had his second medical almost immediately after his release and it wasn't long after that when the three of us had that first meeting I told you about.

'Probably we each received our call-up papers about the same time, and I heard no more about him until I was told in a letter from home that he had been killed defending the beaches at Dunkirk in a rearguard action during the evacuation that allowed time for others to get safely across the Channel.'

Some of the guests were not sure whether that was the end of the story, but Tom spoke again.

'A short time before I was married my mother asked me if my father had ever mentioned anything about his younger years. I told her that all I knew was that he had started work in the locksmith trade before the Depression made him change to being a riveter, then, through wartime necessity a welder. She persisted in asking it he had hinted at anything at all about those early working days of his. I knew she was going to tell me something very important. Then, in a conspiratorial quietness she told me that my father, in his younger days, was considered to be extremely efficient at opening safes, and gained a reputation in that field which stretched out to other cities. Various unsavoury people employed him. All that was expected of him was to gain entrance into a protected area or open a secured container and then depart from the scene as soon as he then wished, leaving the others to do or see what they wanted with the contents. Dad charged a service fee and a customer would pay it. It was as simple as that. I suppose it was only a matter of time before he was arrested and the police finally found evidence against him in someone's house during a raid. Later on, following the chain of events that followed, he was lucky on leaving prison to have been directed to, and given an honest job which he gladly took and never looked back. A few years later on I appeared on the scene and was given the opportunity to follow a career of my own choosing. Please do not think that our lives were easy for I must assure all of you that it was a pretty hard grind for both my parents to achieve what our family now has.

'Let me say as a soldier and a chartered accountant, that once we have righted the wrongs which brought about this war and put the fighting behind us, then what I want to see is a second chance with a clean slate for everyone who earns it. In other words the law being fair to everyone. It would also be nice to think that colleges and universities would expand to give all genuine students, including those from poorer backgrounds the opportunity to enrol in them.'

After a slight hesitation he added with a grin, 'It would also be good to think it would all happen in my lifetime.' He ended with the pleasing impression that the listeners happily agreed with what he had just said, with perhaps one exception amongst the guests.

Even Mr McGrith's face had flushed slightly before Tom had finished speaking, yet as usual he was the first to speak. This time he reminded everyone that there were always casualties and losers in any form of governing. He continued, 'What had just been said qualifies the point that Britain truly cares for ordinary worthy folk and especially victims of crime. Its law, its order and its punishment of crime is the envy of a world made truly aware that the British Empire stands for all the things that decent people live and die for.' With a theatrical flourish of his arms he demanded, 'What on Earth would happen to all those unfortunate coloured people in the colonies without the Empire?' Then, pointing a finger around the room he asked, 'How would these poor countries who depend so much on us for their present and future economies possibly survive in managing their own affairs?'

He turned towards Mrs Bacall and asked very politely what priorities she would have for the future if she wielded the necessary power to make them come about.

Mrs Bacall rose, but headed towards the door, intent on making her departure. 'All I want,' she seemed to say through rigid jaws, 'is that husbands are returned as soon as possible and assume the responsibilities of their families. I have not been out anywhere worth speaking about for almost a year, nor have I been able to buy a thing to wear except for the cheapest and plainest of clothing. The biggest sin in this country seems to be in trying to live a normal life, and how "one" goes about that now just seems impossible. Who "one" is nowadays apparently doesn't matter any more. The quicker this war is over with everyone back to their own station in life and everything else back to normal again, the better it will be for all.'

It was very obvious that she did not care to listen to what other people had to express in the way of opinions.

'I will say good night.' She left the room and a short time later the front door was slammed shut.

Strangely enough, most of the guests present had the feeling that Mrs Bacall had lost something which neither money nor privilege could replace, and that she had come here quite alone because she had permitted no-one to become close enough to her with whom she could share anything of a personal nature, maybe even grief. Spoilt she had most certainly been and selfish she most certainly was, yet somehow at this moment they all felt sorry for her. There was the one exception and that was Mr McGrith.

Edna suddenly appeared after having somehow crept in at some point and was now down on one knee in front of the fireplace. She struck a match and lit the paper of the prepared fire. After a few moments she removed the decorative front piece from the ash-collecting area beneath the grate, then stretched a newspaper across the front of the fire. This caused a rush of air to be drawn in at the bottom and travel up through the fire into the chimney. There was a slight rushing sound for a few moments while she held the paper and the fire burned bright. When she was satisfied the fire was well alight she took away the newspaper and replaced the ashpit front.

Recovering from the unexpected departure of the lady, the permanent boarder wondered if it had to do with anything he had said, then very quickly decided against such a possibility. He surprised everyone now by asking Edna what special 'something' there was that she hoped would or should not happen after the war.

Edna spoke. 'I would not want to see a future where there was a secret police force or ordinary people spying on each other or where political youth groups were indoctrinated with what other people thought. Equally it would be terrible if everyone just suited themselves and scrounged off their family or some charity. That would be another terrible road to follow. I want people to be allowed to do their own thinking in their own time and in their own particular way. I would also very much like to see certain people in public office being reminded periodically that they were public servants. The worst thing that could happen would be for authority to be removed from home and classroom and placed in the hands of others who could wield it politically over young impressionable groups and manipulate them as easily as one could control that wireless on the table.'

She pointed to the object in question, then continued, 'They could be switched on and off when it suited them to do so, or they could choose to make them listen only to what others most wanted them to hear. They could change their output capabilities with a flick of a switch and adjust their volume to suit the occasion.'

Edna promptly finished and theatrically bowed to the applause then instantly vanished from the room.

The atmosphere was warming as the guests were steadily becoming more relaxed and showing greater interest in what was being said as the evening wore on.

Bob Farrow tried to catch the self-appointed chairman's eye and, failing in this, after a few moments started to speak. 'I think we all agree with what has been said by Edna.' There was a pause that allowed the sounds of general assent for his opening remarks to be heard. Then he swiftly carried on speaking. 'If I may pick up on what was said just prior to the time when Mrs Bacall was asked to speak, I would like to remind the listeners that many great and mighty empires have come and gone in times past and I fail to understand why any of the countries that Mr McGrith has in mind cannot govern themselves. After all, they seemed to have managed for a long time before any of them had ever seen a white man, even allowing for an error on the Creator's part.'

He continued after the short silence which he hoped was caused by the audience thinking over what he had just said. Addressing the senior resident he said, 'I think the generation of your class draws a curtain of respectability over the cracks and flaws in your society.'

He turned round to look in his fellow boarder's direction. 'Tom has mentioned one of those cracks already this evening. Let me tell you of another flaw. I am a Jew who, like so many others, is quite willing to fight for what I think is correct, and being peaceful by nature should never be taken by anyone as a sign of weakness. But loyalty to the country of my birth is never in question for I would still be in this room if Hitler had not raised a finger against my race.'

He stopped for breath before resuming in a rather abrupt fashion. 'What I have said gives me the right to ask why it is that some of the most reputable golf clubs in this country bar Jews from membership? I think there are a number of undesirable symptoms in our society that will have to change, and the first break with the past must be the removal of the false prestige which so much wilfulness and bad taste can hide behind.'

The sound of Anne Ziegler and Webster Booth could be faintly heard coming from the kitchen wireless. They were singing the love duet from *La Bohème*.

Mr McGrith was now decidely uncomfortable and, looking directly at Helen, blustered out, 'If there is any such curtain in our society it is to protect the embarrassment of those whose behaviour falls short of that expected from them.'

He was going to say more but Edna appeared silently carrying a tray laden with cups of tea and a plate of plain biscuits through the unclosed doorway.

'Who knows?' she claimed. 'I might dream tonight about spending a fraction of all that wealth made from the Empire that wasn't thrown out of tenement or golf club windows to impoverished singers.'

She must have overheard what was being said before entering the room, but with apparent ease and disinterest moved from person to person before prodding the fire with a poker and placing a few pieces of coal on top of it. Then she was gone, and this time the door was closed firmly behind her.

Jean broke the silence by stressing the hope that after the war there would be greater fairness to the women who would be left without a husband to support them, and especially those with young children. 'Perhaps,' she said, 'this free medical help for everyone that has already been talked about tonight might be available in their lifetime. Wouldn't it be nice if war pensions were made more generous for widow and wounded alike? Paltry pensions are demeaning and a constant source of resentment.'

Bill had moved across the room and was now standing beside Helen.

The oldest guest thanked Jean in a light-hearted manner that gave the impression he considered what she had said 'pie in the sky'. The listeners had already detected a feeling that he now wanted to return to his original tack, and no doubt at the same time endeavour to win at least someone to his way of thinking. He then briefly mentioned the young Scots of both sexes who had gone out to the colonies to work and help to prepare such places in adjusting to the modern world.

This was the perfect time now for Bill the Canadian to speak. 'My father came from Scotland, but he was not one of the young men that have just been mentioned. In his case he had been one boy of a quota that had been sent over to Canada from the orphanage that had been the only home he had ever known. He was given no choice in the matter. The system was such that a number of the children were sent to Canada while others were dispatched to each of the other Commonwealth countries.'

Molly had entered the room and taken up a position standing behind one of the easy chairs, mouthing a silent apology and signalling an encouragement for Bill to continue.

Bill carried on. 'My dad tried at various times to find out who his parents were and if he had any brothers or sisters, but he received little or no help. Sometimes he claimed it was of little importance but I'm certain there was a hankering to know if he had any family at all back in his home country simply for his own peace of mind. It don't think that could be considered very unusual. It might sound silly of me to say that I'm fighting for what my father missed or thought he missed in this country, and I rather like to think he's both pleased and proud of me for doing so. He married a bonny Canadian lass of Scot descent and through their sacrifice and insistence I studied at Hamilton University where I met Bob.'

He nodded toward his friend. 'And from discussions with him and others I now believe that people fight for personal, as well as political reasons. There seems little doubt that most of us are influenced by the attitudes of those closest to them.'

He stopped speaking for a few seconds as though deciding to finish. 'What I would like to see after the war are closer ties with the Commonwealth and all its peoples and markets. It would be a great pity if it were to be otherwise.'

The general nodding of heads indicated that all the present company thoroughly agreed with him.

Mr McGrith now had the ghost about Mr Farrow and his visit to Hamilton well and truly laid to rest, but he still had to say something. 'It would be unthinkable to contemplate that the special place held by Britain for the Commonwealth countries could possibly be set aside in preference for trading with any other single or group of countries. In any case, there is only one other English-speaking country, namely America, and any special trading alliance with them at the expense of our traditional English-speaking countries would be totally out of the question.'

Molly gave the impression she would not be staying very long, and was asked by her permanent boarder, who sensed she was soon to leave, 'What change would you like to see, Molly, when this is all over? Mrs Wilson has just suggested there should be free medical treatment for everyone regardless of one's social station.'

The very thought of such a thing was summarily dismissed by him with a patronising, exaggerated, patient smile and a carefree flick of his wrist. He then said in a gallant fashion, 'I'm sure we would all like to hear what you have to say.'

Molly gave a hearty laugh and said, 'Well! You mean around here? I would like to hope that an awful lot of people would want to fly Tiger Moths or Avro Ansons to keep our aerodrome busy, but it will probably go back to the farmers to grow potatoes in. It would be nice to think that maybe some day I might have a prosperous commercial and international passenger airport on my doorstep.'

She paused as though not knowing whether to stop or carry on. 'From a more serious point of view, and one I shared with my late husband, I hope that the level of assistance to the most needy inside our community will steadily rise. The super-rich have reached a peak where they can get nothing more out of each twenty-four hours than the wealthiest did fifty years ago, or in each and all the fifty years before that, whereas, the worst-off have very slowly bettered over the same time. The word "poverty" will remain, but what I hope will happen is that its living level during each current generation will steadily rise. If war does anything it brings change and I just hope the end of this one will mean a greater fairness in the way people live out their lives. And now I must check that the black-out is all right and attend to the hot water bottles. If I don't I will be in trouble from both outside and inside these walls.'

Ignoring Tony, Mr McGrith asked Sina what she thought about the future and what it would bring, which was taken for granted by all to mean – 'After we have won the war what would you like to see happen?'

Sina wasn't used to being asked for an opinion in front of strangers and quietly replied that she thought Britain would simply return to what and where it had been at the time before Hitler came along. She presumed the country would be in a much stronger international position after winning the war.

Mr McGrith nodded in full agreement and gave the impression that at last the conversation was coming round to his way of thinking.

Sina continued, 'To be quite honest with you, geography was never my best subject, and that includes the Commonwealth. For instance, I have never known or spoken to an Indian. Several times I have seen one around the suburbs, carrying a large suitcase containing fabric goods of Indian origin that he was peddling around from door to door. I have heard people call him Indian Johnny.'

She looked down at her feet for a few moments as though slightly embarrassed at what she had said. It also gave her time to think of what next to say. 'The only black people I have seen have been on the screen during visits to the picture house and the impression I am always left with is that they all appear to be good faithful servants and workers outside Africa, and mighty warriors inside it.' She stopped before loudly stating, 'What I would dearly love to have is first hand knowledge of what foreign people are really like and what life is really like inside their own countries.' She paused long enough to make her listeners wonder if she had finished, but started again. 'Our church had a group of women who, up until the outbreak of the war, both made and collected what was called, "Clothes for the Heathen", to which I as a young girl contributed several semmits that I had cut out and sewed up myself.' She gave a guilty look. 'I have often wondered who wore them. I am well aware that the Hollywood films we see are all part of a make-belief illusion, but they must give us some inkling of truth about what the countries they were filmed in are like. Those travel films that always finish bidding farewell as the sun sets or sinks in the West acts as a sort of magic carpet that carries me away to distant places where I could otherwise never manage to go. It would be nice if the world could be made small enough to be seen in my own front room.' She smiled at such a thought, then continued, 'Travelling is so slow and terribly expensive and that's not likely to change, but in any case even if it were financially possible for ordinary people, I don't think the average person could ever find the time to visit foreign places.'

Her eyes seemed to darken and the tone of her voice changed slightly, which brought an immediate quietness to the room. 'We have reason to be ashamed at much of our treatment of peoples whose culture differs from our own. I hope that social morality, legal morality and commercial morality will one day mean the same thing.'

Her face was still slightly aglow. Then, in true Gallic fashion, she shrugged her shoulders and spread her artistic hands in front of her as a sign she had finished what she had to say.

The listening group all nodded in total agreement with what Sina had said. Mr McGrith reminded them that the only purpose in going abroad was for a restful and cultural visit to some interesting place, and therefore there was very little likelihood of working class people crowding out the popular resorts abroad. 'If that happened, then the gentle folk would have something to complain about. It's rather like saying that everyone will some day have their own motor car.' That thought apparently amused him.

Edna reappeared and moved towards a corner of the room, telling everyone about a young local man who tried to shoot himself when he received his call-up papers, and as fortune favoured him, he apparently missed. 'The Army,' she insisted, 'still took him, saying they would teach him to fire a gun properly and accurately.'

She retrieved an ancient one-bar electric heater from the corner and placed it on the hearth rug, then pushed its two pin plug into the nearby socket fitted into the wide skirting board running round the room.

Sina asked, 'Did you ever hear what happened to him?'

'Oh!' Edna replied after she had straightened herself up and retrieving the tray. 'The last I heard of him he had knocked down and nearly killed a major while learning to drive one of those American jeep things.' She deftly and quietly collected the supper items and gently closed the room door behind her.

Perhaps it was the look of the thing that had just been plugged into the electric supply or perhaps it was the dying fire, but somehow or another the room felt a few degrees colder.

Tony reminded the attendant guests that his origins had a culture developed long before the rest of Europe had developed theirs, and in those early days the soldiers of Rome appeared to have been competent enough and very much aware where they were going. He added lightly, 'You can laugh at that. It was meant to be humorous.'

Tony continued, 'I'm as Scottish as anyone here, and proud of the place where I was born. I will wear a uniform and fight if I'm asked to because I think our way of life is second to none. I have been well educated and have degrees in science and chemistry. Some people find something derogatory in my name or my Latin looks. They make jokes about the shape of my nose or some other feature but most of us can tell the difference between underlying menacing humour and landlady jokes. I have had my share of spaghetti and pasta sarcasms from stupid uneducated strangers. Nevertheless I would always proudly wear a British Forces uniform to fight for our style of living and all the various methods and means there are on this island of doing it.' He waited as though he expected a remark of some kind but none came and he carried on. 'When I was a child in the days before the war, one of the spin-offs of being British and having an empire was an adequate supply of cheap rice in the local Co-op. At the same time many Indian children were emaciated and others dying because of famine. It don't want any child of mine getting a second course of rice pudding at that cost.'

Tony then looked into the faces watching him, and continued, 'Sina and I are leaving tomorrow, but if I were given a wish for the future it would be that the men and women who fall in this war will be the last names ever to be placed on a war memorial.'

Mr McGrith noticed Helen looking at her watch and, as though anticipating her next movement, he asked her in a patronising manner what it was that she would like to see happen or be changed after the war.

Helen looked around in a confident manner before starting to reply. 'Single women with children have already been mentioned this evening, but in the cases I'm referring to I would like to mention the hope that the churches, along with society in general, would lower the sights of their ideals in this matter and stop the continual repetition of first rushing to defend the high moral ground or whatever at the time is more important to them, and stop behaving like campaigning politicians who like to be seen on the surface as honest, untainted and sunbeam-splashed. I'm not going to argue over rights or wrongs or good and bad. What I will say is that it is difficult, if not impossible, at present or any other time, for something as old and natural as producing a child to be placed neatly between two orderly lines on a behaviour pattern. Saints or sinners rarely differ when they reach a sexual point of no return.'

Mr McGrith seemed to be experiencing great difficulty in finding a relaxed position in his easy chair. He was very obviously finding what he was hearing to be disagreeable to him, but the lady continued. 'No-one in their sane senses condones irresponsibility, yet there always appears to be so much confusion over loose ends which seem to differ with each case one hears about. Who would have thought there could be so many versions of the same old story? Some will blame the unmarried mother and give plenty of reasons for so doing; others will blame the absent father and give endless cause for holding such grounds, and of course parents will be criticised for being either naive, lax or even uncaring. Whichever way one is orientated on this subject surely no-one can lay any part of the blame on the child of such a union. Why then must a birth certificate be produced when applying for certain jobs if not to weed out the illegitimates?'

Helen paused for a few moments but only to change her tack and enjoy the continuing anguish on a certain mature face. 'I have the feeling at this moment that I'm speaking like a schoolmistress, but whatever you think, there will be times when each one of us here will become very vulnerable, and therefore fallible to a gender situation that might appear without effort or design on your part.

'It would be over-simplifying it to say that no father should desert the mother carrying his child. What would happen, Mr McGrith, if a winning army suddenly ran off after a successful battle? I suppose I could say that's what happened to my niece's father who supposedly ran off to sea. The whole story of what happened I will never know, and I will tell you why, but first, for those who have noted I'm a single woman, let me also tell you that I'm a qualified schoolteacher who, if ever she decided to marry, would have to give up her profession, as school boards do not employ married lady teachers. Not only do we have to contend with that, but there are a large number of silly bigoted people who do not even think it is correct for unmarried ladies to be in charge of a child that bears her maiden name and whose father is unknown.'

She looked about her defiantly then continued, 'My younger sister made the age-old mistake of falling in love with the wrong man. She gave birth to his child but by then he was well away from the area and could not be traced. It might have been the pointing fingers and innuendos outside her home or the shame of the guilt concerning the child's future and the anguish brought upon her family being carried constantly in her mind when inside her home. Either way it will never be known for certain. No! She was never told by her father "To go and never darken the doorstep again," but nevertheless she wanted to wash herself free of a "something" she just could not rid herself of. Perhaps she might have finally accepted that the man she loved had merely used her and would never return.

'One night she took a sharp knife from the kitchen, after having run a hot bath. She locked herself in the bathroom. Later, as she lay naked in the water, she cut deeply into both of her wrists. That was how she found her final peace of mind.'

No-one attempted to speak during the long pause that followed. Helen continued, 'I've been asked what I would like to see happen when this war has ended. It would be nice if a lot more people developed a greater understanding and compassion towards those in need of comfort and support. I'm not endorsing selfishness or lack of thought, nor downright badness. I'm talking about the person who has been let down by someone who was trusted – and that is the difference. If damnation or accountability there must be, then leave it to juster and safe hands on a much higher plane than our mortal one.'

She looked at the clock on the mantelpiece, then stood up saying that she had to meet her niece who had been at a youth activity in the church hall. She gave a brief nod to the company, adding a quiet, 'Good night.'

Bill called to Bob in a stage whisper that he would meet him shortly later on. He was pointing somewhere in the direction of the window, which apparently made sense to his fellow countryman. He went out into the hallway, somehow having managed to get himself between Jim and Jean and listening to both of them who were talking to him at the same time.

The other Canadian followed Helen out of the room and patiently waited until she put her coat on and the other guests had discreetly gone their separate ways, leaving one person who still remained quietly seated. It was there, in the privacy of the cold hallway with some rather grim people looking down from prints hanging on the wall, that he asked her quietly if it would be possible for him to write to her as he would very much like to keep in touch.

Someone passed them and a voice rather like Edna's was heard to say something about there being plenty of married female teachers in Canada.

Back in the front room the sole occupant appeared to look very small sitting in the large armchair. It may have been fluctuations in the voltage due to one of the numerous power surges, caused by emergency demands, or it may have been a trick of the light but it seemed as though several spotlights had been trained on him, and were now being switched off one at a time.

Mr McGrith could not remember a time during any of the evening discussions held in this same room since he had been at the house when there had not been at least one person who agreed with him in what he had thought. After all, what he had said and stood for in the past had always been proper and correct. He thought the whole social muddle was because the classes had never been so intermixed as they were today, due, of course, to the war. He still convinced himself that these new attitudes and the talked about changes would sort themselves out once everything was back to what it used to be. His mind flitted back to that brazen woman's outspoken comments about sex and being in charge of young children. Some people just didn't know where to stop and are nothing but troublemakers. The thought passed his mind that the sister who got herself into such a mess most likely had herself to blame.

Edna suddenly appeared. 'You're the last one tonight, Mr McGrith,' she said, then added cheerfully, 'You're also looking very tired. I remember once working for a lady whose face never seemed to change no matter how she felt or what she was doing. One day I asked her what the secret in her make-up was. "My dear," she said, "there's no mystery in my make-up, it only takes longer to put on." '

The mystified guest just looked at her in alarm. 'I'm, er, yes, having an early night myself, but after I stretch my legs first.'

'Hope it's not too busy. It's a dark night so don't walk into a lamppost on your way back,' said Edna. She quickly wandered about the room, checking that nothing had been left, then pulled the electric fire connection from its fireside wall socket. Before leaving she added softly, 'Good night, Mr McGrith.'

The elderly gentleman remained seated, casting his mind carefully back again over the evening. He recalled how each of the guests, as though by prompting, had said something which struck a sensitive chord somewhere in the back of his mind. He thought again and then corrected himself for it hadn't been only the visitors but the staff as well. He felt slightly drained by the events of the evening. It was as though all the persons present had been cast in a prepared production and the entire evening orchestrated by some outside influence. The fact that they each seemed to be an average cross-section of ordinary intelligent people caused him more than a slight irritation. With a feeble shake, or was it a shudder, he decided that he was beginning to imagine things. He consoled himself with his vision of a future peacetime Britain after the Allies had finally given the Hun and their Axis allies a well-deserved thrashing that knocked some sense into them. The country could then return to the same manner and standards of living that he had been reared in. Yes! Back to the good old days of what used to be. The image of Mrs Bacall momentarily flitted in front of him and he thought the evening would have been better for him had she not left so early. Like her he still could not think what was wrong with each person keeping to their own social station and obeying the laws of the land. He started to feel a bit tired and just wanted to remain sitting where he was for a few minutes longer. Strange, he didn't usually feel this way after one of his organised discussions.

Outside in the hall Helen started to say something, then paused as though to choose her words carefully. 'Please try to understand that my first thought must be for . . .'

He never let her finish for he insisted rather urgently, 'That's not what I asked you.'

Helen capitulated. 'Yes,' she said. 'I'd like that very much.'

At least one thing had not been changed by the war, and as if to prove it, the couple had the feeling that the framed faces on the wall actually smiled down their agreements and approvals.

There was then another unusual occurrence. Edna suddenly made her appearance, walking through the hallway. She gave the young couple an exaggerated knowing look, and passed on without saying a word.

4

Father firmly believed that each young man should make his own way in the world and expected him to produce the necessary effort that would be required to do so. He also believed that parents should supply the assistance and support that any of their children required during their school or university years. Failure was not a word he ever used and he would have discouraged any of his family ever thinking of it. Having said these virtuous things about my father, I must mention the one big flaw in his attitude. He expected to be asked for his assistance in any school homework that wasn't understood by his offsprings, and schoolchildren being what they were was itself the weakness. Father became impatient if any one of us did not grasp his explanation quickly. Mother was more helpful with homework than Father was. He certainly gave support in the sense that none of his family had the distress of a cold home, empty larder, lack of clothing to wear, or games or books to read. No, I could not fault him in supporting his family, and that in turn automatically made it easier to mould the May children into the shape and direction he wanted.

Mother did not hold any strong political views, and as far as I know she voted Unionist at the ballet box, as I know Father did. With her ideas of compassion, cleanliness and neatness I'm afraid her politics would have appeared rather over-simplified to Father, although their underlying political themes must have been compatible. Mother was busy in many other ways apart from her dressmaking. The whole house was her workshop, and this she managed with apparent ease. Food and feeding were made to seem so simple. She had always supported her church by attending regular Sunday as well as mid-week services and contributed goods (mostly baking), along with her personal time to the various church functions. She had her social life in visiting and being visited according to some age-old schedule worked out between her and friends of long standing.

Not so very long before the war started I spent a long convalescence at home, and during that time I met most of her friends when they came to the house, and whom I had heard of only as names up to that period. There was Mrs McBride, a widow who called regularly and who seemed particularly able in obtaining anything from a mangle to a wash-hand basin. She was in the business of getting items of this and that cheaper than others could, and I think she must have had a treasure trove of bits and pieces at home. It says a lot for her that of her three children the eldest turned out to be a minister of the church and other two became schoolteachers.

Both Mother and my godmother had been seamstresses together as girls and were both now married with my godmother staying in Blackpool and running a guest house with her husband. She never forgot my birthday or any other particular event. She visited me during my illness when she brought me a jacket and short trousers for when I was fit and well again. I never saw her after that as she died during the early part of the war. Shortly before her death I received a book from her. It was a large beautiful red and gold bound 'Waverley Illustrated Shakespeare' bearing the inscription 'To Ian with love from Elizabeth Linton, 1940'. For some reason that I never found out, I thought she knew we would never meet again after that pre-war visit. I learnt much later that my godmother died from cancer.

During that enforced stay at home I also got to know Mrs Burke who came once a week (I think) to help in the house. She was Irish and probably in her fifties. She wasn't very tall but what she lacked in height she made up for in width and good humour. She would say something funny that would be followed by a great roar of uncontrollable laughter. I was told that her husband was blind; later I learnt he had a drink problem. Apparently he liked to spend all his cash on drinking and betting, and no matter where she hid any money at home he would always manage to find it. My only early conception of a blind person was Poor Blind Pew from the pages of *Treasure Island*, and in my imagination this is how I pictured Mr Burke, rummaging around the household as though searching for pieces of eight. Mrs Burke told me she had to carry all her money on her person each day, and I seemed to have been left with the impression that she kept it all in a large knicker pocket. She must have been a poor woman in the material sense, but she had a sparkle that riches alone could never buy.

Mother was an early riser and was ever the lark of the family as Father was the owl. She was always up between six and seven in the morning with the kitchen fire ablaze before the rest of the family were out of their beds. Plates of porridge were often put out on the window sill to cool, depending on the urgency of the moment at breakfast time. We had our dinner at midday, which was the usual time in each home to have it; probably it was thought that children needed a warm-up at that time. During the afternoon Mother would come in beside me for a 'wee rest' as she termed it, and it must have been just that, for she would be speaking to a visiting friend or be dressmaking by three thirty, and a little while later the family would start arriving home in penny numbers shortly after four o'clock from school. Then she would slip into her role of homemaker to her children. Father, as I recall, must have arrived home just before six o'clock and that was then tea-time (a substantial hot meal with bread and butter including biscuits or something similar).

I hope the reader doesn't think that my parents were dull, for that is the last impression I would like to give of them. Father was straight and strict, yet the family was quite relaxed in his company. Mother had a serious and artistic side to her nature. She was also good fun.

Mother was good at sketching, a gift she passed on to each of her daughters. During one part of her career she occasionally visited Paris to catch up with the latest ladies' fashions, which I assume she sketched and brought back to her employers Simpson, Hunter &

Young of Buchannan Street, for their clientèle. There was an impressive sketch on the wall at home that Mother had done as a young woman of the family dog and it was often admired.

Wartime is not the best of times to recall the role of men in the household through young eyes, but first I will draw on my earlier impressions of the female gender. The role of women is much easier to recall. As a young boy I was brought up at home by Mother and on my first day at school was handed over to a Mrs Moore. Later on I was a Cub under the watchful eye of Akela (Mrs Boxer). The church Sunday school that I attended had all female teachers, and the church choir included both sexes, so even there I was under the eagle eyes of both soprano and contralto. A matter of a week or so before the war started I was handed over to Mrs Dunn, and later, when I stayed in digs, I was once again in the hands of a woman. After that it was back to Mother and all things being normal and equal I would have remained with her until being handed over to a wife. Such was the early pattern I followed during my innocent years, although it did alter later on, during my latter school days. I do not think such an upbringing harmed me. In all probability it was just the influence a young male required, providing the correct balance was struck, and I would like to think it was, by me respecting each of the women in my formative years. Good women teachers at an early age also make it more normal for a male to heed what is said by the opposite sex when he is into manhood.

Any activity in the home was carried out by the women of the house. All mothers appeared to be the mistresses of their own home; family affairs, budgeting, feeding, cleaning or any other function was her business. As a little boy I would always have to ask the mother of the house I was in if I could use the bathroom. I would never have dreamed of asking the father of the household. Men tended to ignore children unless specifically introduced to them when visiting a home of a friend, but this was rare because they were usually at work. The smiles of welcome and any interest shown to me in other homes always came from the woman of the house, and no visiting child that was without parents was important enough to be given more than a cursory polite nod from someone else's father whose arrival was usually the cue for young playing friends of the family to leave.

Children were firmly supervised and controlled by women and when I left those childish years behind me, this all-female world of teachers and tenders must have shaped some part of what I am today.

Since moving up from the Cubs into the Boy Scouts in early 1939 which was only a matter of months before being evacuated, until the time I now speak of (1943), I had increasingly entered a man's world. Comparing the men with my earlier memories of their pre-war counterparts, I recall the latter seemed in their homes to do an awful lot of sitting down by their fireside. They were seated when they read, listened to the wireless or when you talked to them. They had naps in the chair when enjoying the fire-side and rose only to sit down again in front of a meal. No-one ever sat in 'Father's chair' if he was in the vicinity or even when expected home. Perhaps this was a woman's ploy to keep him from getting under her feet. They seemed totally redundant. I cannot remember any one of them being enterprising or energetic enough to fill a kettle with water or place coal on the fire; such domestic chores were done by others. It may well be that the home in those days had to be a sanctuary for those who went out to work. I think it would be safe to say that the treatment Father received set the scale or tone of the general social pecking order of the working sons and daughters with the children being fitted in somewhere at the bottom. Mothers not only ran a home – they ran a refuge as well.

It would be very naive of me to think that my parents never had an argument. To have had a perfect father and saintly mother would have been very dismal indeed. Whenever they did have a difference between each other, it was never within hearing distance of the children, or if it was it was explained away. This protective behaviour did me no harm, and probably gave me a sense of security at that time, and developed in me for later years the attitude that family business was family business and part of being a responsible adult.

By some means I cannot recall I started to learn that in some other homes there lacked a stability which mine appeared to have. It was probably a mixture of subtle motherly teachings, having an older brother and mixing with other school children. Excessive alcoholic drinking, with its numerous spin-off effects, was well-known to young adolescents, and it was 'big stuff' to talk about it. I must confess I don't recollect much sex around at the time, but the lid was kept pretty tight on that subject in those days.

About that same time I started to hear about the drink and violence which was prevalent in certain deprived areas of my own city, which I was mercifully spared. 'No Mean City' appeared and disappeared as it flitted its way from before young eyes. Middle class children heard about slum conditions but never saw deprivation, and I can only report here what I remember of that time. Many books have been published about the seamier side of Glasgow by much more competent authors than I.

Father, for all his Conservative leanings, had a great admiration for the Socialist leaders of the thirties and forties, and spoke affectionately of Manny Shinwell in particular, whom I think he knew personally at one time. He talked of the intellectual, out-spoken men that formed the nucleus of the Labour movement. It must have taken some doing on his part to say that, considering his views about making one's way in this world by hard and loyal work, and if one also played a good round of golf, so much the better.

Back in Glasgow and now a young adult I felt I was still living, energetic-wise, in the same mode as during my final year at school. When I found time to study I just don't know, though I do remember doing homework. I'm sure everyone remembers the carefree hours rather than those requiring persevering effort. Maybe burning off our energy as we did was not discouraged.

Up till now I had taken so much for granted but slowly I was beginning to realise that family and homes just didn't happen. The freedom I had enjoyed was the kind of freedom a wild young animal has but for a young human adult that freedom was curtailed by what was called responsibility. Now I was discovering that family and relationships were moulded and each took effort.

Before I left Prestwick I had already chosen to be a marine engineer. But I had two years before my call-up was due, which would be ample time to find out if I had made the wrong choice. Shortly after my return to Glasgow I wrote to Barclay Curle &

Coy, Ltd, Ship & Engine Builders, Whiteinch, which was a well-known Clydeside company. I did this on advice given by Dad after he had enquired of an engineer colleague who, as it turned out, had served his apprenticeship there and recommended that I apply to them. There was also a lady in the same office who had a brother employed at BC, which more or less settled the matter of which company I should write to.

I was more than pleasantly surprised and excited when my application was acknowledged; my interview was for ten o'clock on the following Thursday morning. I arrived at the office in South Street with half an hour to spare. There was another applicant about the same age as myself and who, like me, was probably hoping that two apprentices were required that morning. We waited together in the reception area for what seemed to me to be ages before he was asked to see Mr Wilson, the works manager. In what seemed to be only a few minutes later, I was asked to present myself, and in doing so I passed this other boy, who gave a resigned smile with a shake of his head.

That day I was lucky. I was accepted as an apprentice journeyman, and told to report to a Mr White, head foreman of the engine works at 8 a.m. on Monday morning. I was to tell the gateman on my arrival at the works entrance who I was and he would give me an employee's works number; then he would direct me to the head foreman's office. I was to be suitably dressed in a blue boiler suit, a stout pair of shoes and a deep sea cap.

I had managed through my first interview for a job and I do not think I said very much apart from a few Yeses and Nos. I think I must have been expecting something like an examination of the type I had at school, and did not expect it to be over so quick. Mr Wilson gave the impression he was a very busy man and was merely slotting my interview in as an added chore to his hectic morning. What he was probably trying to do was to let me know that apprentices were on the bottom rung of the engine works social ladder.

Up till now my slight hearing loss had been of little significance as I had more or less always been in the company of clear speaking voices. The only time I experienced any inconvenience was when there was background noise, or when the direction of the voice sound was not travelling towards me, as when someone spoke when they were walking away from me. Sometimes in the shops and certainly in the swimming pool where the background sounds were bounced around from tile to tile, I often had to rely on the expression in the face as to where the voice came from and to know whether to smile or otherwise, and I think I became quite apt at this guessing game. I did it because I found out a long time ago that if I kept on asking people to repeat what they were saying too often, then as sure as not they would shout with a shake of the head that it was of no matter, or tap the side of their head and call out that they had a terrible memory and had forgotten what they said. This behaviour led to the possibility that their performance would be repeated in some other place where I heard every word they spoke. I could hear quite well where wood or soft fabrics were about me, whereas it was difficult for me to tune in properly inside a stone church, and I found it hard not to let my mind wander when I could not follow the sermon. The one situation I tried to avoid, and still do, is to be landed with the sales girl with the dull accent and the high pitched voice; but apart from what you have just read I wouldn't change my ears for anyone.

In later years I sometimes wondered what happened to the young man I spoke to for these few minutes at my interview. Unfortunately he spoke with what was called 'that terrible Glasgow accent,' or, inferred with a knowing look, 'You know the accent I mean.'

During our brief meeting I had great difficulty in making out what he was saying and what I did understand sounded pretty awful to my ears. His voice was impoverished of tone or melody and with scant pronunciation. It was difficult for me, an inexperienced middle class boy, to understand why some parents, no matter how poor they were, could not at least insist that their children speak with an acceptable accent which would allow them to communicate and compete with other youths from any part of the same land. How innocent I was! Accents are extremely attractive and Scotland has an Aladdin's Cave of that particular commodity, spoken by rich and poor alike, but somehow or another a part of Glasgow did have this inability to use the tongue and lips, causing a lazy language malaise at one end of the speech scale in stark contrast to the first class Scot's speech quality which the city can boast at its other.

If I ever came out with any Glasgow slang or slurred my words, I was immediately chastised by my parents at home, or by my teacher at school. I could never quite understand why such a progressive and cultural city did not go to the heart of the problem in all its schools, especially then, when discipline and control were in the hands of the teachers. Looking back at that particular time it may well have suited a certain group that this should have been so, bearing in mind that 'academic born losers' make a reliable work force in the low wage work places.

What I am writing about is speaking and learning by ear. Nothing to do with split infinitives or the ending of sentences with prepositions. It wasn't until later in life that I found out – or stumbled across – the useless or otherwise information (to me) that Latin has neither prepositions at the end of sentence nor splitable infinitives. I suppose the insistence on having the same rules in English survives from the days when Latin was taken as a model for English grammar. To me that seems an absurd reason to cramp the style and colour of speakers and writers.

What I have just written about accents I hope will not be construed as snobbish, but I must point out here that there is an immense difference between slang and Old Scots Tongue. There can be no confusion between the two. I never considered myself advantaged at my first interview for a job in the sense that I was better equipped than the other applicant. I do not think I thought that for one minute, but looking back – I was.

It may sound strange if I tell you that the use of Old Scots words had a greater impact on me than the use of modern English. I learnt at a very young age, that when Father said, 'Be quiet,' he really meant, 'Quieten down,' but if he came away with, 'Wheesht,' then it was a command for instant silence.

Children have an inbuilt impertinent habit of answering back, as it was called, and no doubt still is, but under such confrontational circumstances I was aware that when told, 'Don't answer back,' it merely meant I was not to interrupt until whoever it was had finished speaking. Whereas to be told, 'Hold your tongue,' or 'Haud yir tongue,' spoken in a sharp tone meant not only instant silence but also to stand absolutely still and listen to what was being said to me or others. It is strange how men revert to their original tongue when they are more than just a little annoyed at something or somebody.

It was at such times that I learnt what such words as 'glaikit' and 'daft saftie' meant, and when one of my sisters was being scolded I got to know the meaning of 'a wee besom'. I probably picked up more Scots words and phrases through misbehaviour as a child, than in any other way.

National Scots and dialect words are not always spoken in a hard voice; far from it, especially when a baby or a toddler is involved, but when someone from Glasgow, in a soft spoken drawn out voice says, 'Ay, that'll be right,' it means the speaker has not believed a single word that has just been spoken.

Talking of young days and schooldays makes me wonder how many people remember having used or heard of the abbreviation of the word 'anybody' used by young potential academics in Scottish schools of which I give the following example. 'Has "emdie" seen Wullie anywhere?' And how often was said. 'Y're just a wee clipe (tell-tale).'

I would like to mention an old practice carried out in schools which permitted an older sister to bring a pre-school sibling into her class when the mother required a few bairn-free hours for whatever reason, and thus allowed her the peace of mind of knowing where the child was. My sisters assure me that I was taken to school several times in that fashion. I have no idea when this custom stopped, but it has shades of early family welfare and the very humble beginnings of the crèche or nursery pre-school class.

Many Glasgow parents made sure their young offspring joined associations where they would meet others of the same age and sex, and where there would be rules which they would have to learn and obey. These same children were expected to do tolerably well at school, before being directed into a future which would demand of them an expected level of education, discipline, loyalty and the giving to an employer of a reasonable amount of honest work in return for a remuneration. That was what learning was all about, a preparedness to allow a pupil to function either in continuing with further study, or applying for a job. In many ways it was hard work being middle class. I wonder how much further the young man would have gone had he spoken in a more up-class manner. Perhaps by the time of my writing this he might well be a contented millionaire. I would like to think so. Looking back I would have had more confidence in his future if he had been able to present his qualities through better speaking.

It must happen in every city but I can only talk of the one where I was reared. I have no intention of carrying or claiming any part of the blame or guilt which should be apportioned amongst the patronising persons of both sexes who call it 'Glaswegian delivery' when addressing those who use it, then call it 'Glasgow slang' in the confines of their home when it is heard coming from members of their own family or some select grouping when they are free to express such a view in an open fashion.

At home it was permitted to use expressions like 'Wheesht' (be quiet) or 'Oh dinna be daft' between brothers and sisters or come out with whatever it was you were thinking of at the time, which probably caused a lot of laughter and embarrassment during the innocent years. But like the young boy's habit of licking his plate after a meal (girls didn't do such things) and always inseparable from a parent's or siblings mild rebuke, it was never done when visitors were present. In this fashion we were taught that a standard of behaviour had to be apparent to persons outside the family and it was expected to be our best.

Two dates must have been important in my grandfather's time: 1865 when Lister introduced antiseptic surgery in Glasgow. The other was five years later when Forster's Education Act was passed in 1870 and put elementary education within the reach of all children. Prior to this a wide range of paid professional teaching was charged for at one end of its scale in guineas and at the other end in pennies. Each parish had by law to build a school at this time and this is still evident today by the date shown over their entrances. This act must surely have opened up another world to many and was ultimately to produce a new and not-so-spoilt greater middle class. With the steady growth of industry and the plentiful manufacture of goods which were to supply the demand of Empire and countries the world over, came the modern middle group of society, stretching from the large detached residence in suburbia to the comfortable council house with each having been dependent upon what fate or birthright decided. I was somewhere in between.

I must add something about the part that females played in the family education scene. Economically it was expected that the son or sons should get the opportunity to receive further education and a place at university, and it was hopefully assumed that a daughter would get a secondary school education as far as she would like. From there on it was expected that she would marry a similarly educated man and between them they would produce an educated family. More than often that was how it would work out, and not necessarily only at the upper educational level. There was nothing to stop a daughter with ability going on to university if the family could afford it. Many did. It was generally a matter of large families and their priorities in which the female played the back-up home front part to allow her brothers the privilege of an advanced learning to enter a profession. The importance of education was drummed into son and daughter alike in the growing middle class structure. It contained the people who worked hard for today and lived for the future with its rainy days, rent or house payment, immediate payment of household bills, the schooling of sons and daughters, medical costs and retirement. Their whole life revolved around what could or might lie ahead. To them the present was a time to use whatever means there were inside respectability and love to achieve the family's assured future.

The high standard of women's education was reflected in the teaching roles they held in the field of medicine and church, school and nursing, along with the popular worldwide popular demand for Scottish governesses over a long period of time.

It would be unfair not to mention the onerous task that befell (and befalls) many daughters and unsuspecting daughters-in-law who, without choice, became the natural candidates to care for the ailing elderly or merely ageing relatives. A great many of those untrained and unpaid carers received little satisfaction or recompense in any way. They sacrificed a great part of their personal lives, a share which some of the persons being cared for and other members of the same family took very much for granted and without gratitude.

But back again to my particular reality and time-spot. I was excited with the result of my interview and couldn't get home quick enough with the news. Both parents seemed happy enough over the outcome although it was some time later that I found out that it was more because I would not be called up for active service the following year when I would be seventeen, rather than because I was going to start an apprenticeship. I think they had something else in mind for me, but wars alter circumstances.

The following day Mum took me to Paislay's, a well-known shop in the immediate vicinity of the Glasgow Bridge, where the boiler suits and the deep sea cap were purchased. I cannot remember anything about clothing coupons, and in any case, Mother handled the whole family's coupon books. Regarding the cap, I found out very quickly that the Barclay Curle Apprentices, for some reason I never found out, conveniently lost their caps within a few days of starting work. I didn't realise it at the time, but the deep sea cap was one of the forerunners of the safety helmet, and the famous bowler hat, worn by managers and heads of departments, served the same purpose. If you were wondering what a deep sea cap, or bonnet is, then let me say that you have probably seen several, differing in style as they have been worn on nautical heads from the *Mississippi Queen* to the *Queen Mary*.

When I walked through the portals of the Barclay Curle gatehouse that Monday morning I did not fully realise it at the time, but I was entering into another world where I was to start learning the beginnings of a trade and profession that would take me across the oceans of the world to play out my small part in a lifetime of contributing towards the carrying of cargoes along their ocean trade routes. The whole world was somehow or another going to be made smaller just for me.

My first employers, then, were Barclay Curle & Coy, Ltd, Engineers and Shipbuilders, North British Engine Works, 739 South Street, Whiteinch, Glasgow W4, and you can take my word for it that they built the best of ships at their Clydeholm Shipyard, and the best of marine engines in the engine works at Whiteinch where I was now employed. None of what I have just mentioned had anything to do with me as far as I was aware. They have held

THE FIRE GUARD (BUSINESS & GOVERNMENT PREMISES) ORDER, 1943.

In terms of the above Order the following information is required by the Ministry of Home Security and The Scottish Home Department.

1. Full name Ian James May

2. National Registration Number S.H.L.B. 115/5

3. Date of Birth 17th April 1927.

4. Private Address 13, Hamilton Drive,
Kelvinside
Glasgow.

5. (a) Name of Local Authority where you are resident ____________

(b) Is compulsion for fire guard duty with this Authority in force? ____________

6. Are you entitled to total or partial exemption and, if so, for what reason? ____________

7. Are you a member of any service (e.g. Warden, Home Guard, etc?) Indicate date of joining No.

8. Check No. or Department 108.

9. Are you employed on

(a) Permanent dayshift Yes.

(b) Permanent nightshift —

(c) Part-time Day and Nightshift —

All males over school leaving age had to register.

an excellent reputation in the shipping world dating back to 1896, and I wasn't around then.

I started work in August 1943, and although I was not then aware of it, it was the best time of the year to work in the engine shop. This was due to the abundant number of high windows, creating a greenhouse effect from a warm sun. However, in a matter of a couple of months or so I was destined to discover how cold and miserable the river area could be. Yes, Whiteinch was very nice during that wartime August.

During the first half of 1943 I was known on the school register by my full name and for most of the second half I had become No. 108 at the place where I was working. This meant that each morning when passing through the gatehouse I lifted a round copper token, the size and shape of a pre-decimal penny, with the number 108 stamped on it from off a similarly marked hook and dropped it into a box. At 8 a.m. on the dot this collection was immediately removed and another similar box was put in its place. Whoever's token found its way into this other container was 'quartered', meaning that a quarter of an hour was deducted from that person's weekly wage unless there was a very good excuse offered, but for apprentices there was no recourse. The fact that you were allowed through the gatehouse showed how fortunate you were and reflected the benevolence of the employer.

At fifteen minutes past eight another box made an appearance by the same sleight of hand method as the previous one, and for apprentices who found themselves this late it meant reporting to the head foreman, Duncan White, and giving him an explanation which you hoped he would accept. If he did then he would give you a written note to hand to the gatekeeper, allowing you entry into the workshop with half an hour deducted from your wage. If, however, no note was forthcoming then it meant going home, or back to your digs, and returning again after lunch. Whether slightly late, or late, or very late the apprentice in question still had to finally report to his own foreman who read the riot act and usually handed out some punitive task, although it was never openly called that. There was no such thing as a sympathetic ear, and the war had nothing to do with it. Lateness and absenteeism in those day, and not just where I worked, incurred strict measures that applied across the board in all manner of employment. I can't remember being late for work at any time during my apprenticeship, and therefore I never had to stand outside Mr White's office until he noticed me, and ask him for a pass-in note.

Now I was ready to start learning my trade, as it was poetically put, and later on I was to discover what the advantages were, or were not, in so doing. I must stress now that in the days I am talking about there was only one way to become a marine engineer, and I had just stepped on the bottom rung of that ladder. There was plenty of work for an apprentice to do, and very little money for doing it, neither of which bothered me at the time, and for that matter the same went for all the apprentices. The pay packet at the end of the week was important, but it wasn't the uppermost priority in your life at that time. One was frequently reminded and left in no doubt whatsoever at work that we were not there for the money, but to learn a particular craft that would be traditionally taught without the expectation of any show of humour or enthusiasm about your future from supervisor or management. This, of course, did not mean that the lowest of the low did not enjoy themselves, because for some inexplicable reason we did. We must have brought our laughs in from outside the working premises because there was a lot of humour about. The Scottish temperament is such that if it's not you that finishes up with egg on your face, then it's got to be someone who deserves it. Glasgow humour generally keeps its feet on the ground, and very often revolves around tenements and the level-headed people that live in them and there is always an added dash of flavour if a wee dig can be made at any seat of power or officialdom.

Whether it's from Edinburgh, the Borders, the Highlands or from the Isles the humour has its own built-in subtle difference, and each of these areas sent their emissaries, in the form of apprentices, to the Clydeside, so there were plenty of smiles.

Very few of the apprentices had their home in the immediate vicinity of the engine works, but came from all over Glasgow and the surrounding countryside, with a scattering from much further afield in Scotland. Many stayed with relatives or lived in digs, and some had quite a journey from their home at the beginning and end of the day. The penalty for being late and not being allowed entry into the engine works had a sting in the tail, as not only was that day lost, but an extra day had to be worked, which meant apprenticeships lasted for five years plus any penalty time.

There were probably fifteen to twenty fitter apprentices at the engine works during my time there and I cannot remember many of their full names, as we were always known to each other either by our Christian name or simply Thingumajig. One of them was called Jimmy Riddle who was the same age as I was and as we got to know each other we became firm friends. Jimmy lived in Springburn and not very far from the world-known locomotive works. His father worked at Singer's, the sewing machine manufacturer in Clydebank, as a machine turner. During the third year of our indenture Jim coughed up some blood at work, and was later diagnosed as having tuberculosis. It took several years of treatment before he received the all clear from his doctor.

Ian Hunter was a couple of years older than I was, and we worked together for over a year, which meant we must have made a pretty good team. I can always remember his works number as it was one less than mine, one zero seven. I could always tell if he was in before me in the morning, which at the time was neither important nor relevant. Ian, I know, went to sea at the end of his apprenticeship.

Ralph Mills was another apprentice in the same year as I was, and who later carried on into the drawing office, as I did. Somehow or another, between moving from the shop floor to the drawing office, and then, later on, going to sea I slowly lost contact with all my Barclay friends and colleagues apart from two: Alex Bankier, whom I kept in touch with over the years, and Tom Gourley, whom I met up with many years later and who refreshed my memory of my working days in the forties.

It was expected that apprentices would further their own career by attending night school and take the subjects covering the Junior National Certificate, which would later lead on to the Senior National Certificate, and finally an Institute membership. Somewhere during this period of study there would be the breakaway point for those who decided to go to sea as marine engineers and they would attend the courses set by the Ministry of Transport. These courses would allow a candidate to obtain a

Second Class Certificate of Competency and later a First Class Certificate. There were certain conditions which had to be met regarding service at sea before permission was given to sit the final examinations. It was possible to avoid sitting a part of the test questions if one had already attained a required standard in certain subjects. This applied to a lot of young applicants, myself included. There were three types of certificates: Steam, Motor and Combined.

These certificates became better known as 'tickets', and with a 'Chief's Ticket' a marine engineer would be allowed to sign on any British ship, and a lot more foreign ones besides, as a chief engineer. If an engineer was so inclined, it was possible to carry on with further study and gain an Extra First Class Certificate which would mean leaving the sea; for no other reason than to get the maximum benefit from such a certificate one would usually have to work ashore. For the Second and First Certificates the examinations circled around maths, engineering knowledge, construction, electricity and engineering drawing, although the latter stopped fairly early on during the years of study. The use of practical technical sketches were expected from you throughout all your studies and during the whole of your working life. Interpreting drawings and technical sketches was a language you had to learn fluently.

As an apprentice nothing was made easy for you; therefore it would come as no surprise when I tell you that on night school examination nights it was necessary to report to the head foreman for a pass-out note to get away half an hour before finishing time, mostly to catch a tram without queuing just to make sure nothing made you late in getting home on exam night. The half hour was deducted from the wage packet at the end of the week and the time lost would be added to the five year indenture time. I cannot be sure that for each half hour lost, an hour had to be served as was the case in some apprenticeships. For an appointment with the head foreman the ritual was to knock on his door, then wait. He could see quite clearly who you were. The office was a large wooden hut with a flat roof and plenty of window space and situated in a central advantageous position on the shop floor. This, then, was where you had to wait until you were finally asked what it was you wanted (as though he did not know); then you would have to explain why you were there, and in detail. Everything was given so grudgingly. The ice curtain always dropped when you wanted something, yet Mr White was really a very nice man who had his job at his fingertips, and on whom, quite possibly, some apprentices modelled their own professional life style.

At the start of my apprenticeship I travelled to and from home on both the subway and tramcar, the former between Kelvin Bridge and Partick, and the latter between Partick and Whiteinch along Dumbarton Road. I have no recollection of the subway being cold and smoky, but I have of the tram. To travel underground was noisy, draughty, shaky and at peak travelling times very crowded. Sitting upstairs in a fully packed tramcar and often hearing the conductress telling some luckless traveller trying to board, 'C'mon get aff', meant completing my journey in a cigarette smoke haze, which I partly contributed to, and listening to hacking coughs and the clearing of phlegm from choked chesty tubes which sounded the normal dawn chorus for many thousands of workers. Today it would be considered an episode from an unhygienic nightmare.

There were at least three good points about the Glasgow trams. There were plenty of them. They always ran to time unless there was some unforeseen reason like a derailment or accident, and the passengers always reached their destination regardless of rain, smog, fog or ice. Everything seemed to be done to keep the service reliable and litter-free. It was not uncommon to see a Corporation employee out in extreme icy conditions cleaning rails and points with a wire hand brush. Benito Mussolini tried to do with the Italian railways what Glasgow Corporation did with its transport. Can I add a wee bit here by reminding people that there was a notice upstairs saying there was a fine of 40s. for spitting, and another notice downstairs stating there was a fine of 40s. for spitting and smoking. I thought I'd mention that one could get better value for one's fine downstairs.

For some reason or another I associate the first part of my journey to work, that is in the subway, and the first ten minutes on the tram along Dumbarton Road with the winter months, and the remainder of the time along to Whiteinch I somehow or another connect with the summer. I do not think that makes much sense, but for some deep down reason the recollection of these two seasons had their maximum impact on me when travelling through these areas.

Wartime Glasgow during the winter months meant a dark Glasgow and very cold. I was always physically healthy, therefore the basic food that we consumed and the limited amount we were permitted must have contained all the vitamins required by a developing body, yet no-one seemed to give it a second thought. This says heaps for the family cooks. On the subject of food and rationing I suppose each family had its potential Oscar winner who played out his/her part over it. As far as I know no-one ever claimed they were about to die or go stark staring mad because of it. For myself I had already discovered that after the age of seven my angelic smile, through a missing tooth or two plus a spoonful of guile, no longer had the same impact. Therefore in common with my generation regarding food rationing, if I had to do without – then tough luck.

The family, since returning to Glasgow, had stayed in the furnished flat at Hamilton Drive, and I was well aware that it was only a temporary place to stay until a suitable tenement flat turned up. There had been no house building or repairs going on during the war, and with each passing year vacant accommodation was becoming more scarce.

The house in Hamilton Drive was the biggest house I had ever stayed in although we only rented the ground floor rooms. It was set back from the road with a long front garden through which we entered and left the apartment, using the main front door. There were three rooms and a small kitchen with one of the rooms being a lounge. The bathroom was downstairs in the basement where there was a back door into a small yard. There were other rooms in the basement that the owner used as well as the rooms on the floor above us.

During the year I stayed in Hamilton Drive I suffered from terrible leg cramp where my affected muscle would turn as hard as stone. I was told that I was growing too fast, the most common reason for cramp at my age. It always happened when I was in bed during the night, and of course woke me up with pain. I was advised (probably by Mother) that the best thing for me to do to alleviate the pain was to place the bare foot of the cramped leg on the cold surface of a tin tray. My faithful bedroom partner from then on was my tin tray but I cannot say if it ever worked for it seemed to me that the cramp lasted about the same time, whether I went through the tin tray ritual or not.

Looking back at that time I know it must have been a mental and physical phase I was going through and which every parent must dread. I could not be bothered with doing anything helpful in the house which included wilfully neglecting any studying. I would often fall asleep in a chair listening to the wireless. I do not think I was particularly sociable at home at that time, and in matters religious I told Mother that religion had not anything to offer me, which I knew full well must have disappointed her very deeply.

I suppose, having lived part of my adolescent years during a war and learning that some countries attack others every so often for one reason or another, I realised that in between these conflicts their over-riding purpose is to arm themselves to the highest standard possible in preparation for the next war. This must have caused doubts and confusion in many young minds, especially when they are assured which side God is on. It appeared to me that if any one species amongst all other life forms on Earth had to be removed to leave this world a better and safer place for the others to survive in then the answer would not be hard to find. Surely after a quick check through the track record blatantly displayed in its own history file, Mr and Mrs Human Being and Family would top the list of candidates.

The Church told me of an afterlife only for people and of a Heaven that is likened to a garden of great beauty where nothing is out of place. My leanings were and still are towards the natural and more rustic type of garden without hysterics over a weed, and not where ex-people sit or walk around wearing a contented smile all day. To me that appeared to have a crucial lack of purpose. I remember seeing several stained glass windows where each showed some kind of creature apart from human beings. Many depicted doves, oxen, lions, donkeys and lambs. Whether they were wild or tame they all came under His dominion. I do not want to make light of what I am trying to say, but by no stretch of my imagination could I think of Him reposed in His seat of power disporting trophies from Planet Earth. I honestly don't know what status the animal kingdom hold in the great overall scheme of things. One thing I do feel sure about and that is, mankind was never expected to get pleasure out of their destruction.

My religious views at the time of my early apprenticeship days certainly were being questioned, with the result that I was stepping away and laying less importance on my religious teachings. I could not possibly believe that Earth was created just for humans to enjoy and that they should care only for themselves and aim solely for an increasingly more comfortable way of living, even though that meant a war during each generation, followed by a further creation of an Eternal Life of happiness and leisure. I could never conceive of a world without the sounds of animals or birds but containing only people. I had found this Earth to be a most desirable place and would hate to change it for a less active place full of grinning humans. All was not lost for I still held what lay behind 'All things bright and beautiful, all creatures great and small.'

In common with a lot of young people of my age group, then, was the feeling I was a pawn in a more serious chess game, constantly being played by unseen but very human hands, whose detached minds didn't give much thought for the pieces they moved, but only for the success of the final outcome as they saw it. All this was mixed up with what was simplistically termed 'Human Expediency' and certainly did not strike a just balance between people, property and human needs on one hand and flora, fauna and conservancy on the other. The number of battle dates that we had to commit to memory without any purpose or reason given for the fighting, apart from a few one-liner explanations, must have registered at the back of a few young minds.

I think the last thing young people want to learn is how to look back or forward in detail at their own lives. Youth lives for now, and now is always. I would have thought at that time that anyone who perpetually thrusted at me photographs of myself as a child or reminded me of what I did as a toddler was quite insane. Similarly I would have thought the same of anyone trying to sell me a pension for my old age. Could it be I was confusing Faith with pension and insurance?

These were days where I expected answers to be available for all my questions. It was the simple growing-up stage that seems to complicate itself through naivety. There was no explanation or earthly reason for a God to place on this planet the source of its own destruction through a slow burning fuse in the form of a continual warring mankind. Was the whole thing merely a cosmic experiment of which we were only a disposable token part? Could the whole thing be some sort of cruel joke? With such innocence it was easier for me to conjure up a Creator not unlike Edward G. Robinson and hear him say, 'I ain't got nothing for you at present, kid, but stick around and play it smart. Take good care of yourself meantime and I just might have something for you later on.'

Nothing in my world during that period seemed to slot into its correct place, and the meaning of 'purpose' appeared to be some abstract development which all young people were expected to understand, but didn't. Apparently it had something to do with attaining a certain level of education and living out one's life with an expected standard of respectability and holding on to certain moral values. It was the standard middle class survival pack for whatever lay ahead in a middle class world.

As far as I know, in Nature's world all the animals, birds and fish are also taught along somewhat similar lines, but somehow or another each creatures goes one step further by fulfilling a clear-cut purpose which is apparently much better defined to them than it is for us. They must at some time get a satisfaction that is quite impossible for us humans to attain.

When the purpose of any species comes to an end it appears that it is removed by Nature itself, with only a very few leaving any trace of their presence. What really is so very special about humans?

If I had been told in some previous life that I would go to Heaven after I died, then I would have agreed now with what I had been told. I could not think of a nicer place than Earth to be on. Perhaps I might have made a few changes. I hardly think I would have removed all the mega-rich people as I didn't resent anyone having more than me. In any case countless revolutions have proved that their money never goes very far when spread over a lot of people. (I did learn something from Hollywood.) The people I would have nicely removed would have been the cruel people and the selfish people. If that included several rich people, so be it. Of course this left me with the question, 'If I can so easily reach an easy solution to world problems, why can't He?'

I certainly am going on and on with this subject. I wonder what brought all this on? Well, I suppose it didn't help any that about this time Mother explained to me most delicately, though did not spare my blushes, about an incident regarding a minister of the Church whom I knew and respected. This man had interfered sexually with a young male member of the congregation and there was to be a subsequent court case over it. Of course I knew about such things, but, like most of these cases when it happens to and about total strangers, it tends to be a two minute wonder that is soon dismissed. It's rather like finding about a road, railway or aircraft accident and only when a name is recognised from amongst the casualty list does real concern emerge. This is how it was in the case I was being told about.

This type of behaviour was beyond my comprehension and shrieked of betrayal, which added to my general confusion. I had no smart reply to give Mother when she was finished because I was completely out of my depth.

Somehow or another it all seemed to level out with me accepting that not to believe in something did not mean that I could not believe in anything. I quite accepted that every now and again there would be countries at war, with a distinct possibility that one of them might very well be my own. I had been brought up to think that being British gave me an edge over all other peoples. It was, of course, the common arrogance held by citizens of most countries in the world at that time. Politically I don't think I was at all sure what party line I would like to follow; perhaps I can save face by saying I was an Independent Something or Other. Glasgow always had a strong egalitarian streak running through it and where no privilege was given to the boast of having an exalted rainbow-coloured blood line. Anything could be hotly debated yet it was both expected and encouraged to use the words 'please' and 'thanks'. All this seemed to me to be cut-and-dried, but for some reason for me at that time it wasn't. Maybe it was having a war to contend with as well as growing up.

My sister Joey married her army lieutenant sweetheart in 1944 under a special licence which personnel in the Armed Forces could apply for during their short leaves at home. She became Mrs Robert Gee on 11th March. Bob had been stationed near Ballantrae in the vicinity where Joey was doing her stint in the Land Army. A romance flourished which, like so many others, was well tested through several wartime separations.

It all happened one morning when Joey came up to Glasgow and said she was getting married to Bob the following day if he could get the necessary licence, and she could get a minister to perform the ceremony. Both were successful in their respective endeavours and so they were together as man and wife at 2.30 p.m. the following afternoon in St Mary's Cathedral.

The bridesmaid was Anne Brittain who had known the May family since our Pollokshields days before the war when she had lived in the upstairs flat above us in Keir Street. Anne was about the same age as Sybil and had been friends with my sisters ever since I can remember, which goes back to the time when they went to and from school together. Anne was as at home in our house as she was in her own. It would therefore not have come as too much of a surprise to be awakened that morning and learn she was to be a bridesmaid at 2.30 p.m. the same day – and further, she had to help Joey buy some clothes and shoes before the wedding.

Anne rose well to the occasion and by three o'clock Bob was married to his bride who had just successfully spent as many clothing coupons as she could get her hands on. No doubt the same was done by many other brides during the first four months of 1944 when, with the passing of each day, it must have been more obvious to the serving men that the Second Front Landing was not so very far off.

On 6th June the Allies landed on the beaches of Normandy, and I wonder how many newly-wedded husbands were amongst the fighting men?

Not long after D-Day Mother finally managed to get a permanent place for the family which suited her requirements, one of them being to have a home big enough to house some furniture which had been in storage since the Mays had left Glasgow for Prestwick back in 1940. Our new home was a five-roomed tenement flat at the very top of Garnethill Street, and it was one storey up. It was a typical type of Glasgow tenement which was entered through a close entrance from the street.

One evening near the end of our stay in Hamilton Drive, when Joey was home from the Land Army, she was given the keys to the flat in Garnethill by Mother. She was delegated along with me to carry some cleaning essentials over to our new home to be. It was a clear September evening and the bits and pieces the pair of us had to carry included buckets, mops and disinfectant along with some other paraphernalia which included a ladder. Both of us started out on our laden walk which was about a mile from door to door and the route lay along the Great Western Road to St George's Cross, then up the hill to number 36. The original intention was to light a fire for hot water and do some house cleaning as well as to 'take the chill off the house', as Mother put it.

It did not quite work out that way. Just as we were approaching St George's Cross the heavens opened up and there was one torrential downpour of rain, and thrown in for good measure came the loud crack of flash lightning that sounded directly above our two heads and was immediately followed by an explosive bang of most unsympathetic thunder. Both of us were drenched with our shoes full of rainwater and looked every bit like the orphans of the storm. The elements were not finished with us yet, for a sudden strong wind came from nowhere and propelled us along in the right direction as though we were both under full sail. The heavy solid wooden ladders of those days which were manufactured to last at least a hundred years, one of which I was carrying on one shoulder, caused me to spin round several times. How I avoided not leaving a trail of human casualties amid broken shop window glass, I will never know.

Joey and I wearily climbed the hill from one of its steeper sides. Horses would have shown better sense, for if they had had a load to deliver to the house we were going to, they would have done so by approaching it from another direction with a lesser gradient. They would have come down Garnethill Street which we climbed if there was a delivery to make somewhere in it, and the cart brakes would be more or less full on during the descent.

We finally made it to the top and struggled up the first flight of stairs, then into the flat, where I'm afraid there wasn't much done by either of us that evening. True, we persuaded the kitchen fire to light and keep burning, and somehow or another we also managed a cup of tea before the pair of us, like the Duke of York's men, marched back down again. It must have been straight home to our respective baths with the permitted four inches of water in them, or in my case it may well have been putting both feet into a basin of hot water and mustard, a remedy Mother was very keen on when it came to cold wet feet.

I just thought I would mention the incident to let the reader know something about the Glasgow weather – if not having already experienced it!

Our new home was surrounded with worthy neighbours such as St Aloysius Cathedral with its college, a synagogue, the Glasgow School of Art, designed by Charles Rennie Mackintosh and which ranks high in European status. There was also the Glasgow Veterinary College, a hospital, various churches, Garnethill School and a cinema. It would not be right to leave out the latter, called the Cosmo, in Rose Street, with the two globes making the Os in its name. It traditionally specialised in foreign films.

We were right in the centre of the city, bounded by four main roads, each serviced with tramcars, making it possible to travel with ease to any part of Glasgow. The roads were Sauchiehall Street, St George's Road, New City Road and Cambridge Street. This central area embraced the two busy tramway crossings at Charing Cross and St George's Cross which are in a part of Glasgow that can claim some remarkable dwellings. Glasgow is an interesting city of tenements and nearby to us at the St George's Cross corner where the Great Western Road meets Maryhill Road there is a tenement with a distinct ancient Greek appearance, while at Charing Cross stood the Charing Cross Mansions, which I had been told was the most upmarket tenement building in the city. I should make it quite clear to the reader that although the Mays lived fairly close by, our flat did not have quite the same status. Our clock was on the mantelpiece whereas theirs is an enormous affair on the outside wall just beneath the name Charing Cross Mansions. I'm sure the people who lived there had a few advantages over us, but give or take a minute this or that we knew the time when we wanted it. After all, who wants to run outside to find out the time? I have the feeling that each and every tramcar that passed cocked its eye towards it to be certain it was in the right place and right on schedule.

A stone's throw away was the jazzy Beresford Hotel (where Joey and Bob spent a short honeymoon!). This had been built for the many expected Americans visiting the Empire Exhibition in 1938 at Bellahouston Park, and was later apparently well used by members of the American Forces during the war.

Surprisingly, I seemed to change for the better shortly after I had settled into the flat in Garnethill. My leg cramps stopped and hopefully I had grown up emotionally as well as physically; I also regained my lost energy. Through some sort of illogical reasoning I can recommend, through experience, to any young male around the sixteen/seventeen years mark and suffering from leg cramps and over-tiredness (sometimes called 'fed-upness'), to go and live at the top of a hill, and if that doesn't work then try a cold tin tray.

Perhaps it was the climb up the hill each day that sorted me out, although a thought did come to me that in some unknown way I had returned to a similar home to which I had left in 1939. But perhaps that's nonsense and it was merely the added physical exertion I had required while my hormones were doing what hormones did at that age to a young male.

While on the subject of climbing I think I'll mention that the height of a Glasgow tenement I have heard said was determined by the early city planners to be the height one could reasonably expect a coalman to carry a 1 cwt bag of coal to the uppermost flats, and this they agreed was two flights of stairs that could be reasonably stretched to three flights; hence the number of three and four storeyed tenements. Now, I have no doubt that the coalman's task was taken into account as would also be the delivery of a piano by the removal men when handling heavy Victorian pieces of furniture. The stair landings (stairhead), would be spacious enough for this purpose as would be the door frames into the flats. I am inclined to think that the number of flights and the height of each step would hardly be decided totally by the wants of tradesmen, but by the tenants. I would guess the criterion would probably have been more how a mother-to-be could manage in the latter months of her pregnancy and later coping with carrying the bairn in one arm and humphing a bag full of messages (consumable domestic goods – mostly food), with the other one. I'm sure there were others like the postman, milkman and leerie (who manually lit the gas lamp on each stairhead), who could also have made a contribution of their own as to why tenements in Glasgow are the height they are.

At the corner of Union and Argyle Street and beside the railway bridge where the trains passed overhead into or out of the Central Station, better known as the Hielandman's Umbrella, there was a corner where the deaf and dumb would gather and converse in sign language. It was known as Dumby's Corner. The name was not derived from any derogatory sense or any other similar source. At the worst the name at the time of writing could be considered tasteless, but it is an example of the straight language used in Glasgow's yesteryears that clearly stated this was their Speaker's Corner now and for always. The Deaf and Dumb Institute was nearby in West Regent Street. I have no idea why or how this particular corner was chosen as their meeting place; presumably because it was in the vicinity of the Hielandman's Umbrella which is a traditional Glasgow meeting place that got its name originally from the Gaelic speakers that used to meet there in past years. As well as being near the railway station it was also at a busy tram intersection that converged from all parts of the city. All I know is that those particular citizens came into the town and had this place to meet and communicate with each other. That was no bad thing, and if it was a reminder to any passer-by of his or her good fortune, then that was no bad thing either.

Looking back, I learned words that were passed down from the class above at school and usually first heard in the playground but never repeated at home. Words like Skelly Een (squint-eyed), Humphy Backet (hunchback or more likely round shouldered), Bandy Leggit (bow-legged), Skinny Willie (thin and probably tall). There were other descriptive and mostly bi-worded terms. What was seen was exactly translated into speech without the slightest thought given to feelings or verbal cosmetics.

The first time I passed this corner, believe it or not, was to visit a zoo in a shop under the railway bridge, and that is where I saw my first lion. Poor creature. Looking back, I shudder to think of it. That was around 1933/34.

Back to 1943 and nearly four years into the war: this time it was a familiar sight in most homes to find someone occupied in repairing or checking something in the house. This ranged from basic home maintenance in the form of early DIY to sewing or altering garments and dressmaking, which was a constant task due to the lack of clothes and choice of what was available in the shops, topped of course, by the rationing restrictions. One the reasons in going to the pictures was for the ladies to get fashion ideas about what was being worn in America. Many of the men in reserved occupations, along with the older and the younger males, turned their hands to basic woodwork for birthday presents and Christmas toys, with perhaps the four by six inch wooden box with a none too round wheel at each corner that was presumably to be pulled by a tatty six foot length piece of string attached it – one of the more popular lines from Santa's domestic production centres. A lot of activity revolved around the various religious centres, involving music, drama or the simple meeting of church friends keeping contact, and perhaps being engaged in some war effort. There was no shortage of things to do, including the usual family and friends to visit through duty or delight. There were also the sad wartime visits to give comfort and support after a familiar name had been officially reported as missing or lost.

I hope you can see the picture I am portraying of that time in the context of wartime Britain where households were run with great imagination. Many hobbies and interests are self created, perhaps by a gene passed down some way or another, but I'm sure that more than just a few were born out of necessity because of empty shops and the disappearance of the tradesman workforce who were then fully engaged in more important war work.

My generation and the others who lived the war out on the Home Front will probably be recognised by how we salvage paper and string from a parcel or by the thoroughness of scraping the butter dish clean and retrieving the last particle of jam from the jar.

I honestly don't remember doing much, if any, book reading for pleasure during any phase of my apprenticeship days. If I had been asked at the time what mental asset I prized most I would have said that I had been better at mathematics than English. Then I might have expressed the thought that something of everything in general had rubbed off on me. Probably, on being pressed still further, I would have said it was most likely to be the something that I have already mentioned which seemed to continually surface in my mind. It was the instruction in mentally removing the over-flamboyant words and unnecessary adjectives in anything that sounded too flowery or suspiciously bland in what I read or listened to. It was also to teach me to write in a language that was easily understood with as little or no repetition of words. At least that is what I would have liked to think, but we can't all be perfect.

What was not taught to me at any time that I can recall was that every book or article contains only the thoughts of the author, which I did not necessarily have to agree with; nor did the substance have to be either correct or even true. I left school taking it for granted that all books, apart from adventure and romantic novels, must be correct in essence with the message it contained having been proven right and proper. That must have left a not quite sixteen-year-old rather vulnerable to questionable fringe group writings and politically-orientated literature. It was fortunate for me that I somehow avoided that particular pitfall.

Novels were different, at least the ones I had earlier read, as they had all been written in good descriptive English which also meant I never had the experience of discriminating between good or badly written material. That was simply because I had been brought up on a stringent diet of literally well-established authors.

A lot of people spent a good part of their spare time reading, but whether for learning, enjoyment or compulsion I'll never know. Each page of a newspaper was entirely read and every type of novel was sought after. Libraries were all well used. It may well have been a wartime disease for information. The same could be said for the wireless and especially when news bulletins were being broadcast, there was a sudden quietness when everyone listened attentively, and no-one dared make a sound. Such programmes as *Itma* or *Take It From Here* were to be laughed at as noisily as one cared to do so, whereas music was played to be heard and interrupted only for very genuine reasons. The background music fashion had not yet arrived for domestic social functions. The nearest to such a manifestation would be a brass band playing quietly in the background at a civic social gathering, or merely playing in the park on a Sunday.

I must make some mention about the resourceful men of Glasgow who attended to the family oddment deliveries when home on leave. These were the men who pushed prams in the fair city, but there was, of course, one important proviso, that being there must be no child, or even evidence of a child in it. They could be seen pushing prams containing the kitchen sink, or the household washing mangle, or coal, or some piece of domestic lumber, but they would all rather be seen dead than pushing a pram with a bairn in it.

Winter for all apprentices meant night school; therefore the weeks leading up to Christmas and Easter included swotting that culminated in examination tension and waiting for results. Like most students I used to question before each of these two church calendar events how anyone in their right mind could use the word 'Happy'.

The picture houses had queues outside along the pavement each evening both in summer and winter. Many of the patrons who found themselves standing in them were lucky if they saw the whole of the main feature let alone the B picture. They would also miss seeing both the 'forthcoming attractions' and the Pathe Movietone News, which for public morale reasons had always to end on a cheerful note, preferably with smiling faces on the Home Front, and never with a scene depicting war damage, which was always screened at or near the beginning of the news. Clark Gable, Spencer Tracy, Myrna Loy, Bette Davis played out their parts as young lovers along with so many other well-known names and familiar faces that constantly appeared as the cab driver, the maid and the butler, barman and drunk. The big screen would show Jeanette MacDonald having another musical romance opposite Nelson Eddie, while a few streets away Johnny Wiesmuller was swinging his way from tree to tree with Boy and Cheetah for a few mumbled words with Maureen O'Sullivan. The film world during the first half of the forties was most certainly an all American market.

I was told that Glasgow in the thirties had over 130 picture houses, and goodness, a time must have been spent on deciding where to go. In reality it was hardly a problem as some would be showing the same film and it was the usual thing for most people to attend their local cinema, especially courting couples.

In Sauchiehall Street there were the La Scala where patrons could view the screen from the tearoom if they so desired, the Gaumont Picture House and the Regal. Just within a few minutes walking distance from them was the Greens Playhouse picture and dance hall situated in the upper part of Renfield Street and directly across the road from it stood the Pavilion Theatre. Fairly close by, in St George's Road was the glitzy Crystal Palace (ex Norwood), owned by the eccentric Glaswegian A. E. Pickard. Whenever I asked what this character did for a living I was given and accepted the reply that he was a 'showman'. I had no idea what that meant but he also at one time owned the (White) Elephant over in Shawlands and I believe he once paid a motoring fine in farthings, being dressed for the occasion in full Highland splendour. His Cadillac, with one-way mirrored windows, was quite a talking point as were his big property buys which always involved huge notices that modestly contained only the words 'A. E. Pickard'. Heaven's knows what he did to be called a showman.

Starting from the Crystal Palace let us take a short walk followed by a trip on a tramcar. First we will make a visit to Renfield Street in the city centre where we will board a No. 8 tram that will carry us to the southern part of Glasgow. On the way I will point out the picture houses along the route. This will not be a cultural journey. Let me put it down to a nostalgic jaunt. But before all this happens we must cross the tram lines on St George's Road which will place us on the same side and close to the Thompson's Ballroom that almost faces the cinema.

Now we start to walk away from the Charing Cross direction and towards St George's Cross where we turn right into New City Road, but not before noticing the Empress Theatre over on the opposite corner. Now we have to start weaving our way along a busy pavement and past the shop windows.

All the main roads in the city have a tram service. We do not have very far to walk before we see the tramway lines separating at a fork to respective destinations but we continue following the road with its tramlines that veer to the right where we find ourselves in Cambridge Street. A mere few minutes further on we arrive at Sauchiehall Street and turning right we leave behind the mixture of small shops and tenements for the shopping world along Sauchihall Street.

Shoppers have always made this a busy hurry-skurry place and from here it is only a short distance before crossing over Hope Street with trams running up and down its whole length. Continuing on we arrive in Renfield Street at the next corner. From this area in Glasgow it is possible to interchange with trams that would take you to any of its outlying districts.

When I write of catching a red No. 8 tram I hope the following short description will allow the reader to get a clearer picture of the transport system. Each standard tram had a broad strip running around its upper deck which was coloured either blue, green, red, white or yellow. Up on the same level as the colour strip, directly above the driver, was the destination board on both the front and the back, and just to confuse anyone who has followed me this far let me tell you that there were dual controls with one set at each end of the tram. In other words, there was no back or front. Travelling one way, the back was the back and the front was the front, but returning to its other destination, or from whence it came, the front was the back and the back was the front. (If only everything was as simple.) Three things only were changed when a destination was reached: the destination board, the trolley at the top of the tram that made contact with the overhead wire which had to be pulled over so that it was sloping away from the direction of travel, and the driver himself who moved to the other end of the vehicle where there was the other set of identical operating controls. The trolley was pulled over by a rope that could be reached from either of the front or rear upper deck window, which was real modern stuff. The trolley type I'm describing was the latest style, shaped like an inverted triangle with the two uppermost angles rounded (angles rounded?). This allowed the uppermost side of the triangle to contact the suspended power line. It also meant that the tram could rock sideways and still keep contact with the live overhead line. The previous type of trolley looked like a fishing rod in appearance and had its end slotted to receive the live overhead line, but I'm afraid they parted company too easily and too often. I recall the driver at the end of the line having to pull it off the wire with a permanently attached rope, then walk around his tramcar and re-connect it again for the return journey. The later trolleys were designed such that a strong spring tended to make them take an upright position but were held back at an angle by the overhead power line itself which gave them the reclined working angle position.

From one extreme to another I would like to mention something about rail level. There had never been any type of stopper or buffer at the terminuses and I never heard of trams leaving the rails because of this. The drivers must have been very careful in fog or snow and well aware of what could easily happen. There were occasions when a tram was derailed but it always seemed to take place at the busier spots. Each tram was capable of pushing or pulling another one and had a long steel link bar stowed on board for this purpose. However, if the following tramcar could not help a derailed casualty then that would soon entail a long line of trams being held up.

Everyone used the tramway system and the city centre was awash with trams. At its peak the system must have operated on roughly a couple of hundred miles of track and overhead power cables. The longest route lay between Milngavie on the north bank of the Clyde and Renfrew Ferry on the south bank, a distance of twenty-two miles, and that was only cut back as a wartime economy measure in 1943.

Having now finished our walk we can catch that red No. 8 at the top of Renfield Street and move in a southerly direction in the comfort of a clean Corporation tramcar. At least we have started in good time before darkness falls and the blackout prevents us from seeing things.

You will notice that the tram is quite busy, with a sprinkling of uniforms amongst the young men. It's strange how you pass men in the Forces on the pavement and pay little attention to any detail about them, yet when sitting down your mind starts to tell the

Czech from the Pole and the Free French from the Norwegian. Strangers in Glasgow are and were quite common, it being a seaport city. What was different now was being able to identify where they were from, especially in failing light.

The tram has just started and almost immediately passes the Regent Cinema on our left-hand side and at the next corner, a matter of seconds, we pass the Paramount on the same side. By the time it takes you to look out on the other side of the street there stands the Classic that can be seen before rattling over the tram lines running along St Vincent Street where George Square and the Civic Centre lies to the left, through a web of tram lines running this way and that way. Looking quickly along to the right the rails can be seen turning up into Hope Street which we are running parallel with at the moment. In the meantime we push straight ahead and find ourselves in Union Street; then, in no time at all, our tram clunks across the lines running at right angles to us in Argyle Street that direct their tramcars past the old town centre on our left and under the Central Station Bridge (Hielandman's Umbrella) to our right and the docks lying on the Northern bank of the Clyde. Once across this busy thoroughfare we find ourselves in Jamaica Street and after a brief space of time we pass a small picture hall on our right-hand side that gives a continuous showing of newsreels and cartoons only.

I earlier mentioned the uniforms worn by the Armed Forces, but there are still quite a few civilian ones to be seen, apart from those of policemen, special constables, nurses, auxiliary nurses, firemen, auxiliary firemen, wardens (ARP) and Home Guard. For instance there are two elderly (to me) railway porters at the Central Station tramstop. They are wearing a heavy worsted pair of dark blue trousers with a matching waistcoat that had linen arms. Both of them are clean and smartly dressed as well as being polished-booted, collar and tied with each wearing a shiny weather-proofed cap. I'm surprised they do not go upstairs as one of them looks as though he would be quite at home puffing away on a pipe. Incidentally a few of the women returning from their place of work are already clicking away with their needles, either crocheting or doing 'one plain two purl stuff' with wool. These ladies carry their knitting in their handbags, although in homes it is often seen peeping out of a canvas-like shopping bag with wooden handles and decorated on its outside with a heavy string pattern. These bags contain all sorts of balls of wool, needles, patterns and, of course, the current project.

I cannot remember if there were any traffic lights in use at this time. They were certainly there in the fifties. I remember that fire engines and police cars had a ringing bell as a warning signal. I also recollect (perhaps it was my hearing) that I could tell quite clearly the direction the sound was coming from in contrast with the siren sound of later years which I could hear but the direction of which I could not identify. There were plenty of traffic policemen wearing their long white coats. At times I couldn't help but watch them because of the confident Sons of the Bookie Manner they had with their arm movements and pointing fingers. Trams and horses between buses and lorries must have been cumbersome traffic to keep moving in some sort of orderly fashion. Now, back once more to our tram trip.

A short distance further on we arrive at the River Clyde (very close to Paisley's) and pass over it by crossing the Glasgow Bridge to its southern bank, leaving behind the city centre with its concentration of busy shops and offices, surrounded by all the normal activity on pavements and roads. I hope I have not utterly bewildered the reader with too many street names and perhaps it will make a little more sense if I explain that so far we have crossed three main streets running at right angles to the one we are on, which has already changed its name three times although still travelling in the same general direction. We will continue to do this until we reach our destination.

Having just crossed the Clyde we are now moving along Bridge Street where we meet up with tenement buildings on our left-hand side while to the right and unseen, due to boarding, runs the main railway line to and from the Central Station. The next street we cross is Norfolk Street that tramwise has something in common with Argyle Street which we have left behind us nearer the city centre. As the tramway system traversed the east and west of Glasgow north of the river using Argyle Street, so did the system operate between east and west of the city south of its famous waterway along Norfolk Street. Do not be confused by the different street names.

Once we have rattled across those intersecting lines the name of the street we are in changes to Eglinton Street where on the left we see two very popular picture houses within shouting distance of each other and called the Bedford and Colosseum, and incidentally, lying not too far behind them but, of course, unseen is the Citizen's Theatre and the close-by Gorbals Cross. I can remember from before the war, and it was most probably Coronation Year 1936 or early 1937, when the school (Melville Street) children along with others were taken to see *The Last of the Mohicans* either at the Colosseum or Bedford. I cannot recall which one it was but we arrived by tram. If that was so, and I am pretty certain it was, then perhaps there was some sort of tramcar hire service arrangement with the Corporation for special occasions. For what it is worth I found out later that the Colosseum had been a theatre until sometime in the late twenties, therefore it must have been standing for a long time.

Back in the comfort of our tram we push onwards, sometimes swaying as though the driver is trying to make up time lost in the city. On our left there are still the three-storeyed tenements and still on our right runs the railway line, well hidden by fencing and a few small businesses, although this now changes as we pass the Corporation Works with its gasometers just before reaching Eglinton Toll.

Do you remember the walk we had before boarding this tram? By far the major part of it was between two theatres. The first was the Empress at St George's Cross and the other was the Royal in Sauchiehall Street which was just round the corner from the tram stop where we caught our tram (trams were caught or left, never boarded or disembarked). Adding that walk to the tram trip we have just completed was the route of the very first tramcar service started in Glasgow in 1872, which ran from St George's Cross to Eglinton Toll. I'm just a mine of information. It's a pity that this particular first stretch of tramlines was not left as a reminder of the men, women and animals that had served during and since in the transport services of the city. The original length was two miles, two furlong and two yards, and in those early days it would have taken rather longer when using the original horse power.

But once again back to wartime times at Eglinton Toll where our tram lines converge with those coming up through the Gorbals in Pollokshaws Road. Both the lines briefly meet over a set of points and then part again. We have now reached the distance from the city centre where the colours on the trams start to fan out to their respective destinations. The White No. 3 turns off here to the right and heads away to Dumbreck and Mosspark and at the points a yellow veers off to the left in the direction of Langside as also does a red No. 11, leaving behind them the BBC Cinerama and the Plaza Ballroom with the Corporation Bus Depot separating them. We continue onwards in our red No. 8, taking the right fork and now moving along Pollokshaws Road. In scarcely any time at all we pass St Ninian's Episcopal Church on the right-hand side where my family (apart from Father) were attendant members until shortly after the outbreak of the war when the Mays left the area.

The church stands on a corner and fronts onto Albert Drive beside the Coplawhill Tram Works. I shall mention here that serious tramcar accidents as far as I was concerned were very rare. There must have been bumps and bangs with a fair share of electrical faults, but I only once saw a tram over on its side. It was a new type tram which means I can date the accident to 1938 (Empire Exhibition, Glasgow 1938) or pre-September 1939. It had been travelling along Kenmuir Street and making a ninety-degree turn into Albert Drive on route to Mosspark when it fell over on its left side. I happened to pass by shortly afterwards and would have loved to have seen how it was lifted back onto its wheels again, but alas, for some forgotten reason I could not wait to find out. That incident made me aware of how large these vehicles were by seeing the land space taken up by this one having flopped over. I had often seen a tram pushing or towing another and have mentioned that each was obviously capable of performing that particular task. There were also one-decker, all brown-coloured trams used by maintenance crews that were very dowdy compared with the much brighter work-a-day tramcars and the only thing they had in common was the Glasgow coat of arms on each of their sides.

Now back again to our particular journey where we find

ourselves approaching the tram lines of Allison Street which for us is the last outer circular tramway route. The vehicles plying along this track that we will be crossing would arc back towards the river on either side while we rattle on a short distance to reach Queen's Park on our left with the Shawlands district shops starting to appear on the opposite side of the road.

A mother with a babe in her lap abruptly signals her young son of about eight years who is sitting at a window seat to stand up while she shuffles over to take his place. This is to allow an elderly person to sit down where the young mother had been sitting. The only sound for this operation is a smiling 'Thank you'. The young boy had known exactly what to do and why; it was really quite normal tramcar passenger behaviour.

The park was created on the site of a battle that had been fought 400 odd years ago, involving Mary Queen of Scots, who witnessed it. Soldiers who fell in the battle are supposed to be buried beneath the spot where the pond now is, where strange happenings and queer goings on have been reported since that time, especially on still and murky nights. I think we should return to the tram.

It won't be too long now before we will be leaving tenement territory synonymous with town dwelling behind us and entering a living area with much more space. But before that we first arrive at Shawlands Cross where once again the line in front of us separates and this time we take the left fork along Kilmarnock Road. But just before that, if we look down Mosside Road on our right, the Waverley Picture House would be easily spotted on the corner with its white entrance steps where one could expect to see a tap dancer going through his or her paces on them. Not too far away from here and in the same direction we are heading in are two other picture houses called the Elephant and the Embassy, standing quite close to each other on our right-hand side.

Passengers have come and gone. Young people have clunked down the stairs as though they had seen someone on the pavement and wanted off in a hurry. There are quite a number of empty seats now. I'm sure it was a conductor when we boarded and it's now a conductress so I think the two original staff must have changed at Shawlands Cross.

Passing through the districts of Newlands and Merrylea we finally arrive at Giffnock where we alight for Dalmeny Avenue which boasts an Italian café at one corner and the Tudor Picture House and Dance Hall directly across the road from it. The tram trip we have just completed was one I did many times (certainly not always for the picture houses) and the distance would be about four miles. Allowing ten minutes for each mile for picking up and dropping passengers and for careful and considerate slowing down for horse-drawn traffic, then the trip must have taken about forty-five minutes and the cost would have been around 4d.

It was just ordinary people who used the trams and it was THE perfect classless area. The last thing one would have thought of was where the person sitting next to you lived. Passengers were mostly drably dressed because of habit and what there was to buy in the shops. We had all learned over the recent years to add our own colour to persons and places. Looking around on the tram there would be the Miss Prims, the young chattering couples, the silent persons and the elderly along with the young. It was a place where each traveller had his or her own spot and it probably reflected a scene played out in every city in the land. The extroverts, the grouches, the humorists and, for a place with a reputation for heavy drinking, I don't recall any nasty drunken behaviour or incidents involving police attendance. Let us continue.

These picture houses I have mentioned are amongst the ones I went to during the second part of the forties, and that was only because they were either at or near a friend's home, or en route to a friend or friends where we could meet up. I should also mention here that the cafés were well used during the forties as meeting places for young people, either before going to see a picture, or having a cup of coffee on leaving a picture house, and before catching our respective trams home. Oh! There was another one. I seemed to have missed out the Ascot out in Knightswood where I sometimes also went, but that lay in the opposite direction in the north-western part of Glasgow.

Meanwhile on stage at the Alhambra Theatre, Dave Willis 'was going his dinger' in the Half Past Eight Show, and at the Kings Theatre Harry Gordon was playing to packed houses. The Theatre

Royal had the dubious reputation of being one of the main 'testing' theatres in the country, and was where the best and biggest names in showbiz played. It was on this stage a few years later that I remember seeing a young smiling newcomer doing an act with elongated balloons by making them with a few swift flicks of his wrist into various designs, including a poodle dog. His name was Stanley Baxter. The Logan family, including Jimmy, were very popular and firmly ensconced at the Citizens Theatre in the Gorbals, and at the Empress Theatre at St George's Cross Frank and Doris Droy kept their audience giggling with what was considered to be extremely risqué for these days. These names were Glasgow personalities and each city had their own.

Glaswegians are proud of and enjoy their museums and cultural exhibitions, all of which were enthusiastically shared by many of our wartime Allies. Concerts of every description were always well supported and I remember with considerable pleasure listening to several Choral and Orchestral Union concerts in the Playhouse Cinema on certain Sunday afternoons.

During the summer it would be difficult to walk through any park without some form of entertainment in progress, usually a brass band or a variety performance. Very few spectators paid to gain entry to the enclosure for a seat, but rather preferred to sit on the grass around the three sides of the perimeter open to free viewing. No-one ever envied for a moment the good patrons seated in the front row of the open-aired stall watching the performance and quite unaware of the hundreds of empty seats behind them.

Travel had its difficulties, as all public transport ran to a limited schedule with the bus and train stations always very busy. The buses catered more for civilians and servicemen and women who were home on leave and there were long queues of contending passengers waiting at each bus stance. There may have been a late night service running on some routes where there were factories on war work, but usually no-one expected a bus after ten at night and was quite resigned to walk.

The main railway stations were much busier than the bus stations, not with trains but with people. The frugal wartime timetable and wartime commitments meant packed passenger compartments and where there were coaches with corridors then they were crowded as well. The general public were not encouraged to travel unless it was absolutely necessary in order to allow the railway system to carry more essential passengers and to cope with sudden rerouting because of enemy action. Every station liberally displayed notices asking potential rail travellers if their journey was really necessary, and as though they knew you were going to take the train in any case there were other notices reminding one about the danger of careless talk and that the walls had ears.

The notices in the toilets were a bit more eye-catching at the time, because they reminded the patrons (the best word I can think of) about the dangers of illicit sex, and then detailed the symptoms of gonorrhea and syphilis. That was as far sex education extended about the dangers of sex.

Servicemen and women used the train a lot in their comings and goings which must have been a nightmare at times for the Station Services Travel Officer when lines and signal boxes were destroyed and trains stopped for an unknown number of hours on the approach to a city or town under enemy attack.

The three uniformed groups I remember in the Glasgow Central Station during the war were the Services Travel Officer's personnel who operated from a large portable room and were the centre of a lot of activity. Another group were the Military Police who were always present walking around in pairs, and the third group was the Salvation Army with its offer of help in any way possible and a friendly smile. Many people passing in or out of Glasgow at that time will remember the soldiers of the Sally Army at the Central, St Enoch's and Queen Street Stations who were always present amongst the to-ing and fro-ing of the thousands of passengers under their sooty roofs, and who had become used to the cold bleakness of railway travel with its Spartan station shops and empty chocolate and cigarette machines.

I seem to remember ladies of the Women's Voluntary Service at the stations, though being a young male I probably didn't have much interest in what they were doing. In all probability their main type of work then was inside rather than in the open station public area.

The Salvation Army was never far away from the people in need, and many a person who survived the continuous bombings in the cities and towns will well remember that first cup of tea from an Army member, amongst other things after emerging from the air raid shelter or underground after the 'All Clear' sounded.

Competent speakers gave lectures and talks on a variety of subjects covering those who had an experience to tell of, or gave advice or an account about their profession. The progress of the war and the lessons that had been learnt from it that must be used in the days of peace were well debated in front of interested spectators. Glasgow audiences at such times were both friendly and supportive to the speakers by expressing their interest in every possible subject, although it has been said of those same citizens that their tolerance was a little lower at political meetings, especially if someone gave the impression of talking down to the audience, for they had at such times the gift of psychologically stripping the speaker down to his or her winter underwear and leaving them wondering what was humorous about such excellent serious advice coming from such an illustrious source. On the other hand, visiting stage personalities told of the 'friendly fire' from patrons with such asides as 'Oh no, not that again. The book's a lot better.' Unnerving, of course, but that was Glasgow.

It was strange how at that time there seemed to be an inbred psychology in many of the working men to dress first thing in the morning into their working clothes, and not to remove them until they returned home in the evening, which is quite all right and tolerable providing the garments were clean. Tradesmen who worked with wood could be said to be in a clean trade, but unfortunately there were other trades where working clothes had a greasy shine to them which must have left its mark on the seats of public transport. Glasgow Transport Department must have had a very thorough cleaning department, as I cannot recollect seeing any dirty dingy litter-strewn trams or buses, and here I should remind the reader that the war was used by some people as an added reason to protect existing standards and used by others as an excuse to do otherwise. Unfortunately none of those explanations could have been of any consolation to the girl who sat down in the seat just vacated by a dirty overall, or other similar clothing.

Clothing coupons were too highly rated not to take the greatest care of work-a-day attire. Somehow or another a certain group of the older workers had to prove to others that they were workers, and through some sort of insecurity, had to display the fact both inside and outside the place where they worked. It seemed to stem from some form of mental conditioning they had suffered from. It was quite possible to carry a boiler suit rolled up under your arm. The men who insisted in wearing messy clothes were from that fringe I later called, 'Medieval Britain raised up a wee bit'.

5

There was a canteen at work which was a recent war feature as such places for workers to eat in clean conditions had never been a top priority for the workforce. I used it periodically although it was more usual for me to have my own sandwiches and a flask of hot water which was converted at the right time into a can of hot tea. My flask could not have had a cup at the end of it as the later models had. Most of the apprentices and a lot of the men did this, and like myself had a small oval-shaped tin with a cover at each end and separated at the centre to carry both tea and sugar. I cannot remember anyone carrying teabags but perhaps they had not been invented then, or maybe it was another of the many shortages.

I, like everyone else, had my own tea can, and it requires no imagination at all to describe it. It was a can, the same size that was to appear later with soup labels on it, and it was bridged across the top with a piece of looped wire, not to carry but to hook it out of an open fire. Every ironmongers sold such cans to boy scouts, hitchhikers and workers alike.

Boiling water in a can over an open fire was permitted only during the lunch break, and I have reason to remember four cans of water not far off the boil during working hours one winter's day, when a bowler hat appeared in the form of the manager, which resulted in four empty tea cans rolling on the ground, followed by a gaffer (foreman), who proceeded to read the riot act to us. It was by a very narrow margin that four apprentices were not sent home that day. Such was the nature of the crime that each of us had to report to the gaffer's office on completion of any allotted task and remain there until given another job, which wasn't very long.

It would be so easy for me to criticise what food I had in the canteen, but I'm not going to. The fact that I preferred sandwiches could probably suggest that the food was very basic and probably not very appetising, but I don't remember complaining then and I'm not going to start now, even with all I have been told about food preparation since. It didn't take much imagination to consider the alternative, but apart from that, most of us were slowly learning the sad fact that what we knew as wartime food rationing was a lot more food than some people amongst us had experienced at any time during the whole of their lives.

My first job was to help Bill and Jenny in the fitter's store. Bill, as far as I knew, had always been a storeman and was in his middle fifties. He was small and wiry with very grey hair, and had a great sense of humour. He also knew the what, the when and the whyfore about the business of running a store, not only on one particular day, but the previous day and the day before that. He was a natural born planner, the type that made any job look easy. He also organised and ran the weekly football sweep where the results were worked out some way or another which I have forgotten from a number or numbers that appeared in the *Sunday Post*. This storeman was an action man and a very much liked character in the workshop. He was one of those people who make you wonder what he could have achieved with a university education.

Jenny was a wartime product in her forties who had replaced some young man who was now serving in the Forces. She was a born worrier who was constantly on the move, not wanting to keep anyone waiting at the counter, and in between serving the callers she would be sweeping an already swept floor.

Both Bill and Jenny were very tolerant people and it was a very pleasant spell for me while I was with them, although I remember thinking at the time that writing out chitties for each piece of equipment handed out and knowing where everything was kept and why it was placed on that particular spot was not exactly what

I imagined marine engineering to be about.

I spent about two weeks working in the store where I learned something about tools and instruments which I had never even heard of before. I also had an understanding of some of the strange terminology used in engineers' daily jargon. The short time I spent there passed very quickly and it was a good start as far as I was concerned because Bill taught me in the best possible way to do my job first, to do it well and to do it quickly, and Jenny would always help me if she could, even though she usually left me wondering what it was she had forgotten to do that was worrying her silly. She was the kind motherly type.

The day finally came when Dave Aiken, the foreman, called me from the store into the main workshop area, and beckoned me to follow him down the passageway between a long heavy wooden workbench on one side, and an area where large parts of the engine were stored on the other side. Finally he stopped and pointed to a large wooden toolbox on the workbench, and told me that it was now mine. He then wrote out a note from his foreman's book and instructed me to go the main store (not Bill's), where I was to hand in his note and in return I would be given one smooth fourteen inch file, one medium fourteen inch file and one rough fourteen inch file. I would also receive a 2 lb fitter's hammer and a flat steel hand chisel. I was now in business with my very own tools and my very own toolbox to keep them in. All the toolboxes were the same size of approximately two feet long by one foot high and one foot wide. The one I had acquired contained only a brass padlock and key, and I had already learnt that I was to allow no-one access to my toolbox and that tools were never shared.

The fitter's bay, where I now found myself working, consisted mainly of long rows of wooden workbenches, with an engineer's vice bolted on to it at approximately eight foot intervals along its length. The individual toolboxes were each positioned at, or close to one of these strong looking steel vices.

The head foreman in charge of the fitter's bay was Harry Blake, and he must have held that position for a long time because the area was commonly known as Blake's Bay. I find it difficult to guess how old Harry was at that time, but I would say he was in his middle fifties. Harry was tall and slim, and I got the impression he could have enjoyed better health; either that or he was always haunted by some sad memory. He never did much talking and his hands were always in his brown foreman's cover-all coat pockets when he walked around the bay, giving the impression he had all the time in the world. Beneath his cap he had a dark complexion which went well with his trusting and sincere face and I think he was of Maltese origins. He was a heavy smoker.

Dave Aiken, the under foreman, was very different from Harry (who were both called gaffers); he was shorter and heavier built. Dave walked with purpose with his arms swinging like twin pendulums at his sides as though they knew where Dave was going and tended to give him all possible assistance to get him there. This gaffer more than compensated for his boss's lack of conversation, and had the habit of starting to talk when he was still a few paces away from the person he was addressing. Do not get the wrong impression that he was all talk; on the contrary, as a pipe smoker he was a very good listener when he wanted to be.

I liked both these foremen and I never heard of anyone who didn't. Their office, or Gaffer's Box, where the business of the bay was conducted, was elevated and positioned above the entrance to the store where I worked when I first started, and its wooden staircase ran against the store wall. The view from the office commanded by far the greatest part of the working area, but I think it was more likely to have been put where it was simply because there was no other space for it. It was the only foreman's office that was raised off the ground in such a manner, and in any case there was always such a perpetual cigarette fumitory fog inside it that I doubt very much if anyone inside could see much of anything.

One erroneous impression that remained with me was that in appearance the older fitters had actually owned their respective toolbox along with the workbench space on either side and the vice attached to it. It appeared to me that such things had been theirs from the beginning of their working life which now sounds terribly depressing to me as I write this, but at the time it appeared to be quite the normal thing and fitted into the picture of what life in an engine workshop was like then.

At a central point in the workshop area there was an upright drilling machine, and beside it was a grinding machine, better known as a 'buff'. The name came from the terminology: 'Buff the metal down to this mark', or 'Buff off the sharp edges.' Every journeyman apprentice will remember being told at some time to: 'Take that chisel to the buff right now and get rid of that mush-room.' The mushroom was the flattened out head of the steel chisel caused by heavy hammering on it which, if allowed to spread out too much could break off under a hammer blow and enter your hand. The buff consisted of an assortment of grinding and polishing wheels and the name in this sense covers not only the soft polishing but the heavy grinding as well. The grinding wheels were made of rough and smooth stones whereas the polishing wheels consisted of wheels with their outward side covered in either rough or smooth emery. There was an additional polishing wheel called a dolly, comprising a handy sized wheel with strong cloth-like fabric that was used as a final polish. The wheels were about six inches in diameter or slightly over, and rotated at a high speed behind a protective glass shield. There were no goggles supplied for the safeguarding of eyes.

Let me first say something about the personal effect of being an apprentice at that time. Thinking with hindsight I can look back and say that those early working days, apart from starting me on my profession, did more than just prepare me for that future. Up till then my father had supplied the stability; Mother furnished the love and my apprenticeship covered that period in every boy's life where the reins on self-control from outside the home must make demands upon you, whether you like it or not. It's part of the process of both growing up and learning. For me at that time everything one did or tackled had to be done properly. If I had been asked then, 'Can you swim?' and I had replied, 'Yes,' then it would be assumed by the enquirer that I was a good swimmer. Likewise if you attended night classes it would be taken that hard study and good results would automatically follow. I suppose it must have been exactly the same with the girls. Student nurses or anyone training for a specific purpose would mean 'great expect-ations' from parents, uncles and aunts, with the daughters and sons having to grin and bear it. Even starting to dance entailed classes and practice in order to glide properly across the dance floor with your partner. My generation and no doubt the one before it had to do things properly, always finish what they started – and no nonsense!

Apprentices learnt their trade from anyone in their working zone; in fact it would be more accurate to say from anyone who was older than you were. I only wore a tie once when operating the buff, and that was seconds before a passing fitter told me what would happen if my tie got caught up in the rotating wheel. He then added that if my common sense hadn't already told me before he had, then God help me in the future, if I had one. He didn't exactly tell me in quite such a nice way as I have put it.

I managed to adjust easily to this type of direct and unsolicited advice which was mostly in my best interest. I also began to understand these craftsmen who appeared outwardly to have little humour towards me and were usually full of complaints, but would never have reported me to the foreman. An apprentice listened to the journeyman he was working under – he had to – and you worked as he told you to – you had to. If any apprentice was stupid enough to find himself outside the journeyman fitter's empire, he would be in a very vulnerable position, for I doubt very much if some members of management would even bother to find out an apprentice's name before sending him home for a misdemeanour. That would be left for someone else to do, but conversely, the management would have taken an identical attitude to any member of the workforce in general, which had not gone unnoticed by them over the years.

The longer I worked with the fitters the better I got to know their funny little ways. Scrap pieces of timber were surreptitiously cut up in order that they all would fit into a certain secret jacket pocket and be stealthily carried home to be used as firewood, and during the weeks prior to a child's birthday or any other such event, then all sorts of basic wooden railway engines and carriages would be secretly made. One thing that stood out like a sore thumb was the inability to act at being secret. It was like a Victorian melodrama; their idea of not being seen was like the furtiveness of a white-coated traffic policeman on points duty at the busiest crossing in Glasgow.

There was a lot of talk amongst them about emigrating after the war and finding a better life for themselves and their families. It became a familiar pattern of conversation to hear the men at work talk of going out to a new country where they already had a cousin or an aunt who would dearly welcome them.

The journeymen fitters were the mainstay of the workforce in the engine shop; in fact they were part and parcel of the building, yet their daily working life as such was not particularly hectic during their time at work. Each one was a specialist and craftsman who had his own special part of the engine to prepare. It meant that their work was repetitive; if four engines were built during a year, then each fitter would have repeated his cycle of work four times. The journeyman in charge of the pistons, who would be known as a charge hand, as were the other senior fitters in charge of an assembly of parts for the engine, would be more repetitive in his work than the charge hand who prepared the camshafts. I don't want to confuse the reader; therefore please accept the simple statement that in an opposed piston engine with five cylinders there would be ten pistons to prepare for assembly, but only two camshafts. Somehow or another the workload seemed to iron itself out, and everyone put in a fairly honest day's work.

An apprentice would be told by the foreman to work under a certain charge hand, and to take instructions from him. He would usually stay with him for four or five months learning that particular part of the engine construction.

At the risk of making engineers out of the few readers I have left I will now explain how an engine works and what happens. Each one consists of moving and stationary sections. The moving parts either rotate or they move this and that way. The stationary parts prevent chaos by holding those moving pieces from going too far in either direction and by bringing them back to the point where they all started from. To crown this, a rather clever lubricating oil shower is installed that sprays over all the moving parts, ensuring that a film of oil separates any two pieces of the engine from touching each other and it also has a cooling effect as it flows downwards, carrying away the heat generated from the moving parts.

If any of my now desperately few readers own a car then allow me to give this piece of advice when you are desperately seeking a garage that is open. Run by all means for as long as you possibly can with your petrol gauge showing an empty tank, but don't dare even to entertain the thought if you just merely think there is a scarcity of oil in your engine.

And now if I have any readers at all still left with me let me just round off about the engine before I return to my apprenticeship days. Man with his knowledge and use of metal ores has copied Nature in her wisdom in producing differing types of timber that can each be safely used for a specific purpose. The same differences apply to metals for the same reason; hard, soft, grainy, rough, smooth and they are all somewhere to be found in every engine.

I spent my first several months 'bedding in' connecting rod bearings using good old-fashioned red lead to mark the bearing whitemetal 'high' points that all had to be gently scraped away. Do not imagine these bearings to be the same size as those in your car for the size I am writing about were of such dimensions that when the two halves were bolted together it required a chain block or the overhead crane to lift them. There was a variety of such bearings and there were plenty of them used in the Doxford type of engine built by Barclay Curle. I must also mention that before I was allowed to scrape a bearing face I first had to make my own scraper from a discarded file. All bearing surfaces (here I go again), are made from a fairly soft white metal alloy that can easily be machined and as easily 'bedded' on to a hard steel journal (round pin) which is positioned through the centre of the bearing. Remember about the luboil keeping the metal surfaces apart? Well, if anything adverse happened to the lubrication in a bearing then the idea is that the soft white metal will melt, giving an audible warning. It is much less costly to replace a bearing by remetalling it than to replace or repair the hard steel pin or shaft damaged inside it.

My next move was into the piston assembly area where the large pistons were received from the machine shop and now had to be prepared and assembled, then tested before being fitted to their respective liners in the engine. I think I spent about six months in assembling these pistons, after which I spent a similar length of time assembling and setting camshafts that would ultimately govern the speeds of the engine through its fuel injection timing apparatus.

By this time my toolbox had acquired quite a number of contents which included a two inch outside micrometer, set of engineer's feelers, a twelve inch steel rule and an engineer's square, all of which I bought. The drill gauge and white metal scrapers I had made myself; otherwise everything else, which was mostly tools, came into my possession through a foreman's line from Dave Aiken. I do not recollect anything being stolen from toolboxes and certainly there were no incidents of forced padlocks or suchlike, even though I had dire warnings, which were groundless, about the honesty of the night-shift and no doubt my counter-part on the night-shift was probably given the same advice about the day-shift. The code of practice was simply that no-one would ever dream of opening someone else's box even to borrow a small item without first getting permission.

Now let me take you on a conducted tour of the engine works as I remember it.

I will start with the building we are going to walk through because it does have a unique feature built into its structure, the brainchild of the German engineer, Dr Rudolph Diesel (1858–1913). It was his idea to build a workshop where the main load-carrying steel columns of the building rested on large steel rollers or pins that would allow each of the columns a slight degree of swaying movement. His thinking was that if there should be any heavy vibration at ground level when the large engines were being tested, then the whole building would absorb this vibration energy and use it up through a gentle swaying motion because of the rollers and thus avoid any structural damage caused through vibration. The thinking behind the idea was quite valid – and worked.

The same applies in the unlikely event of a natural earth tremor or the shock pressure from a strong gusting wind, which is very important because the type of engine intended to be built at Whiteinch stood very high and required a tall building to be assembled in.

The pivot bearings can be easily seen from inside the engine works at the base of each main structural column at the ground floor level.

Dr Diesel is better known as the man who thought out and demonstrated on paper the sequence of successfully and economically burning fuel in the cylinder of an oil-powered engine without the use of any electrical system, and fittingly left his name to what was to be called the Diesel Cycle in the study of 'heat' and the internal combustion engine. He patented his findings in 1893 and five years later displayed the first internal combustion engine that generated its own energy from the combustion of its own fuel.

There were a number of international business interests that could see the commercial advantages of the good doctor's findings and used their resources towards the manufacturing of oil-burning engines. One of these interests was in the production of marine motor engines which could do away with most of the costly ancillary plant required by a steam engine, thus allowing more space for the carrying of cargo. Liquid fuel would be much easier and cleaner to handle than coal, and was fast becoming more readily available in ports around the world. Oil was to prove cheaper than coal, and with a ship burning ten tons of fuel a day, it was a considerable saving.

The reader might well want to know why giant car engines were not installed in ships. I had better explain that a ship's propeller in those early days rotated at the same speed as the engine crankshaft, which was in the region of 100 rpm, being considerably less than the revolutions of any motor car crankshaft.

The expansion or explosion in a car engine cylinder is caused by a spark igniting a low pressure and fairly cool petrol/air vapour, and is operated by an electrical timing device. The marine engine, on the other hand, raises the air temperature inside each of its cylinders by the mechanical means of allowing each piston a longer travel inside its respective cylinder, compressing the air and at the same time raising its temperature to a heat that will ignite the fuel injected into it.

Before concluding this topic I should mention that the air compressed by the pistons is very important, for not only does it assist in the economical burning of each charge of fuel, but it also has a coolant effect on the internal walls of the cylinder. One further point I should mention is that the petrol used in a car engine would pre-ignite if used in a diesel engine, but in any case it would be too volatile to carry about in large quantities with its high rate of evaporation, and so another less refined or down-graded fuel is used. It is called diesel oil.

In 1913 Dr Diesel, aged fifty five, disappeared from a cross-Channel steamship in which he was travelling as a passenger. There were many rumours as to what might have happened to him, but the truth was never discovered and the investigation into his disappearance was closed. But what is known about this man is that he left the technical world with his heat cycle and the internal combustion engine, and amongst other things he left Clydeside's Whiteinch with a unique building for its time and a similarly constructed main railway station in Hamburg.

Something that I must mention about an apprenticeship was that it was designed purely for a practical training. There were no educational lectures, talks or tours as all that was left to the apprentice himself to find out through study and attendance at night school. The nearest anyone got to theory would be learning from some little snippet that came your way by chance like how to make a well-used file into a magnet in the electrician's shop or being told that brass is non-magnetic and non-ferrous.

The total ground area of the engine works is divided into several different working bays while upstairs is a single gallery containing the light machine shop. This consists of a line of lathes that operate from several overhead common rotating shafts connected with driving belts to each machine. There is also a large store which supplies the whole of the workforce with nuts, washers, bolts and any other basic requirements, but of course these bits and pieces are a small part of what the lathes upstairs produce or machine. The heavy machining is carried out at ground floor level on reinforced flooring.

Most of the workforce enter the building through a small door situated in a much larger doorway which could be opened by its two halves sliding apart to allow a steam locomotive to shunt goods wagons inside for unloading. The company ambulance room is situated to the right of this door as one enters the building, and there is an ambulance man in attendance during working hours, although I feel he has some other job to do at the same time, (even though my mind to-day thinks this other job must have been connected with safety and safe working practice). At the same time let me assure you that there was no safety man or officer in the sense of today's.

I remember two serious accidents. The first was when a gas bottle exploded in the metal cutting shop, and a number of burners and labourers were taken off to hospital with burns and shock. The other occasion was when a large pot of paint fell from the outside roof and crashed down into the store in Blake's Bay. Bill and Jenny, whom I have already mentioned, had a very close encounter with serious injury or death. The store had originally been added at ground level and jutted out like an outhouse from the main building. The pot crashed through the store roof and then proceeded to smash its way through some heavy timber shelving, leaving no doubt whatsoever in my mind as to what would have happened to any human being in its path. It must have left a lasting effect on Bill and Jenny who were in the store at the time, and we have heaven to thank that Molly and her friend Kitty were not having a tête-à-tête at that moment on or near the spot when the damage was done.

I visited the ambulance room twice during my time in the engine workshop or 'at the tools', as it was better known. I managed to get a piece of metal in my eye which couldn't be removed so I was sent to the Eye Infirmary in Berkeley Street, not far from the Mitchell Library and St Andrew's Hall, where a no-nonsense lady doctor removed the splinter of steel from my eye.

The other occasion was after I had taken a long length of angle iron to the burning shop to be cut into shorter lengths, and foolishly grabbed an end that had just been cut with an acetylene gas torch. My idea was to push the angle iron along the trestles to assist the burner with his job. My fingers weren't too badly burnt but remained bandaged for a few days, and I still attended work.

There were four women employed in the fitter's bay. There was Molly in the store whom I have already mentioned, and there was Kitty, the sweeper-up, who was never without her brush of office. She was probably between the age of fifty and sixty, petite, grey-haired and always wearing a whimsical smile which left one thinking that she had lots of patience. There was also that nuance as though she had just heard of something that she would like to talk about. Then there were two much younger girls called Isa and Kate. Isa worked in the brass cutting area, making brass liners or shims and tying them up into sets which would ultimately find their way to rest between the two halves of the large bearings I mentioned before. The idea behind these thin pieces of brass was that if the bearing became slightly worn, then one or more of these brass liners could be removed to close around the shaft that was rotating between the two halves. (Too much gap would cause a fall in luboil pressure.)

Kate operated the brass nameplate printing machine. There were a lot of small nameplates required when you consider that each valve, wheel and lever in an engine room had to have an identity label or nameplate attached to it. Each of these identifying tags or discs was finished off by hand and the lettering filled in with red wax before their final polish.

Let's start our grand tour from the bottom of the gallery stairs in Blake's Bay beside Bill's store and underneath the Gaffer's Box. If we start in an upriver direction we move into one of the heavy machine shop areas where massive connecting rods are tediously machined and shaped to their final drawing dimensions. Part-lengths of the huge ungainly engine crankshaft are also completed in this section, and what an exacting job it is to set up these weighty and awkward parts into the huge lathes! Other heavy engine parts that are also machined here are the lengths of main shafting which one day soon will be rotating between the engine and propeller of a brand new vessel. The final operation on these shafts before leaving the lathe is to give each a fine skim by the turner, leaving them with a polished appearance that would last throughout their working lives.

All the heavy machines on the ground floor have their own electric drive motor which is driven by DC current, which I hasten to add will mean nothing to most people, but a few will recognise that I am merely dating the era when all those machines were installed. Up to the time I worked there, and probably many years later Barclay Curle produced its DC electric current from its own generators and to supplement this when required they bought in AC current from the Electricity Board which was converted into the old type DC for their workshop motors.

Like some pre-warning in the vicinity of these big lathes and slotting machines, indeed any machine large or small that dresses metal, there is always a kind of antiseptic smell in the surrounding air. Maybe that's too strong a word to use, but it originates from the mixture of oil and water that is continually running over the cutting tools as a coolant. This whitish-yellow liquid is circulated by being pumped back up from a tray under the lathe into a small header tank above the machine. This tank has to be topped up now and again as it is slowly depleted by both spill and being carried away in the metal cuttings. They are constantly being collected up from around the working machines by labourers and taken to an outside area where all the scrap cuttings are stored until an open railway wagon appears on the scene and carts it all away.

Walking around as we are, we're not exactly touring a carpeted mansion but at least it's clean, orderly and litter-free. One advantage of a long apprenticeship is the indoctrination of tidiness. It is inconceivable for an apprentice to crumple up a piece of paper in his hand and carelessly throw it on the floor. Cigarette ends – yes. Cigarette packets – no.

The next bay lies towards South Street (running parallel with the river) and is separated from the one we are just leaving by a wide passage which allows space for large bogeys to operate along rails that are used to transport heavy items along their length. These rails also run outside into the yard and are used to collect basic engine parts from outside and deliver them to a particular bay or point that is within reach of one of the inside overhead cranes. The bogeys are pushed or manhandled by labourers.

Across this passage is another heavy machine shop area similar to the previous one. Here the cylinder liners, inside which one day the pistons will play their part, are patiently machined to their blueprint size. To give some idea of the dimensions of these liners let me say that it would have been quite easy for Sydney Greenstreet to stand unseen inside one of them with Peter Lorre having to stand on his shoulders to look out from the top, and if the former of the two gentlemen cared to give a burst of his sinister though hearty laugh, his ample waistline would still not touch the inside surface of the liner.

The pistons that are to operate inside these cylinders have their circular ring slots cut out in this bay. Nearby can be seen the work being carried out on massive gear wheels and other heavy items being machined to their final size.

Before we move any further let me briefly explain about a lathe. It has what is called a 'chuck' at one end with jaws that can be altered to grip round the end of an object that has to be machined. It looks like a round cave on a sheer mountain side with four steel doors, all being at right angles to each other, completely encircling its entrance. These doors or jaws as they are called can be adjusted by the operator to either open or close at the same time as though they are trapping or releasing their prey in or from the centre of a fantasy web. In reality the 'chuck' rotates with whatever it is holding at a pre-selected speed when the turner switches on the electrical power to the machine. At the other end there is a 'tailstock' that does not rotate but which has a strong centre-pointed pin that fits into a pre-made recess in the central axis of the item being machined, thus keeping it level in the lathe and supporting its weight at that end. Operating these lathes is a trade on its own that combines patience with skill to produce the finished article. The machinists work to very fine limits using a variety of instruments to achieve this. To give some idea of the dimensions of what could be machined under this roof, there is one particular lathe whose chuck jaws operate inside a 12 foot diameter face plate.

Before leaving this bay let me mention that at the bottom right hand corner there is a large general store that caters for the working needs of all the workforce, and on one side of it is a wide wooden swing door built in two halves that opens inwards or outwards. This leads into a wide passage space used mostly for store purposes and leading through into the outside yard. Just off this passage is the engine shop managers' office, occupied then by Mr James (Big Jimmy) Wilson.

The impression I am left with about 'Big Jimmy' is that he was tall, slim and bore a facial resemblance to Bela Lugosi and I mean that in the nicest possible way. If I were to think back for anyone at that time who actually smiled it would have to be him. Do not get me wrong for he was a very strict man and had the reputation of being one, but I would place him as being an honest and fair man. He did of course, wear a bowler hat which was the symbol of authority and only managers and the upper echelons were entitled to wear such an adornment. One of his habits was a regular walk around the workshops and upstairs to the light machine shop.

On the other side of the store from the manager's office is Alphie's toilet. Alphie was the one-legged lavatory attendant who timed one's stay in his particular province. I was warned about how he would throw open the unlocked half door of any occupied cubicle for either of the following reasons; he considered that one had spent sufficient time where one was, or he suspected one was reading a newspaper. The toilet was the great leveller between journeyman and apprentice for in Alphie's eyes there was no difference. The one good thing his patrons had to their advantage was the early warning system given by his peg-leg on his approach. 'Clunk-pad, clunk-pad.' Whenever I try to visualise anyone's lifestyle I usually get it totally wrong; therefore, while I imagined Alphie arriving home at an upstairs tenement flat just after all the immediate neighbours had checked their clocks at the unique sound of him climbing the stairs, was it possible that before he could place his foot (no tasteless comment intended) across the threshold, he would be greeted by a beautiful wife who would immediately attend to his every wish?

My lasting impression of Alphie was that the lavatory had been built with him in mind as its keeper. There was an aura about him that suggested that somewhere from his dim past he was being haunted by a great white toilet that owed him something which he did not like to talk about. He was quite a character in his own right and one of those people who, if you wished him a 'Good morning, Alphie,' would give you a look as though you had said something quite offensive.

Now we can retrace our few steps to where we halted our tour, and on making them I have to admit that I have no idea where the female toilets are, and with that bit of useless information we can continue our perambulation and the keeping of our minds on much nobler things.

If we move across a comfortable sized walking passage that has been running down on our left-hand side, as we move through the heavy machine shop we find ourselves in another rectangular area situated at the bottom of Blake's Bay and used partly for heavy industrial machining and partly for the assembly of steam turbines. This area boasts of having one of the largest slotting machines in the UK and probably Europe. It is into and through this bay that the majority of the workforce enter the engine works from the gatehouse entrance in South Street.

Let's take a wee pause here before we push on again. After knowing now how much big stuff was handled under this roof for marine use would it surprise you if I said that aircraft were made and assembled here at one time? Yes they were, and just a war away. It was part of the building's effort in 1915 during the First World War to produce seaplanes and airfield landing aeroplanes under its roof, and during that period of time there were around 500 flying machines manufactured and placed in service.

I wonder how many people have stood where we are standing now, trying to imagine the countless manufactured pieces that have been required over the span of its being for huge diesel engines, steam engines and steam turbines, including also the fiddliest of pieces for those early airplanes. One has to admit that much has been created within these walls that has been the envy of people all over the world. All done, and done well through local thought and skills. Some day the marine activity here will move into history to mix with the ghosts from its past and look down on what has replaced it. I would like to think when that time comes, if one listens very, very quietly, within these walls its early echoes will still be heard.

Let me move forward in time to the Second World War and hope I can tell you more about the ladies themselves than I can about their toilets.

I cannot say how many women were employed amongst the inside total workforce, but it was a very small sprinkling fairly evenly distributed in all the departments. All females had to keep their hair tightly covered with a headscarf or hat as a protection against any of it being caught in a moving part of machinery. They had to wear sensible shoes and gloves would be worn if they were working on anything with a sharp edge. I seem to recall that industrial gloves were supplied for certain work but no protective clothing was provided by the company.

It wasn't a working environment that attracted a great many of the women caught up in the web of war where other choices seemed a lot more attractive. Having to persevere with tough metal in a cold draughty semi-Victorian workshop did in no way guarantee soft hands with manicured nails and rosy cheeks. Having said that, there were a lot of women machinists and welders who did excellent work in the workshops and shipyards all over the country.

Coming back to engines for a moment there was one thing about the engine test programme that always made me think about the heart attack I never saw happen or even heard about. The Doxford diesel engine is tall, long and lean and when it is running it looks like an experienced athlete performing a well-rehearsed part. Suddenly the innocent onlooker and attending staff would practically jump out of their skins when a fuel valve stuck in the open position, causing an almighty 'crack', 'crack', 'crack' sound coming from the respective cylinder relief valve, and this was accompanied by a sheet of flames shooting out from the source of the noise. During the ship sea trials I was to be later involved in and during the early part of my life at sea I had to learn to duck down pretty fast when I found myself in the firing line. Looking back I thought it was strange that legislation to alter the direction of the flame took so long to come about.

Right! Back again to the walkabout. This bottom bay, containing the entrance and ambulance room, is the biggest, and it is here that the head foreman has his office ... He was a silver-haired, stockily built man called Duncan White who always wore a dark suit, collar and tie and never without his Crown of Office which was a deep sea cap jauntily worn. He reminded me of W.C. Fields playing the part of the master aboard the *Mississippi Queen*. I'm sure he was very efficient at his job, as the business of building engines appeared to run smoothly enough and with good results with the deadlines always seeming to be met that proved he was an efficient engineer and organiser. To the apprentices he was known as Dunky White, and I never knew of him giving a smile. Carrying the mantle of the head foreman was a very serious thing indeed.

Facing the top of this bay and across the main passage with the bogey rails is the area that comprises Blake's Bay to the left, with the stairs at the top end where we started our walk, and the erecting bay over on the right where the diesel engines are built and tested. It was interesting for me to see the daily progress and assembly of all the pieces of these huge Doxford engines that were so aptly called cathedral engines because of their height and finally watching them run on test which was termed 'test bed trials'.

It all started with a very large empty space; then one day the sturdy base of an engine appeared, quickly followed by upright columns that gave the fanciful appearance of a laughing, moustached strong-man. He was then dressed with all the other parts with the competence of a troupe of acrobats springing on and about him with apparent ease. The final product was then ready to be tested.

As size is a relative thing I will give the following analogies: as a rabbit is to a motor car engine, a mule would be to a turbine; a horse to a steam-reciprocating engine; an elephant to a diesel engine, and a row of several giraffes to a Doxford engine.

To me there is still no mechanical movement more graceful than a Doxford engine running at slow speed. The upper pistons and their connecting rods, which can be seen, seemed to bounce majestically up and down, as though they were attached to a rubber band. To open any one of the crankcase observation ports, or circular windows, and look inside is to observe a quiet Swiss watch motion, with the short centre rod sliding in the opposite direction to the side rods under the command from the rotating crankshaft, and all this seen through a magic waterfall of escaping lubricating oil tumbling down from every bearing and returning to its original starting place beneath the crankshaft bottom.

Continuing our Grand Tour we find, in the downriver direction from where the engines are built and tested, that there are another two bays, one on either side of the main passage with the bogey rails along it. Both these areas are given over to welding and burning. It is from these areas that the sole plates, crankcases, columns and a myriad of other metal parts are prepared and fabricated into a required item.

Overhead in each Bay are the travelling cranes which are in continual use, either lifting, carrying, positioning or gently lowering to the ground some heavy item required by fitter, machinist or welder. The crane and slingers are at everyone's beck and call. Some of those weights range from a few hundredweight to ten tons and very much vary in size and shape. I will leave it to your imagination as to how they are positioned so exactly for a particular operation where a machine working limit of one thousand part of an inch was about to be employed on it.

The lifting, or slinging work is carried out by riggers (slingers), and like the welders and fitters they worked under a separate foreman. These men know exactly what size of rope or wire to use for any particular lifting job. They also have to be quite sure that a lifting wire, or strop does not chafe, mark or damage what is being lifted. It was always a near heart-stopper for me watching the outside preparation of attaching immense wires to half an engine, followed by a team of riggers taking up their various stations, and then the big lift from the jetty into the ship. These men do a great job with everything under control, with the overhead crane driver getting his instruction from one man by either a whistle signal, or an arm movement. The weather plays a major part in the head rigger's decision of whether to commence a heavy outside lift or not.

One heavy part that always seemed to be on the move was a length of main shafting. There were plenty of these around because all vessels built at B.C. were engined midships which required a line of this shafting to run between the engine and the propeller. (At that time only the tankers were engined near the stern, although this later became the standard practice.)

I would like to dwell a moment on the shaft that leaves the ship's hull on which the propeller is attached, and mention that the steel is manufactured to a certain strength, but unless protected in some way, it will rust – unprotected steel in salt water, for example, rusts very quickly. Now let me tell you about the operation that protects it from rusting: The stern shaft (steel propeller shaft) has a non-ferrous (brass) shroud or sleeve shrunk around it – this operation always created a deadly hush among the witnesses. I always watched with a certain degree of tenseness. The steel shaft, approximately 18 inches in diameter and 20 feet in length, was stood upright while the entire length of its brass shroud was heated with gas rings. When its internal diameter had expanded outwards to a previously calculated reading (a matter of thousandths of an inch) the shroud was lifted over the shaft and then lowered down around it until it completely encased the shaft. The brass sleeve then shrank itself firmly onto it during its final stage of cooling, leaving the steel shaft with a permanent protective coat against rust and wear. It should not be hard to understand the silence during the time when the sleeve was descending around the shaft, as we wondered whether someone had got their sums wrong and it might stop half way down – which it never did while I was there. I was learning that in my working world, all things were calculated. Such is the alchemy of engineering, where there is no such thing as chance.

The boiler house is outside the engine shop, and situated fairly close to the main office. Each summer the main boilers which supply the steam to the entire engine works are shut down at different times for maintenance and cleaning. This work entails removing each and every steam and water valve along with the boiler external fittings like the water level gauges and test cocks, which are all thoroughly cleaned and examined, and brought back to good working conditions. In other words all these parts are made like new and before being replaced on the boiler they have to be examined by a Lloyds surveyor who has to be entirely satisfied with the condition each item is in before giving official approval to replace them.

The boilers have to be overhauled separately to ensure a constant supply of steam. Somehow or another I was landed with this work on two occasions when I worked under an old fitter called Bill Jones who was in his seventies. You can guess who had all the climbing about the boilers to do. Old Bill wore his deep sea cap all the time and permanently puffed away on a well-used pipe which emitted smoke which I could have sworn was a product of old socks. He had spent a large part of his life at sea as a marine engineer and had been working at Barclay Curie's since then which was a fair number of years. Every journeyman in the engine works knew old Bill Jones. I learnt a lot about Scotch boilers from old Bill, plus a few horror stories about what had happened on board some ships when these boilers had been neglected by personnel who just did not know or understand their potential dangers.

Next to the boiler house is the electrician's shop which houses the generators and produces all the electrical power and the type required. It also contains the electrician's workshop for the repair of motors and other electrical equipment. It was here I was sent in my early days with an old file that I had 'buffed' down to a handy shape to have it magnetised. Each apprentice had such a magnet for the removal of any small pieces of metal that required clearing out from some awkward space where fingers could not reach.

The next building is the blacksmith's shop where the thump, thump, thump of the big steam hammer can be heard some distance away, beating a hot cherry-red piece of metal into something that more resembled some required engine part after each 'thump'. A short time afterwards, that same piece of metal will be placed on the steel marking-off table in the fitter's bay to be whitewashed and marked-off to the dimensions shown on its blueprint drawing. The machining lines that are inscribed on the whitewash are then permanently dotted or dabbed with a steel hand punch with a sharp point. These punch marks are a guide to the machinist who will later carry out the final shaping to the exact finished size of the part.

When we leave the blacksmith we find ourselves back in the open where we can walk round the outside of the engine works. There are two options. The first is going via the front where the railway engines shunt waggons in and around the large forecourt, though circling in that direction would mean passing the entrance beside the ambulance room. Alternatively, we could meander in the opposite direction round by the jetty and under the shadow of the huge crane, then past the immense sliding doorway leading into the erecting bay which is almost in line with a new ship's hull that waits to be engined, or perhaps there is a completed vessel waiting in preparation for its dock trial in a few days time. Let us continue our circle in a downriver direction along the berth to the end of the building, then turn right away from the river, from where we can now see the canteen that I sometimes used. Pretty close to it is a low brick building which, if I remember correctly, was used as an air raid shelter and a store for fire-fighting equipment and appliances. A little further towards South Street and we find ourselves back on the broad forecourt with its myriad of railway lines sunk into its cement grounding. From here we have a choice of two exits leading to South Street. On the right there is the gatehouse alongside a large double entrance for heavy road transport and down to the left there is another double gate used as a railway entrance and it is here the railway lines lead out on to South Street. This gate is always opened at the end of the working day and is the one most used for the mass workforce exit and rush to the tramcars that are waiting in Primrose Street ready to fill up and away, turning either left or right into Dumbarton Road and speeding off along the tram lines in whatever direction its colour code claimed its direction lay. But! Before the workforce pass through the exit gate they have to pass the pattern shop where the wooden patterns or shapes are made to make the fireclay moulds for all the metal castings that will later appear in the machine shop.

The types of work I did during the four years I spent in the workshop ranged considerably, covering the use of a hammer and chisel, which were required usually as a first means of attack, before the dressing-up began with file or scraper and feelers. From fairly basic work to lapping fuel valve spindles, (making the operating spindle in a valve the correct fit) to fitting and setting the cams on the camshaft in order that each fuel valve would start to open at the correct time. A particular job I did on occasions was to fit melting plugs in the cylinder liners, which meant two fusible plugs with a low melting temperature were placed in a drilled hole, which was then plugged and dressed up in such a way as not to be noticeable. These plugs might well have to be examined at some later date by the builder to determine whether the liner, or call it a cylinder, had at any time been overheated after it had left the engine works.

During the summer months most of the Apprentices spent their lunch break outside the engine shop premises on the grass verge overlooking the River Clyde.

If anyone has a river then mine must be the Clyde. I probably first saw it as an excited little boy crossing his first river bridge, and peering down from the parapets, being given the answer to my unasked question that the river flowing beneath me was called the Clyde. It could only have been a few years later when I sailed 'doon the watter' (humorous Glasgow term) on board one of the railway paddle steamers. This river had never been far away from me when I was evacuated and immediately following that period I lived once again beside it at Prestwick during my formative years. It seemed to me at that time it was following me from place to place and pretty determined that if it could not follow me along its exact chosen path, then some mystic part of it certainly would. Here it was again beside the very place where I was to learn a trade, from which I would be able to compare it with many other famous rivers which I would some day visit during the years that I would make my living from the sea.

Let me bring in a spot of history at this point. It is only a matter of some 200 years ago that dredging started on this part of the river, an on-going process to allow for the ever-increasing size of vessels, and to permit them to sail up the river as far as Glasgow. The city then lay much further to the east where the oldest preserved buildings still remain. Glasgow Cross was the centre of the town at one time, but since then Glasgow has flourished downriver towards the deepened waters of the Clyde.

I will now take that as a cue to pause for a moment and change my style, at least, after the following few paragraphs.

Every country has beautiful and ever changing scenes throughout its land and around its waters, if such there are. Each has been created and preserved through Nature's own special efforts and gifted to mankind. Unhappily this endowment all too often is little heeded and as our ability to kill, maim and destroy not only ourselves but our planet increases, so this special legacy to future beings becomes less and less.

The following are two poems which I would ask the reader to read and compare. They have been twinned for effect and are two enduring experiences that are all too frequently worldwide. They are written in English only because it is the language I was born into and is of little matter. The writing is merely an attempted translation of what must have been spoken a million times in as many dialects and tongues.

The first is a personal example from the many natural wonders that are woven into the design of what incessant means. Each person reading this will, I'm sure, be able to identify something as special and personal to themselves. It might be a hill or a mountain, a moor, a valley, a desert, a special vista or perhaps it's a tree.

The substance of the second poem can only be created through the wit of man. Its last verse has been deliberately inflated and is not an oversight. I want to give the impression that conflict between two countries should be by no means a local thing but of worldwide concern.

THE FLOWING LINE

In breeze blown floating laden sail and with heaven's sagely spell,
This special task was long pre-planned, before first droplings fell.
Then rainspots formed fresh puddles that storm-splashed into pools,
Then by stringing each together, spun a thread of pearl-like jewels
That won-wandered gaps and gullies to win-wind a path through wood,
Carrying great stamina substance and share-spreading what it could.

True kin of Caledonia's earth, twinned blend from bleak upland mint,
Its multi-moving scattered shades shows all season's coloured tint.
Four pageant linns like omen's spell display their splashing spill,

For nought could check nor stem the flow, nor hold its waters still.
And enchantment's haze sly softly sings, as impish haunt-heralds do,
'Of Nature's created great wonders, it hand-tailored this for you.'

It closely caressed a sainted place, on being called back to the sea,
That merged the doomed Molendinar, nigh where Monk Mungo chose to be.
Who preached nearby this river spot, where soon would stand his town,
That prayed its roots he'd flourish as they spread more deeply down.
Its lifespace crossed the water width and both banks helped it grow,
And serving soil in rural realm became not sole reason for its flow.

Silver-skirting its way under moonlight, or flaunting beneath the sun,
Reflecting back the weather's mood, decrees tight-reined or rapid run.
It magnets and mirrors all creatures, when each sups as welcome guest,
Blink-bushing the courting couples, odd a'spelled with cupid's quest.
Oh! and it ended noble discord, after serf-salmon returned royal ring,
Earning errant Languoreth's atonement, and chastised her jealous king.

It heard the reels and the lassies sing as the clumsy laddies pranced,
Flowing-floating the lively strain while its shifting sparkles danced.
But now sings Scotland's scenic songs, though laments in

past time sung,
When once amongst its glen hid hills saw sore hurt as claymores swung.
Each morn now greets new dreamlike dawn, where families live full free,
Causing someone-somewhere-somehow to sigh, for its here one longs to be.

Steel ships spawned its deepened verge, from parts that made them sail,
Proving their worth in monsoon swell, or in duel with a force ten gale.
And nearby grew tall lifting frames, for lading safe stowed on the ebb,
Fae neat wee bits to grand rail things, made to puff on a far wynd web.
But more precious cargo ever shipped, was rich emigrant cultural drain,
Fine folk and family taking nocht, but their God-gifted body and brain.

It will flow where fancy takes it, whether to sail or stroll its bends,
Often travelling on much further, from the place where its journey ends.
Where earth's turn fades sun's coloured scene, if braw the ev'en wills,
And great kingdom ocean welcomes home its child from the Celtic hills.
Whose guidness sweeps green fertile path, where kith and beast can bide,
From its finest threads to fairest Firth, ever flows clear caring Clyde.

Caledonia/Scotland
Linn/Waterfall
Molendinar burn/Stream that flowed into the Clyde & now practically non-existent
St Mungo/Patron Saint of Glasgow

Salmon & the ring/Legend of Languoreth's Ring & part of Glasgow's coat of Arms
Languoreth/Queen to King Rydderch of what is now known as Strathclyde

Claymore/Sword
Nocht/Nothing
Braw/Good
Kith/Friends, neighbours
Bide/Reside, stay, live
Fae/From
Wee/Small

THE MOVING LINE

Each stood in line to sign their name, both called and volunteers
To fight for Home and Country, mid the sound of a country's cheers.
For tact and tongue had lost their sway, and reason turned absurd,
With bigot's ears to deafness tuned, bar dire dogma's chosen word.
Though nought was said two dozen times, had not been heard before
Again nigh two decades and five, green shoots will hear arms roar.

And the line moved slowly on.

Some heard the deep down whisper, that warned from foresight's face,
That extremes will be demanded, with this line their starting place.
When wrongs and pride are on parade, and sense won't put them right,
Erupts the leader who lays the blame and whose answer is to fight.
But in the calling forth of fighters and the firing of their guns,
Homeland children lose their fathers and the mothers forfeit sons.

And the line moved slowly on.

Recruited voice now spoke with pride, 'How Fabled Fathers Fought.'
And inward asked feared question, all warring ranks have thought.
'If I should win a foreign grave, or battle-bear some spectre back,
Will I be remembered as what I was, or mere seen for what I lack?'
Unspoken thoughts of what could be, were ones most hard to share,
The fear what fate had written, was faint spoke in private prayer.

And the line moved slowly on.

Youth now formed the moving line and of doubt they showed no trace,
Their manly looks could not betray their frightened school-boy face.
They differed when their pulses beat, in graves they sleep the same,
No second choice grant-given them, even home-heading blind or lame.
See combat wounds feel battle pains, witness what each country lost,
Young muted tongues and empty eyes, just a part war's dreadful cost.

And the line moved slowly on.

Each earthly tribe at fleeting times will show its tarnished spots,
When beast or bully makes the choice of 'who is' or 'who are nots.'
But Briton, Gael, Celt and Saxon on these islands now mixed as one,

Yet no different from close cousin, the Viking, Gaul, Latin and Hun.
Is there a special trouble tree, where its branches all must fight
Or angered stream return uphill from raged river's offhand slight?

And the line moved slowly on.

When this drama's curtain final falls, on all its war-touched cast,
With tragic start of intrigue first, and ends with all things last,
Of darkest dark its acts will tell, to cause conscience sap to flow,
The hurt and harm and damage done, will tear-touch all in every row.
No prompt required for unseen list, of womb-gender war marred minds,
Or maimed-disfigured guiltless young, nor effect their future finds.
Each one a scar sinned living proof, yet just part of what lies hid
Of fast fading untold foe-crimes, safe sound lost beneath war's lid.
But saddest sad stood centre stage, the end scene-set all could see,
The hungered lips denied love's kiss, with caress that could not be.
This final finale starts the flame, to be lit in each audience mind
To stark remind they play their part, with what finer feelings find.
To foremost damn war's warlocks, dream drunk glut with ego's praise,
And prayer plea that line now stopped, won't start some other place.

There was plenty for the apprentices to see on the river during their lunch break, and our interest was always heightened when a gaping torn hole in a passing bow could be seen just above the water line in a listing vessel on its way up-river to discharge cargo. In our imaginations we could see the crew pumping one tank and emptying another to alter the trim and bring the torn bow plates above sea and river water level. It would most probably have berthed inside the more protected areas of Queen's Dock on our northern side in the Anderson District, or across the river in either Prince's Dock in Kinning Park or Kingston Dock in Kingston itself. Later on, after the cargo was discharged, it would make its way to a repair berth where the damaged part would be cut away by the burners with their acetylene torches. When they were finished it would be the turn of the welders who would weld on the new parts of the hull structure. The new plates would be fitted on with the riveters who made such a decibel racket. By far the most of the vessels were flying the Red Ensign and registered at one of our own major seaports. There must have been ships from all the Allied countries coming and going and we would try to identify the flag flying with the name of the ship and its port of registry, though not always in that order. There were some funny sounding names and many of the places where they were registered none of us had ever heard of.

The attraction of the day might well have been a launch in the vicinity which could be heard more than seen from the noise of the drag chains, which always seemed to bring the new ship's hull to a stop just in time for the tugs to get their ropes secured aboard and take control. On occasions this could be a tricky job in a river where strong unpredictable winds can blow up or down its length. A hull with little or no ballast in it floats on the water like a bubble and is in its most vulnerable condition regarding the elements.

The ships that were engined at Barclay Curle Engine Works usually came from the company's own Clydeholm Shipyard which lay further along South Street towards the city, but still in Whiteinch. There were several other shipbuilders whose vessels were engined alongside the engine works. Connels Shipyard next door to us built some lovely hulls and a number of these came alongside our berth. Connells had a proud and hard-won reputation of helping men who had spent time in prison to rehabilitate themselves, and as far as I was led to believe, had a high success rate.

It was never very long before any new arrival alongside the berth was being inspected by critical young gentlemen who considered themselves leading experts in marine shipping, ranging from naval frigates with their cramped spaces, to the luxurious mercantile ships that carried cargo as well as having a limited passenger accommodation. Time allowing, we usually finished our ship's tour on the monkey island above the bridge deck where we had a spectacular view of the Clyde and along its busy industrial banks and beyond where the greenery lay. From that point we could determine where the next launch was due to take place, and also fairly accurately determine when that would be.

There was a watchman on board who never caught a Nazi or Fifth Columnist, but kept his hand in by sometimes chasing us off the ship. Most times he wasn't sure whether we were working on board or not.

The naval corvettes were engined with steam-reciprocating engines, whereas the cargo ships were each powered with diesel engines, which were proving much cheaper to run. It was in a corvette engine room that I first acquired a 'something' which was to remain with me all my life, but first let me explain by taking you through the hissing sound of escaping steam mixed with the hustle and bustle of attendant staff to-ing and fro-ing, and allowing you only the time to clear the warm condensation from your glasses and catch your breath. It is also quite noisy so I will have to shout.

The first test of any new engine on board a ship is called the dock trial, and there has to be a lot of preparation before this can take place. On a steam-propelled vessel, regardless of whether it is engined with a reciprocating engine (pistons and crankshaft type) or a turbine (steam blown on to blades fitted round a shaft causing it to rotate), before steam machinery can be used steam must be produced in the boilers first. Boilers can be the first and last line of defence in any engine room and for that reason the very best water is used in their filling and chemical tests will be taken normally each day of their life to ensure against various forms of damaging contaminations. From the very start the boiler water has to be heated with intermittent firing of the burners to prevent any uneven metal distortion or stressing. Air cocks on the top of the boiler are open during this process and usually the manhole near the boiler top is left slackened back to allow leakage past it. This is to let the heated air out of the boiler and when steam starts to appear then the cocks are closed and the manhole tightened on to its steam joint. Air contains oxygen which causes corrosion in metals. (One of the contaminants).

Steam pressure is then raised by continuing the same slow method until there is a 'full head' of steam in the boiler and it's after that the tricky part starts, when beginning to supply this steam to the engine. Again, the first thing is to make certain that all the drain cocks on the steam pipe leading to and on the engine are full open and that the valves along the line are operable to allow the passage of the steam. All these steam drains are simply openings along the passage that the steam will travel and lead into the bilges beneath the floorplates you are now standing on to be sure that no one gets scalded. All the hissing you hear coming from beneath you with steam raising from it are not leaks in the uncontrollable sense, so please don't be alarmed.

Steam drains are strategically placed at the lowest points along any steam line, the reason being that any water forming in the steam will fall due to its greater weight and exit to the bilges via the open drain line. We already know it's noisy and steamy, but it is essential that only steam reaches the engine and, of course, once the whole plant is warmed through and operating, all those noisy drains are closed and there is a delightful quietness. The first rule that any engineer learns about steam is that water cannot be compressed (remember that first dive into, or more correctly, on top of the swimming pool when you flop-landed flat on top of the water?) If there is any water in a steam cylinder where its piston is moving along its length then something is going to give. Luck is a word I do not like using; therefore let me say it would be fortunate if the excess pressure device (relief valve) lifts and copes with the amount of moisture present, but if it does not, then there is every chance of serious damage being caused such as a cylinder cover being smashed or a bent piston rod and probably an impaired crankshaft. A costly business indeed, apart from any physical damage that may have taken place.

With diesel engines, the engine warming process and the time taken is practically the same as for a steam engine, except that it is the circulating water that is heated as it passes through a steam heater, and in this way the metal of the engine absorbs the heat, slowly avoiding the sudden stress of changing from cold to hot which could cause a crack in the metal. The major difference between a steam and motor plant is that the former requires a much larger steam generating plant. I should mention here for my more advanced technical reader that the boilers I have been describing are an updated oil firing version of the type used in the old *Mississippi Queen* that most of us have seen at some time, compliments of Hollywood. The Royal Navy's larger ships have another type of boiler in which the steam pressure can be raised much faster, as were some of the passenger liners.

Another important part of the preparations is to put out extra mooring lines to compensate for the extra pull that the ship will give when its propeller starts to turn in the water. The river pilot is in charge of the vessel, and when he is assured that the necessary ropes are out and secured to the berth, and that the tugs are ready in case they might be required, then, and only then he will move the telegraph to the Dead Slow Ahead position and the engine will be started for the first time on the ship. The pilot will ring for the engine to be run at slow speeds both ahead and astern to an agreed schedule. The dock trial usually lasts about two hours to allow for adjustments to be made and readings taken.

I mentioned in a previous paragraph about a certain 'something' that I first acquired in a steamship engine room which was to remain with me at least up to the time of writing. Steam and oil mixed together in a warm engine-room produces a rather pleasant and unique odour. If I were to be asked what two smells I would like to take with me to a desert island, I would choose the fragrance of burning pinewood and the aroma of a reciprocating steam engine plodding away under a full head of steam.

Well, that has finished the look-around for the first engine test. I should really mention here that the first sound a ship makes when it becomes alive and independent is the roar of one of its generators when the electrical power from the shore line is disconnected from the main switchboard and its own power is loaded on. Conversely the very last sound from any vessel is the stopping of its generators, followed immediately by an eerie silence, and then you suddenly become conscious of being able to hear someone talking quite clearly from the other end of the engine-room.

Barclay Curle had an enormous crane on its berth at Whiteinch which is still there today, and a well-known landmark. Its great size and strength was primarily used to engine the ships, but was regularly used for lifting many other heavy parts on board.

I would not like to even hazard a guess how many apprentices tried to work out how much it would cost to lift a specified weight a particular height from a certain distance out along the jib, then make one complete turn before lowering the load on the exact spot where it was lifted from. A group of us tried out this exercise on a number of occasions and the various costs ranged from £15 to £80 which might have been a good insight into the stuff that the future captains of the marine industry had between their ears.

The nearest shop to the engine works was a well-patronised newsagent and tobacconist near the bottom of Primrose Street. It also sold sweets and a little of this line and a little of that line to cater for the neighbourhood needs. Outside the shop and whenever the weather permitted there would be a large bird cage comfortably suspended about pedestrian head level and containing their pet parrot that specialised in 'wolf' whistles and calling out, 'I'm Celtic, I'm Celtic.' Many people will recall this parrot as he (?) was a popular feature in the area. Just why I mention Polly (if that were her (?) name) at this time is because I have no doubt whatsoever that it (?) could have shouted out a more sensible answer to what the apprentices came out with on their academic forays involving the big outside crane – and they were using slide rules.

Wartime holidays or breaks from home were fairly basic affairs, with perhaps a short stay at a Bed and Breakfast, or what was more likely, a stay with a relative or friend. During my stay in Prestwick I went to an Army Cadet camp; otherwise I had no holidays during my school days which I must say did not bother me in the slightest. When I moved back to Glasgow I was lucky in managing to stay two weeks on a farm near Colmonell in Ayrshire on two consecutive years in July. Joey had been working nearby in the Women's Land Army, and billeted along with some other WLA girls in a large country residence called Knockdolian House. She had arranged for me to stay at Knockdolian Farm, run by a young farmer, David Telfer. I stayed with a Mrs Eaglesham whose cottage joined David's. My hostess was a warm-hearted country born woman and I can remember to this day the hearty laugh she gave when I handed over some dried egg powder which was amongst the goods in a parcel that Mother had made up for me to give her that contained the usual sugar, tea, tin of corned beef and such-like.

She was a widow and had a son called Alex who I think would have been in his mid-twenties then, and who had been crippled with polio as a young boy. There were two other children much younger than Alex, a boy about twelve and a girl who was a few years younger. For some reason I think that both the two young children were adopted. I can't remember their names.

There was no electricity or gas in the cottage so it was a matter of oil lamps at night along with a warm fire. The cooking was done in the kitchen and the fuel used was a mixture of coal and wood. The toilet was outside in a shed and was a dry soil affair with a seat over it which offered the minimum of privacy. The room I occupied was upstairs and I shared it with a mouse; at least I think it was the same wee beastie. The pair of us got on well together and finished up on speaking terms with each other. On my second visit I was with a friend and I can't remember if Mousie was still there.

On certain days of the week there was a visit from the baker or the butcher or maybe it was the fishmonger, and that would be when they were doing their rounds of the farms and the farm cottages.

There is also a river, but before I give its name I must say it is very beautiful where it flows by Knockdolian House. It was popular with fishermen and is called the Stinchar. It source lies in the Carrick Forrest at Shalloch which is not too far distant, and on its way to the coast it has tributaries from the River Duist and Muck Water before reaching Colmonell. There is also the remains of a castle that is a left-over from the violent earlier times. Here the fighting was over a fertile region and its nearness to the English border, but that does not mean very much because there was fighting all over the country and it didn't take much to start it. It was more or less a cottage industry, and really not so long ago.

Young Farmer David, along with his wife Greta and an almost brand new infant son John, lived next door in the adjoining cottage with the same amenities. David's father owned the neighbouring farm, which meant I had plenty of land to explore or help where I could for both of these activities I enjoyed doing. I could not understand David when he said he envied me the fact that some day I might go to sea and travel the world.

I was not the only outsider staying at the farm. It was a distinction I shared with two Italian prisoners of war. They were genuinely very amicable people and quite trustworthy. If I had been a POW I would have hoped to be farmed out to a family like the Telfers.

I started my apprenticeship in August 1943, by which time the threat of enemy air raids was a thing of the past and we were only reminded of them by the practice sound of the weekly siren test. I honestly cannot recall what the workforce was supposed to do in the eventuality of an air attack. I can only reiterate that I remember a windowless low brick building fairly close to the canteen which I associate with having been the shelter.

Victory for the Allies was certain now that the Suez Canal threat had been removed by the 8th Army's desert triumph, and the talk now was not if but when the Second Front would commence. My first apprenticeship year seemed to pass very quickly as it appeared no time at all before the landings along the Normandy Coast, that took place the following year on 6th June, were announced that Tuesday morning. It was, of course, no time at all before the wise pundits of the fitter's bay had our boys in Paris by lunchtime (or was it shortly after). They might have been a little bit out in their assessment of the situation; in fact if either Monty or Eisenhower had briefly paid us a visit at that time instead of being elsewhere they would have left a few shades greyer and feeling a lot older than they had on arrival. On the other hand, it was far better then for the country that the men of

Blake's Bay built engines and were not on the Armed Forces General Staff.

Working where I did meant that I met a lot of different people amongst which were a few characters. Overall by far the most I liked and a few I didn't. By nature I managed to get along with most persons I worked with. One aspect which was new to me was working alongside Catholic boys. Religion was one thing that was not talked about because for some silly reason it was considered divisive and one only found out another's belief by chance. No one would ever ask directly another's religious views, which would be considered with suspicion as having an ulterior motive behind it. Having said that, I remember one labourer who would talk jokingly about his priest, who I am sure did not share identical feelings towards him. This fellow worker looked quite a lot older than he really was, though at that time most of the men appeared middle-aged to me. Perhaps he had just had a carefree life with all that such a living could conceive in his case. He would introduce a topic, mostly in a public house or gambling scenario, in a casual way and then start on a subject which led the listeners to make their own connection as to the final outcome. One time he mentioned to me in an offhand way about it being time he paid his priest a visit. Then, after a long pause, he continued by saying that if there was anything he wanted to get off his chest (another touching long pause) he would first go to his chemist and if that didn't cure it then he would visit his doctor, and if that didn't cure it then it was time to see his priest. I suspect he saw a lot more of his priest than he did of the other two and had little knowledge of any doctor. I also think it was a long time since he had set foot inside a chemist shop.

There were no actual barriers between me being a Protestant and anyone I worked with being a Catholic. No one in my house spoke against any other faith. There might have been, and probably was, a subtle form of family brainwashing against the possibility of opposite sexes with differing religions becoming too friendly. If there had been, it was not obvious. There were ambiguous and doubtful statements said about many facets of life, including mixed marriages between religions and the future problems they may encounter with their offspring. This, I should add, was responsible parent guidance stuff as both my parents would have stood by any of their children in such a decision.

One thing the May children were blessed with was coming from a home where the word 'hate' was never heard, let alone preached. Looking back we were a very pacifist family with my parents having very pacifist friends. Perhaps it may have been the case of 'not in front of the children,' but I don't think so.

*

Wartime is a strange time. I was never made aware either of anyone being poor or of people paying taxes. Such information just sort of filtered down that in normal times working adults paid taxes and local rates and that some people lived in dire straits. These were topics a young person tended to overlook when most of the population was away in the Armed Forces and the remainder was in the business of supplying them with their wants and needs. Nevertheless the impression I was left with then was that contributions had to be made first and foremost to Government and local council and after that had been attended to one was free to spend what was left on his or her immediate needs and their families, if such was the case, providing some part of it was put aside for what was universally known as 'a rainy day'.

Up till this point I thought there were a lot of 'classes' and to talk of just three didn't have a ring of truth about it, at least not inside the city where the 'middle class' divided itself up time and time again, depending on wealth, attitude, dress, speech or mode of travel and a lot of snobbery. It wasn't like that when we visited friends outside Glasgow. The families and friends in the rural or smaller towns seemed to be identical to ourselves and I was always left with the impression that everyone in those areas was socially equal. It was, I suppose, to some extent the same in the 'working class' group. I knew that poor people could be very proud people and would go short of necessities in order to pay what they owed or somehow would do without in order that someone else didn't. They were also well versed in helping others. Where they lost out and split their 'class' was because it was so easy to focus blame on them for the transgressions of a few.

Politicians and councillors had an abysmal record of helping the genuine needy, partly because of the noisy phonies who by their own effort seemed to have sifted down to the social level that offered them the best cover. Some day a method will be evolved that will show the difference between the financially struggling poor and those who have no intention of making any contribution towards the enrichment of their society. It will probably come too late and in any case will be difficult to activate because again and again the innocent will be used as a shield against their exposure. Glasgow had its share of very rich and very poor and each class produced their quota of selfish and irresponsible persons. Those who came from financially secure homes were medical problems while the others from the poorer districts were social problems. Take your pick. I wonder how they managed when wearing a uniform. Remember I'm not talking about those who tried and failed for they were thought highly of, nor am I including the tiddly, improper and sometimes infuriating actions that are to be expected through frustrations. I would have been just as guilty as anyone else of such behaviour had I been born into a much poorer home than I was and would have had to suffer the finger of respectability being pointed at me.

Looking back it seems to me that having pride in the Empire and remembering the debt we all owed to its builders was extremely well stage-managed. Poverty and riots at home during the same period were somehow overlooked.

When Glasgow spread westward along the river, attracted by its newly built docks and building yards, it looked after the northern side by building fine civic buildings in proper settings and business premises connected with good roads. Directly across the river it built homes that somehow got left behind in the movement westward. This area was called the Gorbals and it degenerated through poverty and disillusionment. Glasgow was and still is the same as any other place where some have more than enough, some have enough, some have less than enough and some have nothing. Not very fair but it's certainly improving, and considering all the solutions that have been offered by the wise and wary over the centuries it should never have happened in the first place. But it did and still does, which suggests to me that the blame must hide behind the apparently most innocent of curtains. Somehow I do not think that I or the people of my city have changed much over its long history.

It is a well-known scientific fact that if Glaswegians get a bee in their bonnet then there's no stopping them, and a rubber hammer sometimes seems the only way to make someone change the subject, done in the nicest possible way, of course. If you could put up now and again with that sort of behaviour then you were 'home and dry' and it was a great place to live in. There was an egalitarian streak that is reflected in its society and which gives an added freshness to that city with its many parks. Unhappily there have been, and still are many Glaswegians unable to recall such things as 'the good old days,' and there were others who have had to leave the place where they were born to find conducive work and raise a family in some other land.

The Glasgow I remember was brassy and dull, grey and bright, busy roads and not so busy roads, quiet streets and green parks, brass bands and quiet Sundays, putting greens and tennis courts, busy stations and horsedrawn carts, Corporation tramcars and overhead wires, steam road rollers and cobbled streets, river and ships, hills and music, tenements and schools, big houses and gas lamps, serious and very serious, happy and very happy, violent and drunken, comfortable and safe. A hard core centred around its poorer areas with well-filled pubs and aspiring Benny Lynches who fought only too often outside the gymnasium and boxing ring.

Glasgow was a lot more soft than savage and underneath it all beat an honest city's heart for every type of mind and stature that could be found in normal ordinary people. Like any other city there were defects and a lot of folk were resigned to living a dingy life of chamber pots and outside toilets. There was a great misuse of cheap alcohol and a raw openness with some lives where argumentative conversation was a normal way of life. There were hard hearts, broken hearts, weak hearts and hearts that just never knew what they were beating for.

One heart works very much like any other but only beats today because of all the inherited genes created and used by its forbears where survival was its ultimate goal. What was done in the past by these genes in order to survive might not bear telling. Nothing happens today to anyone that has not happened somewhere in the family tree of all of us. In many ways each person is a city with all the good and bad that can be found in it. It only depends on the home you are born into and what in one's personality swamps out what. Respectability comes about with hard work and sacrifice by someone else, or by a lucky knife-edged accident.

The reader may well be thinking how this young middle class product remembered about such poor people and my answer is simple. I met and heard about them at work and also at night school where the students, or pupils as we were called, then came from every part of the city. Later on I was to meet Glaswegians of my own generation in Singapore, Middle East, Hong Kong, Australia, New Zealand and without exception it was my good fortune to meet them. Do you remember the parrot at the bottom of Primrose Street? Thirty years onwards in Quebec a chief engineer and a Lloyds surveyor were enjoying a chat after putting aside the business of the day. From that conversation it came out that the surveyor's aunt owned the bird and ran the small shop it belonged to. The engineer was the writer. It's really quite a small world.

Perhaps the following poem might say something that I otherwise could not do.

THE OLD GORBALS
(BETWEEN THE WARS)

Dulled stars blinked down upon them, though not from heaven's space,
Meted means lit-leaked quarried stone, from a Gorbals tenement face.
Gaunt night survived each setting sun in this bleak unpleasant spot
Where its youthful saplings hardened on roots that lived on nought.
No tinted leaves from summer's shroud would dance about their feet,
Each month showed its autumn sign with damp chills in every street,

The firefly's light was never seen, gas lamps bared all they sought
Beneath high host of phantom towers, black crowned with chimney pot.

Where baggy breeks and mended dress shrunk puny wean still smaller,
And hand-down worn with darner's dream, a mite fills fat and taller.
While king's jester bore queen's summons through nanny to the heirs,
Here jeelie piece calls tea-time, but without the 'grace and airs'.
Where free freedom stops at stairheid, ending panto-pavement's reign,
In innocent sure no rich bairn's play 'cud in no wey match wur ane.'
Those lively laughing children, creatures conditioned to this place,
Could spice fantasy with humour, quite unchanged from parents ways.

Deprived all the privileged waters, except their family's oasis well,
With but little shield or shelter, from veiled vested outcast spell.
Sated sorrow mimed 'wants' sad shadow, midst this harvest of despair,
Whose sons and daughters quickly found, been born here was so unfair.
And enticed by cheap elixir myth, only proved balsam brew once drunk,
The tempted taster slum-sore woke, with tomorrow's hope worse shrunk.
Some would lie or some would steal, and some showed streaks of cruel,
Manner marred and squalor scarred, styled in home or gangland school.

Tram-clippied-cars track-traded here, full-fed by floating web wires,
While charity food-fueled the needy, in quenching force-fasting fires.
Grey elders peered with old fox eyes, craft-gift through social flaws,
For living here bred deadly bite, yet most hearts bore harmless claws.
Where needs-must made most traders sly, with no less a rich man's wit,
Like caring breast beneath worn slate, differed not the slightest bit.
Had 'betters' wished to truly find, folks lair-living in cramped cage,
Here then was raw life's live theatre, with this place its open stage.

Some fleeting priceless moments found, in the darkened sanctuary hall,
Where filmed fiction's ushered dreams fled dreich tribal prison wall.
To fancy live another's life, brought whisped shade of an arcane rose,
That might its fragrance later haunt, romance in a clean cavern close.
That 'chance' shone much on others, but haughty-piqued passed them by,
It surely did not seem so wrong, they should ask that question – why?
One wonders what its gardener thinks of this failed far fallen bough?
From good-green branch proud-pruned, furthest far from what shows now.
Yet hope dreams here a summer scene, with cheer of the Gorbals reborn,
When spring sponsored swallows check its chill with a mild mint morn.

Gorbals/District of Glasgow (The original stone tenements were demolished during the sixties and replaced with modern brick buildings.)
Tenement/Large stone buildings, three to four storeys high and each divided into flats.
Breeks/Trousers.
Wean/Bairn, child.
Hand-down/Clothing previously worn by an older child who had hopefully outgrown them.
Mite/Child that for some reason pulls at the heart-strings or conscience.
Jeelie piece/Bread and jam sandwich
Stairheid/Tenement stairway landing at entrance to respective flats
Cud/Could. Ony:Onie/Any. Wey/Way. Wur/Our
Clippie/Public Transport Conductor/tress
Dreich/Dreary. Dull. Boring. Uninteresting
Close/Common entrance and stairway of a tenement

I must tell you about a door. No! THE DOOR. Between the inside engine erecting shop or bay and the outside jetty, and looking straight on to the river was an enormous sliding door. It was opened when an engine or a large section of one was moved outside to be placed within the safe arms reach of the great skyline intruder, the giant outside crane. The part would later be lifted from its fresh isolation and gently placed on board to become a working part of the vessel.

When this huge door was open in winter the temperature inside the whole of the engine works would sometimes drop to below freezing, and this condition was made worse by the icy damp draught from the perpetual chilling wind blowing along the river that somehow was always attracted by some enticement in through the gaping open portal. The total work force must have been very tough as I do not recall any absenteeism due to running noses during winter; in fact I don't think that word had been invented yet in conjunction with working people. Perhaps the truth is more likely to be that we were the survivors and the weaker persons had already been weeded out.

Now and again there was a rush to keep up with a time schedule which meant carrying on working through the night until 6 a.m. There were two working shifts from 8 a.m. till 5.30 p.m. and a night shift from 6 p.m. through to 6 a.m., although some of this time was covered by men on overtime. Saturday mornings were part of the normal working week, but the afternoons were covered by men working overtime. When I was told to work an 'all night' there was just time for me to get home, have a quick wash, collect some sandwiches and a flask of tea and get back to work. There was no such luxury as a canteen service during the night. That kind of overtime, where I was paid extra for it, really tired me out as everyone was on the go the whole time. The rush could be the repairing or renewing of urgent parts which had been delivered by lorry or train, and the transport was arriving at a certain time to collect and return whatever it was back to the ship that was waiting for it.

Once back home again it was straight to bed, and even though I had a clear day and night to recover before starting at my bench again it always took me several days to get back to normal. I did not like doing two shifts in succession, even for the extra cash, but I was never given the choice. It was only a mention or a hint during the afternoon of the day before which was confirmed the following day that I would be working all that night.

I have already mentioned that some industrial workers in Glasgow went to and from their workplace wearing greasy or oil-stained overalls or work clothes and I have to say that the older age group bore most of the guilt for this. No doubt more from force of habit than anything else. It might not be very fair of me making such an accusation when the younger men were away at war, but the true reason, I am sure, lies back somewhere well before the men away in the Services were born. Somewhere in amongst the heap of Victorian industrial relations disciplines I think one would find that the wearing of well-used work clothes to and from the workplace carried with it the stamp of approval from a feudal upper businessman's class. Such habits linger for a long time before terminal decline. The constant hope is that they are not displaced by similar updated ones.

Most of the fitters and all the apprentices that I came in contact with changed into a boiler suit and an old pair of shoes when they arrived at their workbench in the morning and removed them prior to going home at night. Like most I kept my overalls, a piece of soap and a pair of heavy shoes which I wore during working hours in my toolbox during the night, unless my working clothes had to go home for cleaning, in which case they were always carried. As for my working shoes, I just took in another old pair when the ones I was using fell apart with oil or paraffin, or with just old-fashioned wear and tear. At the time I am writing about I had never heard about safety shoes or such things that were resistant to oils and acids. They may well have been around in the coal mines or other such occupations, but not in the industry I was in.

Near to Bill's store in the fitter's work bay there was a cold water tap that opened into a deep well-worn and badly chipped genuine Victorian basin which was used amongst other things for cooling small heated metal parts. Here we were allowed to wash our hands outside working hours; otherwise such a thing was strictly forbidden. When the stopping time siren blew at the end of the working day it was then only a matter of joining the queue for a very quick hand wash and changing out of my boiler suit before plunging into the mad rush for the tram. I usually wore an old pair of trousers and jacket, and later on at one point I wore my brother-in-law Frank's outworn ex-Home Guard tunic and trousers which had been discarded, so perhaps some things haven't really changed all that much for me in my manner of dress.

Mentioning the rush for the tramcar reminds me of something else. I think everybody knows of a dear old lady who suffers daily and bravely from a variety of aches and pains, some of which the doctor (keeping a straight face) tells her would make interesting research. Men, on the other hand, seem to be denied the ability to talk about personal medical matters; therefore the male equivalent to the Dear Lady acts out his misery. When he sits down he mimes terrible agony, and likewise when he regains his feet. Lifting, pulling or putting on a jacket was done with the ritual of a ham actor. However neither Lourdes nor the magic sponge at the football match had anything on the note sound of the 'finish work' horn. These same partially crippled men could be seen to very ably keep abreast the mainstream mob and even succeed in climbing to the upper deck with apparent ease and agility. Having convenient twinges was one thing, but doing without the comfort of a smoke in an upstairs seat in the tram journey home was something quite different.

Working clothes were important and the cleaning of dirty

overalls was crucial because of the soap rationing, so it was a good thing when a boiler suit exchange system was introduced to the workforce. It was a weekly service with no soap coupons involved where a dirty pair of overalls could be exchanged for a second hand clean one. There was a charge for this service, which I think was Government-sponsored, and it must have been very reasonable as most of the apprentices used it, and I would guess the cost to be about a shilling or 1s.6d. a garment.

I do not remember in detail how much money I earned during each year of my 'time' but around 1943 the average weekly working wage would have been in the region of £4 to £4.10s, and in that year I would have received less than one pound in my Friday pay packet. Let me try to compare this to the price of a man's suit which appears to be about the one item that has kept pace with the average weekly wage.

The Thirty Bob Suit, when it was introduced before the war, cost the same as what Mr Average earned weekly, and for some reason the price of an ordinary suit seems to have reflected the average weekly wage that Mr Average has earned since then. Now, by using a gentleman's suit as my yardstick, I will put it to the reader that in my first working year my weekly wage would have allowed me to purchase a pair of jacket lapels, and during my second year I could have blown a week's wages on two jacket lapels plus a jacket arm. In my third year I could have gone out one weekend and bought two jacket lapels, a jacket arm and a trouser leg, while in my fourth year I could have asked a distraught tailor for a jacket front complete with lapels and arms, along with two trouser legs. In my fifth and final year my weekly wage could have bought me a complete jacket and two trouser legs, and at the end of completion of that last year when I received my indentures from the company and I was at last being paid as a fully fledged journeyman, I would be able to buy a matching suit with a waistcoat. Of course, for appearance's sake I would not be able to wear it when I went out with my begging bowl during the whole of the following week.

Mentioning begging bowls and food and drink brings back another memory of those now far-off days. Gambling and drinking were pretty rife amongst some of the unskilled labour force.

This masculine habit was heavily underlined each Friday when there was always a group of wives waiting outside for their husbands to hand over their pay packet there and then as soon as they stepped on to the outside pavement from their place of toil. I was left with the impression that none of the wives thought it unreasonable to relieve a loved one of his hard-earned cash before a publican or bookie got to him first. I don't think that any of these particular husbands thought along those lines, although none of them seemed to object, at least not at the time in public.

There were no football pools during the war, although some matches were played. Most of the professional footballers were in the Forces but games were played with players who were in reserved occupations. I think if a keen player found himself in a part of the country away from his own team then he would play for the resident team. Big companies had their own football teams, and there were also friendly matches. There must have been a Government department that kept sport going as best as possible from a morale point of view. Most horse racing events were cancelled. None of this stopped the bookies runner taking bets from 6d. to a couple of shillings at the works which was strictly illegal. I never did know what or who the bets were on; perhaps someone will find the subject interesting enough to write about it. There must be plenty of scope for one on that topic.

During the winter months in wartime Glasgow, with the coal rationing and black-out conditions, came the cold dark nights along with the constant reminder that Jack Frost was never far away. Everyone had to adjust their living style accordingly by taking what simple precautions that were thought to be wise. These ranged between warm outdoor clothes and a small pocket torch to a hot water bottle in bed at night.

For families like mine who were tenement people the main talking and sitting place was in the kitchen in front of the fireplace. The seats were rather Spartan, typical wooden kitchen chairs, with probably two slightly more comfortably designed seats with cushions on them which belonged to the parents. On very cold evenings it was not unusual to have my face and the front of my legs practically burning from the heat of the open fire, with my back as cold as charity, and any reason at all to leave the fireside was put off for as long as possible. From what I can remember, the coldest place in the home during the winter was the bathroom.

The kitchen fire had a double purpose, apart from giving off warmth and glowing comfort. It heated the oven at its side, and the concealed boiler behind it gave the household its source of hot water. Due to the coal restriction it was usually the only fire that was lit or used in the home. The day started with the kitchen fire being lit and finished when the 'good nights' were said in front of it. It was lit first thing to give hot water from the kitchen and bathroom taps ready for greedy family demands before breakfast. There was usually some sort of guard around the front of it where wet or damp clothes or towels were dried out in a hurry; otherwise they would be hung on the overhead pulley which normally consisted of four equal lengths of wood slightly longer in length than a bed sheet. The wooden shafts slotted neatly in line into a metal coat-hanger type bracket at each end from which an attached pulley rope ran up and over small wheels anchored to the ceiling at each end and then fastened at some convenient place where the handler could raise or lower the four shafts. The rope arrangement was such that it required both a single pulley wheel on the ceiling and a double pulley wheel where the two ropes met at the lifting and lowering end.

Around the fireplace at floor level was the fender and between this and the fire was where the poker rested alongside perhaps with the flat iron which would be used on the clothes hanging overhead. Somewhere in this vicinity there would be the toasting fork which was a long fork-like gadget which could be extended out to about a two foot length, not unlike a trombone action and used to toast a slice of bread in front of the open coal fire. It allowed the holder to keep a comfortable distance from the source of the heat. The kettle and teapot were never far from the fireside area.

Away from the kitchen the rest of the house was cold and any heat given off from a single or twin barred electric fire was soon lost in the high ceilings and large windows. Trapping heat meant wearing jerseys or a hot water bottle beneath the blankets at night. There were no central heating radiators scattered around Mr Mac

Average's home, simply because for some reason such a luxury in the home was never dreamt of let alone being considered as a necessity. Coal was plentiful, easily obtained and cheap. My standard method of avoiding morning feet freeze, as I recall it, was to get them covered as soon as possible making sure neither foot missed the small carpet separating them from the ice cold linoleum. Sometimes I had trouble finding my socks in the morning from the depths of the bottom of the bed where I last wore them before wriggling them off my feet when at last they were warm enough to do so.

The one room in the house that did not have a window with a view was the bathroom. It contained a small high barred window that looked out on to the gas lit close landing or stairhead, that separated our main entrance door with our neighbour's. Temperature-wise, the bathroom in winter would be equivalent to a modern day larderfridge.

Having mentioned the larder takes me back into the kitchen again where there was a large cupboard, which we called the food press. Ventilators were cut in the door and on the sides which were covered with fine wire mesh to allow for the circulation of air, yet would keep out anything smaller than a fly. This was where the bread, milk, butter, sugar and suchlike were kept, along with the cups, saucers and plates in everyday use. There was also a cupboard for dishes and glasses of all sorts, and around the kitchen wall there ran a heavy wooden shelf that could be reached only if you stood on a kitchen chair. Carefully placed on that shelf was the best dinner set and pieces of kitchen china.

On the opposite wall to the fireplace was the dresser, part of which opened into the coal bunker. The coal was delivered by horse and cart and the 1 cwt. bags were carried on the coalman's back from the cart to the bunker. The coalman wore a heavy leather protective shield on his back that was harnessed to his shoulders. It was the sort of thing that Hollywood led us to believe the gladiators of Rome wore to protect the front of the body in combat.

The kitchen bunkers used to hold about five sacks of coal and preparation had to be made in the kitchen prior to its arrival because of the dust. The same would apply when the chimney was swept.

I cannot recall ever visiting a doctor during my apprenticeship, apart from a National Medical I will mention later. Having said that I must also add that there was no chance of a running nose with coughs or shivers warranting a visit to the doctor's house. Most mothers would have gone to the chemist first and discussed the symptoms with him, and the bottle he recommended would be purchased and taken home for the patient.

I have already mentioned that a good friend of mine who was also apprenticed with me developed tuberculosis and later I will tell of a close girl friend who developed the same disease. Fortunately both Jim and Marjorie recovered after a long drawn out treatment period. These two victims of that particular illness came from secure and healthy home environments. They were lucky, if that's the correct word, compared with others who either suffered from or were developing TB as it was generally known, and were living in damp overcrowded rooms in the same city. For some reason the illness was not talked about and when mentioned it was in a quiet voice that was almost a whisper, presumably because it was considered incurable.

One can make light of Glasgow's average winter weather by saying that one day could be icy cold with dense fog and not a breath of wind, when even the trams seemed to be coughing their way through it with each driver continuously using his footbell. The next day could be one of clear blue skies with a gale force wind blowing heavily on everything in its path and at times bringing down some roof slates and the occasional chimney pot. By adding these two types of days and their happenings together and dividing by two it would mean that one could be half killed on a semi-foggy day by something neither too hard nor too soft landing on one's head. The reader may well smile but unfortunately there was such a superior attitude held by a few people in their reasoning towards those less fortunate than themselves. A penniless couple having four healthy children and two dying of TB would be measured against the same yardstick. Six healthy bodies and two sick bodies meant that three quarters of the family had a lot to be grateful for.

Apart from the more serious ailments where high body temperature, extreme pain or notifiable illness were involved, a good ratio of mothers in consultation with their selected chemists seemed to handle the run-of-the-mill medical matters with competence. Most homes had a medical handbook, Gregory powder, caster oil, syrup of figs (all mothers I think were paranoid over their children's bowels) linctus syrup or Fisherman's Friend for the hacking cough, and for cuts and scratches iodine, carbolic soap, lint and bandages.

Those long cold nights did not stop young people like myself getting out and about. In this we were little different from previous generations, the only real difference being that the youngsters of yesteryear knew where they were going to spend the evening whereas the wartime breed didn't because of the blackout. If cash and opportunity allowed the pictures or dancing were never more popular. If your group 'missed out' because of reasons given or otherwise then you found a café and later wended your way home. It never entered our heads to go to a pub.

Alcoholic drink was no problem to those who drank it in excess. They knew exactly what to do with it. The problems of drink in the city belonged to others. You didn't have to look very far for a pub, and depending on your circumstances you could drink in grand comfort, glitzy comfort, comfy comfort or in the comfort of a crowded sawdust strewn floor. Such places were well sign-posted, and incidentally so were the pawn shops with their brass balls. Very few parents would thank a young man for taking their daughter into a pub or anywhere else for a drink, but apart from that most pubs didn't allow females in (probably because of lack of toilet facilities) and such premises had to be emptied and closed by 9.30 p.m. No one under eighteen could be served with alcoholic drink and anyway it just wasn't our scene. At that time you became a liable adult at twenty one.

Talking about signs, there was also the barber's red and white pole and you could always spot the young boys who had never seen the inside of a barber's shop by their haircut where an inverted bowl had been put on their head and any hair outside it was chopped off. They would be wearing the short baggy trousers boys used to wear then. How I remember those earlier years and chafing inside my legs just above the knee level during cold spells where the trouser hem used to rub against them. Mentioning short trousers also brings to mind these horrible horsehair seats we all had to sit on at some time or another where the horse found its revenge by sticking a wire-like hair into your legs, and you daren't complain.

My sister and her husband had been staying in Largs since 1943 where Frank was working in the Barrfield Aircraft Maintenance Workshop. Their first child Maureen was born one year after they arrived there, and a proper little Colleen she was.

I spent a lot of weekends with them, being the family carrier cum messenger between the two homes, as Mother typically always seemed to have something she thought Sybil would be in urgent need of. I always travelled there and back by bus and both the errands and weekend breaks suited me fine. I enjoyed these stays 'doon the watter'. Sometimes Frank managed to borrow a large rowing boat from the base and go out fishing. The boat itself took a lot of hauling on the oars due to its size and when anything like a strong breeze came along it meant some hard pulling. On one occasion a sudden strong wind arose, and it became a struggle to get back to dry land. That was the last time we went out sea fishing which was just as well, as I could never get used to killing the ones we caught, and the weather had taught me what was meant by 'getting the wind up,' when it had nothing at all to do with babies.

The three of us were all fairly keen walkers and walked together whenever possible. Usually after each outing we finished up in Nardini's Café during the season when it was open. Somehow, during the winter when Nardini's was closed, Largs seemed that little bit gloomier, but thinking thoughts of summer drums up the scene I have always carried with me since my early fishing days of the blue Clyde water, white Nardini's and the red of nearby St Columba's Church. Sounds very patriotic, but they were certainly a part of the general view of Largs sea-front with the hill completing the background. Coming back to winter there was also the Viking cinema to while away a long dark evening.

Not very long before my parents had decided to leave Prestwick I had been given an old rabbit from my friend Johnny Duxton in Monkton, and Sybil and Frank had agreed they would look after him for me, so he finally settled in with them at Largs. He was not very popular when he escaped into the next door vegetable patch now and again, but otherwise he was a very well-behaved little creature, and was only there for just over a year before he died. Most of his life had been spent before I got him, and just by chance I was there when it happened. There was a good reason for Johnny finding him another home at the time I got him, although I cannot recall exactly what it was. I missed Bunny during my subsequent trips to Largs.

Early one Sunday morning I went off for a walk along the coast to the north of Largs. It was a lovely clear morning which allowed a spectacular view of the Clyde, and I came to a spot where I suddenly found myself looking down at the *Queen Mary* lying quietly at anchor. She was by herself and I could see that her bow was badly damaged. I recognised her easily with her three funnels, but in any case I had seen so many pictures of her, I knew I wasn't mistaken.

I returned to the house as soon as I could to tell Frank what I had seen, but both he and Sybil thought I was exaggerating and said that it had probably been some passenger ship which had struggled in from the Atlantic after hitting a mine and had been told to anchor there and to await further instructions. Frank was certain that I had made a mistake about it being the *Queen Mary*. To make matters worse, when I took Frank to see for himself, the passenger ship had sailed without a trace of her anywhere. Returning home to Glasgow in the bus that Sunday night I was still convinced that the ship I saw had been the *Queen Mary*, but after that it seemed to fade from my mind.

Some time after the war I was to read about a manoeuvre made by her naval escort *HMS Curacao* which went terribly wrong on 2nd October 1943, resulting in the *Queen Mary* ramming the *Curacao* and cutting her in two. On that occasion they had left the Clyde estuary. The accident happened a few hours after leaving the Clyde estuary on the Saturday before my early Sunday morning walk.

Looking back to these particular years it seems to me that the streets and public parks were kept cleaner, and there was less litter about. It would be nice to think that the reason for this was that the general public were more critical then than the generations that followed. There was a sense of 'belonging to' and, of course, with larger families, the parks and public places were more commonly used. It could be argued that I was recalling the past through a young pair of eyes, and only saw and remembered what I thought was relevant. The other line of reason that could be applied was that during wartime, when all forms of sweets were rationed, or just plain unobtainable there would be less confectionery wrappings and empty cigarette packets to discard. One other simple reason was that people had less to throw away. No one can get rid of what they have not got.

I must make the point that the authorities during my early school days must have had a great concern over litter and road safety. In school as well as at the Cubs and Scouts the message was well drummed home to us never to leave any trace of litter behind whenever we went on picnics or camping. Any fire had to be absolutely out before leaving the scene and the dangers of broken glass causing hurt or fire by the sun were very early instilled into our minds. Sometimes at school someone, I think from the police force and accompanied by a uniformed policeman, who no doubt added authenticity to the occasion, gave a talk about road safety. This was when the roads were a lot quieter than they would ever be again. The Highway Code was printed on the back of all the school jotters and this was before the war.

There was always someone around, whether it was the policeman doing his rounds or the parkies (park keepers) and, of course, the weekend night watchman where there were roadworks or buildings in progress.

Explicit sex was never mentioned in the classroom and the closest we got to it was plant life in biology or the life of a tadpole. Perhaps it was more subtly expressed with periodic lectures about hooliganism and wilful behaviour with a mention of us (boys) being at the dangerous stage. We were never saints, but hooligans – hardly. In the education system in Scotland there have always been mixed classes and these mini-lectures were always directed towards the boys. Girls were well above that sort of behaviour. The time was coming when detailed sex would be brought into the classroom and it was never to be clear to me whether it was joyfully welcomed by most parents or grudgingly accepted by them. No one could ever have predicted that in years to follow there would be such a show in public of so much debris from litter louts, public safety shattered by street rioting and the behaviour pattern of the new-found sexual freedom amongst some of the young.

I hope the press barons will not read too much into my moving from litter and such things to newspapers. The daily papers were used for quite a number of purposes after their reading was finished. Yesterday's news, apart from being briefly read again in the bathrooms and toilets, would more than often finish up wrapped around the ashes of yesterday's fire and carried down to the back green where the dustbins were waiting for them. This was the common method used to prevent ash dust being blown or scattered about. During cold damp weather Mother insisted we put newspapers that were cut and shaped to our feet into our shoes before we went out. It did keep our feet warm and if a shoe was leaking then it absorbed the damp.

Paper was always wanted for salvage and recycling, but after three years of war the number of books to be given for this purpose had dwindled to almost the point where they could be likened to the metal railings around the schools, parks and churches, which by now had long since gone for scrap to help the war effort.

One aspect of public places that still leaves me with the shivers is the memory of the communal metal drinking cup that was connected by a length of chain to the drinking fountains in the park. Each of these fountains was a monument to the Victorian cast iron industry and many came from Glasgow's own world-famous Saracen Foundry at Possilpark. They displayed the intricate, flamboyant metal workings which that period was noted for, even down to the small water trough at the foot of it to cater for thirsty domestic pets. The trough was filled from either the overflow or spillage from the faucet which was very often in the form of a lion's mouth. The designers got it right for the animal part, but I dread to think of the germs and diseases transmitted from mouth to mouth amongst the chattering and playful two-legged drinkers who shared the cast iron mug on a summer's day.

The standard medical protection against harm from any shared public drinking vessel was neither in the form of an inoculation nor a medicine bottle, but by placing a finger around and over the rim and drinking the water that flowed over it. The 'clang, clang' sound of the discarded cup striking against the fountain's metal frame was a familiar park sound during the summers before these cast iron cups finally disappeared.

During the wartime days and the long winter nights when there was no street lighting nor bomber's moon, two people remained who took the fear out of the darkness. The first was the close lamp lighter who always arrived before dark with his lit lamp stick which probably operated on acetylene gas. It had a duel purpose in that he used it to turn on the gas tap and then to ignite the various lights. He also carried a little ladder in case he had to change a lamp filament. Everyone in the close knew who he was. The gas pressure had been permanently reduced to permit a duller light as a black-out contingency, and if a close was lit by electric bulbs then they were painted over with a blue colour which still left sufficient light for anyone coming in from the street, and for those leaving it was usual to switch off the hall light to accustom their eyes to the darkness outside on the stair landing.

The other person was the road sweeper who was the man with the full-sized sweeping brush, a very large shovel and a very special hand cart that looked like just what it was, two large sized portable dustbins into which went all the refuse from the pavements, the gutters and the streets. Included in his general sweeping was the horse manure and dog droppings, and in those days there were many more horses and a lot less dogs. His occupation made it hygienically safer for the girls to play hop-scotch on the pavements, boys to play 'jorries' in the gutter, and the older children playing in groups to play 'release-oh!' across the roads.

Of these two people, the lamp lighter and the road sweeper, the former has completely disappeared and the latter, even in an updated form, is a rarity. The former we knew as the 'lampie' and the latter as the 'scaffie' though neither of those terms would be used inside the home, only outside when we were street-brats.

Before I leave the pavements and the children who used to play on them let me recall the words that some little girls used to chant when one of them was skipping by herself and another would jump in beside her and both would skip together before one jumped out again.

A lady went out for drinking gin,
now drinking gin was a very bad thing,
so you go out and I go in.

The other game they played was called 'high and low water', where there was a girl holding the skipping rope at each end and they would raise it while the other jumped over it.

Please don't get any ideas about me, and I didn't get it from my brother either, but I did have three sisters.

The war caused a lot of changes in social habits, one being that picture houses were permitted to show films on a Sunday which a short time before would have been more than sufficient cause to bring down on ourselves all sorts of fire and brimstone if some members of the Kirk were to be totally believed. Their dire predictions that it would lead to further dark sins like whistling, unrestrictive drinking laws and making merry on the Sabbath was not entirely inaccurate.

One Sunday afternoon both our parents were out, leaving sister Joey and myself at home. Joey was on leave for a couple of days from the Land Army, and on that same afternoon in our truly wicked ways we decided to go to the picture house in Sauchiehall Street. It was broad daylight at the time and we passed the cinema three or four times to make absolutely sure there was nobody we recognised in the vicinity or anyone at the ticket office who could cause us any delay on entry. When all was clear we dashed in like a scene from an episode from Keystone Cops. The film we saw that Sunday in 1943 was *Gone With The Wind.* I cannot remember the reaction when we told those at home where we had been. It could not have been too bad.

The war against the U-Boats and the Battle of the Atlantic was finally won with merchant ship losses fast receding. The sights now were already set on a building programme that would keep shipyards busy for decades to come in making up the devastated fleet numbers. The great changes that were to take place in future size, speed and operation were not even dreamed of then, but where I worked everyone knew there were a lot of marine engines yet to be built.

Almost a year following the Normandy landings the German armies surrendered in Italy and Western Europe. It came as a relief, but not as a surprise as it had been fairly obvious that the Allies would win the war. There was nothing which at that time could possibly stop the two mighty waves of retribution crushing in on Germany from both sides, bringing down the closing curtain on Europe's bloodiest conflict that cost the lives of 20 million people.

The terrible scenes we all saw of the fighting and the destruction which had taken place in Europe paled somewhat into a smaller dimension with the Pathé Newsreel pictures and accounts that came back from concentration camps which were shown on the screens in the cinemas.

I could add nothing new to what has been said by much better writers than I. Perhaps I can say it another way.

THE PREY

Red Danger streaked shalom's clear sky, as Spectre's dark dawn broke,
And Havoc rained blood droplets down, as its fated quiet quarry woke.
Total trapped in Wanton's whirlpool, their whole world was spin-spun,
For Taunt's tidal ethnic emnity's, race-rant-raged tempest had begun.
Then Frenzy turned against them, dread-dressed as a wild maliced mob.
Urging charlatan cheats of Chaos, to bait-blame then revile then rob.
Betrayal's beast rode wicked winds, blew cruel-cold that Jewish morn,
On 'Fate's' chance choice of Mother, who gave birth when each was born.

From laws of stone and rock strewn paths, their stable strength depends,
To face the harsh hate of racism, and basalt backs of faithless friends.
Blessed and bred with Zion's gene, and caste-cursed as a wandering race,
Worked well in a schemer's satanic mind, to guise guile's smirking face.
It jeered Jews blitzed and broken, then taunted with new names to mourn,
And yellowed-star seen as unequal, a show symbol full forced to be worn.
Then ruled all penned in a ghetto, till scorn-summon-compelled to start,
Allowed only what could be carried, or push-pulled in a hasty made cart.

Their doom mark flaunted that fatal form, of a twisted counterfeit cross,
A sinister shape beaming badness, finding favour with each victim's loss
Though terror was honed in horror and hurt, to finish in poison and fire,
No Final Solution was ever found, in the smoke from their funeral pyre.
Their nemesis appeared on either side, from where the sun rises and sets,
Ending 'death's head' dreams of 1000 years, exposing its deeds and debts.
Remember them fairly in future years, tell of their treks to those tombs,
No rite or robe or reverent respect, just numbered tattoos amongst fumes.

When quiet returns comes awesome test, a calm choice for those who live,
Between thought of rightful vengeance, or live-think the word 'forgive'.

Having lucid learned that human hurts, cause by far the longest sorrows
With hard linger legacy leaving behind, its full lake of lost tomorrows.
Yet from each camp's cram-crowded hell, time took what loved one's lost
Where justice judges each callous chill, placing blame to bare the cost
No hid-havens here for profaned past, nor ill suffered sore shrink-wilt.
With right rules to measure goodness, and stern scales to balance guilt.

Sense Ghost guilt-glimpse of holocaust, feel why it reached its spate,
Heed Hades haunting clean the minds, of bigot's faith and racial hate
Feel Phantom fight vile ethnic abuse, and shape earth equals complete,
Let Conscience wail-warn of apathy, with gutter law ruling the street.
Fear Shade's sad-sighing of progroms, leaving worse stain than before,
Hear Spirit say now nothing lies hid, and badness is seen to the core.
Ask Astral find fear-flairs and flaws, beneath each new flag unfurled.
See Soul watch-wither search each lie, of the elitist night-mare world.

6

It took a further three months and two atomic bombs, that caused the total destruction of two cities along with a vast number of their populations and the genetic twisting and distortion of countless human genes, before the total surrender of Japan during the following August, and the final celebration of peace in the Far East on 2nd September 1945.

Hitler had been a good enemy to have fought and beaten as under the scrutiny of democracy everything he had thought was working for him and had been in his favour now stood against him. Our ex-servicemen returning home were proud of what they had achieved and only wanted to get back into 'civvy street' and start reliving their private lives in a style of their own choosing. It hadn't gone unnoticed by the free governments of the world that dictators old and new had always shown that whoever ruled the streets held the political power. It therefore made good sense that no government would want a horde of young men lounging about with no jobs to keep them busy, and everything was geared to prevent this contingency.

Women had made an excellent contribution to the country's war workforce and now they returned to their chosen profession or work routine but by far the most returned to their traditional role of the family's upbringer and guardian of their morals. I do not recall any objections or murmurings against this move for I believe that what most people wanted above all other things at that time was a return to what was for them normality.

The rebuilding programme that had been so much talked about did appear to start as soon as the servicemen and women came home and were 'demobbed'. Assurances had already been given that there would be plenty of work for everyone and a shared prosperity lay ahead for all the population to enjoy. Although such words had been echoed before, it did appear that the wartime coalition government had laid plans for swift action for employment of the returning numbers of job seekers. However, an important change had taken place and that difference was to be found in the forming of the country's labour force. The men arriving home to their own front door wearing their new 'demob' suits had been doing some serious thinking about the future. Many of our young soldiers had been called up from deprived homes and their demob suit had been the first new suit they had ever owned. They had done their part well but in some there was now a resentment showing. Nothing had seemed very fair to them. Where they had been born hadn't been fair. The war hadn't been fair, and their future didn't appear to be fair if it meant returning to live in a poor or worse area to merely be called on when next required. What they wanted was a fairer method of working and where their voices could be heard. They were not alone.

There was an industrial dispute involving engineer apprentices throughout the land and certainly in all the shipbuilding and repair areas. I cannot remember the cause or reason or even if we were being manipulated. Neither can I remember any apprentice who I knew personally having zealous feelings either for or against it. However, it did mean that we were all called to take a medical prior to being called up to serve in the Armed Forces. I had my medical in September 1945; then, like all the others, returned to work and the whole thing quietly petered out and life very quickly returned to normal. I think I passed my medical and all I seem to remember about it, apart from the vague usual examinations, was a woman in military dress who insisted I had indicated on a form that I could play the violin. I told her I did not play the violin and apologised if I had ticked the wrong box. She did not show me the form but went on and on about playing the violin. I still think to this day that she was quite insane.

Many of the returning men and women wanted social change and went about it in the sure and intent manner of one having survived the war that was to end all wars. In the 1945 general election a different party won the majority of parliamentary seats.

That's enough about other people and politics which I will now lay aside to tell of what I recall from that time.

I might sound a little disappointing when I say that I must have very quickly become used to the street lighting and bright shop windows. Looking even further back, and at the risk of repeating myself, I'm fairly certain I accepted the black-out in more or less the same way. I suppose everyone accepts then gets used to anything when it has to be.

The big night was the victory in Europe, celebrated with bonfires in the streets and church bells ringing out. It was just like New Year's Eve with everyone behaving just as they would have done at that time, except the following day was not a holiday. Following that, life continued more or less the same and still included rationing and shortages. I suppose it was 'first in, first out' with service personnel getting back into 'civvy street'. There were so many decorated doorways and windows to welcome someone home. For some it must have stirred sad memories at seeing these happy homecoming preparations: I should know.

In 1946 Sybil, Frank and Maureen went out to Northern Rhodesia where Frank had found a job working in the Copper Belt. Not long after they had left we had a heavy black telephone installed at home on the hall table. I very rarely used it as none of my friends had one, and in any case it would have meant asking permission every time I wanted to use it. I don't think Mother used it very much either; perhaps a call now and again through to Clara in Giffnock. Both these phones were used for business purposes which was the reason they had been given a measure of priority for their being supplied, and both were shared lines. Father mostly used our phone and the family were constantly warned against using it in case it blocked any incoming call. During that time everything was a matter of priority.

National Service was introduced in 1945, which meant that all healthy males reaching the age of eighteen had to do two years conscripted work. It could either be carried out in any of the services, the Merchant Navy or the coal mines where the name Bevin Boy was created from the latter group, included as a National Service option by the then Minister of Employment and National Service, Ernest Bevin.

Ronald Neil, whom I have already mentioned, a friend and classmate at school, had continued on to Ayr Academy to take his 'Highers', after which he went straight into the Army where he survived two years in the Military Police, spending most of his time in Malaya. Going by the PCs he sent me he enjoyed every minute of it. When Ronald returned home after completing his National Service he chose to join the police force. After making an application he was accepted as a cadet at the Glasgow Police Force College. He later rose to the rank of sergeant in the Glasgow Police Force.

I think it would be around that time that I developed a nagging doubt about what could very probably have left me with a sense of guilt, or betrayal. Up till then my father figure was someone who had taught me to play golf, introduced me to music, usually criticised what I did with my time but I never forgot that it was he who paid me my Saturday fourpence when I was a young schoolboy.

Father was of the old Scottish male mould. He was the established head of the house and supplied the family income to his wife on a regular basis and left the running of the house and household entirely up to her. It was accepted that mothers stood one full pace closer to their children than fathers did and as this was thought of as normal it did no harm. I don't think he ever stood on a ladder in the whole of his life or had ever held a paintbrush in his hand. Nevertheless, for all that, I would never have wanted any other man for a father. I think Mother would agree with me for she was left in peace to get on with whatever she wanted to do at home without anyone getting under her feet.

I can understand partly how this came about for it takes no great stretch of the imagination to guess what it must have been like earning a living during the twenties and thirties, in strict no-nonsense offices and workshops where the working of long hours was the reward for company loyalty. I can also see that there must have been times that it would not exactly be a blessing to return to a home full of children after a day when things didn't go exactly right. There must have been times when waiting until they were all in bed would be justified.

I am sure no one enjoyed a glass of whisky more than Father did, which must have had repercussions on Mother, but she never complained about it, at least not to either Eric or I. With me being the youngest it must be borne in mind that my parents and their friends were not young people. Mother had passed the forty mark when I was born. How Father helped or did not help when the first of the babies arrived and thereafter I don't know, but I should think he wasn't much of a help to Mother. He was a good father but hopeless in the home. I have a lasting impression that if asked whom he thought should be allowed back to this world for a second chance he would have replied, 'Anyone who had not taken a confidence or secret with them!'

Towards the latter part of the war and the beginning of the peacetime years, it was not unusual to hear of an increased number of spiritual séances, and of mediums making the usual mystic claims. I had little or no experience or interest in such matters, but I would like to tell you of one occasion when my mother and I attended a meeting at the St Andrews Hall where Helen Hughes, a well-known medium, was appearing on the platform along with a minister of the Church of Scotland, and as far as I remember being told, it was the first time such an encounter had taken place between the two churches. To many people this had an uplifting effect, and raised the hopes that this show of religious tolerance between two sects of Christians would grow. I have mentioned before about the lack of angels and saints in Glasgow, but that does not mean there were no religious beliefs about; on the contrary the city groaned under the weight of them. Maybe this meeting I attended was the humble beginning of a long uphill road in a quest to remove unholy bigotry and sectarian-based suspicion from what otherwise is a lovable city.

The service followed the usual ritual of hymn and prayer. Then Miss Hughes was introduced to the audience in a manner which showed a friendliness between the churches. The medium displayed a quiet easy personality, and gave out her messages without any theatrical mannerisms, and my lasting impression of her was of a very thoughtful, genuine and sensitive person. There was no message for the May family that day which was not surprising as every seat in the hall had been taken. What she said was comforting, and apparently accurate to those people she had a message for from amongst the audience, but nothing was received from any loved one lost in the war.

One of her more comforting messages was given out in the following manner. Miss Hughes walked to the edge of the stage, and pointed over to a certain area amongst the audience.

'There is a very young girl wanting to speak to a lady in that part of the hall. No, a little further back. Is there a lady there who lost a little girl a few days before her birthday? She is telling me something, and pointing to her face. Oh! She tells me she had burns on her face.'

A lady in the vicinity stood up.

'Did you lose a little girl?' asked Miss Hughes. 'Was it boiling liquid that fell over her?'

The woman replied, 'Yes.'

'I have to tell you,' said the Medium, 'that there is no mark or sign of a burn on her face, and she is very happy. she is a lovely, happy, well-cared for little girl, and you must now always think of her like that.'

That and another incident, albeit to a lesser degree, remained in my memory because if there had been questionable practice involved, or even good guesswork, then it must have been pretty slick. The medium had stated, 'a little girl', determining both the sex and the age group with the further knowledge about the fatal accident happening just prior to the child's birthday, and this left me with something to think about.

The other incident was when she told a lady about a damaged carpet shortly after her husband's death. She also gave an accurate description of him that was confirmed by the widow with a comforting message from him and a humorous denial that he had anything whatsoever to do with it this time. Apparently there had been a history of carpet incidents in their household, for which he had been mostly responsible.

Once again the lady had managed to get the sex and object correct. I cannot remember any of the other 'messages' and they were most probably what are called the run of the mill stuff. I have always wondered why on Earth those in Heaven don't sent more detailed information of where they are, rather than always some vague shadow of some past irrelevant incident.

The reader will draw his or her own conclusions about this area of human thinking, but I mention this clairvoyant for two reasons. The first is that I do not think that spiritualism developed in any serious proportions due to the war. It has always been with us in some form or another and it's more than probable that some are drawn towards it for the wrong reasons, following a bereavement. Certainly it is a religion that has attracted its fair share of charlatans and well-intentioned chimerical persons operating on its fringe. I appreciate what I have just said must make it difficult for its genuine members to achieve credibility and purpose.

I have always been rather shy of mentioning the other reason I attended this particular meeting. A few weeks before I was seated in the sitting room at home reading what was probably a newspaper when I thought Mother walked past me. When I looked up I could see quite distinctly a slight elderly woman dressed from neck to feet in a long dark grey dress that somehow covered her arms. She wore a dull yellowed embroidered sort of waistcoat that was made with a see-through stitch. She wasn't Victorian in appearance, a bit more modern. She did not wear anything on her head, nor was she carrying anything. I never got as much as a glance from her as she walked into and through the wall about two yards along from the fire. I never saw the lady in question again. Mother didn't seem at all surprised, only mentioning in her quiet way it was a harmless affair. (As a young healthy male it wasn't exactly my idea of an affair.) Some years later I had a somewhat similar experience on board a ship called the *Lucellum*, and, yes, still another time, though by then I was retired. I could hardly have made a living out of three incidents and I honestly do not know what status one should place on such incidents, but there you have it for what it is worth. Perhaps it merely proves that my imagination has only worked three times in my lifetime up till now. Funnily enough, I have never heard anything go bump in the night. Most of us will have had a vivid dream at some time during our sleeping hours. I wonder if it is possible for one to wander into the conscious area for a few seconds before realising one's error – just a thought.

The visit of mother and son to the St Andrew's Hall that day left us with a talking point for some time. It had been interesting to see Helen Hughes in the flesh, if I may put it that way, and appearing in front of a multi-religious congregation. It did not matter a fig if no one changed their belief or otherwise in spiritualism one way or another. At least there had been an open show of tolerance to and respect of the belief of others, and that was important.

I must have been going through that nasty growing-up phase about that time where I had to question and doubt all things that authority stood for, which included the Church. It must have been a worrying time for my parents, especially for Mother to have an ungrateful know-all for a son. Up till then religion had always been a one direction affair. In other words, if I spoke to God it was called prayer, but if He spoke to me then I was in need of a psychiatrist. At least in spiritualism their flow of direction seemed opposite from the normal, though it did not give any more information than my own religion. Unfortunately, it was just about that time when Mother very delicately told me about a minister of the Church who had been found guilty in court of 'interfering' with a young boy, member of the congregation, which had a cold sinister effect on me. I could not think of a worse character combination than that of betrayal and sexual deviation in any person holding a place of trust. I was then at the age where I had heard about homosexuality briefly from the small talk amongst friends but I could not understand such behaviour; therefore it had to be some form of mental inadequacy and I was against it.

Mother didn't tell me about this incident for any other reason than that it might appear in the newspapers. It was more a forewarning than a lesson to be careful about some of my own sex. In matters sexual I was left to discover what lay inside that particular area by myself using a slowly-slowly method that would not bring any harm to my good name. I was never seriously warned about the sexual chemistry that could change a man into a momentary fool or create a lifelong deviant.

I suppose sex is the one subject within my world where I received only a very hazy base line from which to build any knowledge of the subject. I was given verbal vague warnings about its terrible pitfalls and that it was a minefield I would ultimately have to walk through on my own, and when that time came I would have to tread very, very carefully. (That was the spoken side of it, and that was it.) It was when the years unfolded that its seamier side was slowly exposed. This at least had allowed me in my younger years a time to believe, 'What kind of Fool Am I?' was truly a magic blend of romance and innocence. Looking back I would not have had it any other way. The method of the day worked in my case and in retrospect I do not think I would have been a better person for knowing too much too soon. With me the meaning and value of the word 'decadence' changed with my tolerance level mellowing as I grew older.

My changing from boy to man was in no way an ordeal or unpleasant experience. Up till that time my body had talked to me only through illness and pain. Otherwise I didn't know it even existed. During and after my sexual awakening it spoke to me in an unfrightening manner and was very pleasant about it. In fact we have been good friends ever since.

A sad and totally unexpected piece of news was given me around that time about a friend of mine since childhood. Sandy Falconer achieved his Highers at Albert Road Academy at the same time as Ronald sat his at Ayr Academy. Like so many others, Sandy left school and immediately started his two year National Service during which time he was sent out to India in the Army. Unhappily, unlike Ronald, who served in Malaya, Sandy never returned home. He collapsed during a game of football and died shortly afterwards from exhaustion and heatstroke. He was buried in India.

Both our mothers had worked together as girls and young ladies in the same dressmaking establishment of Simpson, Hunter & Young, Buchanan Street, Glasgow, and had, since that time, kept in close contact with each other. Both attended the same Church where Sandy and I had been raised through the Wolf Cubs and Boy Scouts together. The church hall must have hosted a different function each night of the week, for Sandy and I would meet up again at choir practice on another evening. All the May children around that few-years-pre-war time were in the choir with the girls being Brownies, then Girl Guides. Sandy's elder brother and wee Anne Britain, who was to stand in as Joey's bridesmaid a few years later, were also part and parcel of the choir. The hall was used for boy things, girl things, amateur things, this and that things and over and above that there must have been church business things.

I was shocked when I was told about Sandy's death for it seemed to have been so unfair. I was at the age when I never thought that anyone could die in the Army in peacetime.

The months raced and the years ticked slowly on. Each year the engine works held a competitive examination set by the chief draughtsman, and any apprentice who had completed four years in the engine shop and was interested in entering the drawing office was eligible to sit the test.

The apprenticeship could be completed in the drawing office. I had already made up my mind well before my fourth year that this was the path I was going to take; therefore I applied and was accepted as a candidate for the exam. The result was that I left the workshop where I had learnt the tools of my trade and how to use them. It was also where I had learnt the hard way in my first few months what was meant to be sent for a 'long stand' or its opposite number, a 'short weight,' or maybe a 'small punch' or a 'bastard file'. The trouble with that latter one was it was quite legitimate. The most important thing of all came later on when I discovered that great pieces of shapeless metal along with iron plates, rough castings, mighty forged steel beams and angle bars could be shunted into an engine builder's yard and then each of these parts could be taken into one or several of the various specialist departments. It could have been any of the following; the blacksmith's, the coppersmith's, the metal burner's, the welder's the marker off's, the machinist's or the fitter's and at the finish they could all be assembled like a giant jigsaw puzzle from a thousand manufactured parts into a beautiful and workable world-renowned piece of machinery that some of the best-known names in the shipping industry would choose to engine their ships with and pay a lot of money to do it.

Now that I was going into the drawing office I would learn how all those pieces arrived on the doorstep in the first place.

I sat the examination on the 15/16 September 1947, and on 6th October I started working in the office as an apprentice draughtsman.

The change from engine shop to drawing office was quick and painless. A little before midday on Saturday I cleaned up my bench and put my personal instruments, which I had either bought or made myself, into a carrier bag I had brought in to take them home. The tools given to me over the four years through numerous gaffer's chitties I returned to the store, and my toolbox, containing only a padlock and key, was left as a legacy to some hopeful new-start. I said my farewells as quickly as possible, and when the noon horn sounded, I left with the mob to catch my tramcar.

The following Monday morning I was one of the young men who reported at 8.30 a.m. prompt to the chief draughtsman, Mr McNeill, whom I later found out was known as Big Sanny. After a very brief welcome, followed by a reminder of the merits of good timekeeping and diligence, we were each handed over to our respective section leader. In my case it was a Mr Blechynden, (Blenchy), who headed the boiler and funnel section.

I settled quickly into the very different type of work from what I was used to, and soon much preferred it to being in the engine shop. I did not have to spend any time getting to know anybody, as I already knew two of the boys who started with me. Ralph Mills now worked in the plant section, and Chris Smith, who must have come out top in the exam for he was placed in the design office, which was in the room next door to where the draughtsmen worked and where I now toiled.

It was in the drawing office that I met Alex Bankier who had the drawing board directly behind me, and who became a very good lifelong friend of mine.

My drawing board was nearest to the phone and closest to the office reception area; therefore it will not be hard to guess who had to double up as receptionist-cum-telephonist in between drawing lines and circles. I learnt very quickly to enquire who was at the other end of the phone after being sent back by several

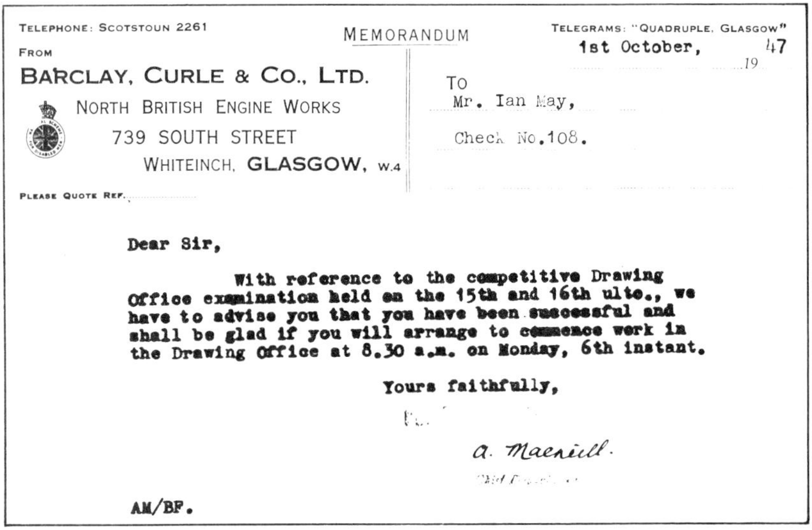

TELEPHONE: SCOTSTOUN 2261

MEMORANDUM

TELEGRAMS: "QUADRUPLE, GLASGOW"

FROM

BARCLAY, CURLE & CO., LTD.

NORTH BRITISH ENGINE WORKS

739 SOUTH STREET

WHITEINCH, GLASGOW, W.4

PLEASE QUOTE REF.

1st October, 1947

TO

Mr. Ian May,

Check No.108.

Dear Sir,

With reference to the competitive Drawing Office examination held on the 15th and 16th ulto., we have to advise you that you have been successful and shall be glad if you will arrange to commence work in the Drawing Office at 8.30 a.m. on Monday, 6th instant.

Yours faithfully,

a. Macneill.

AM/BF.

draughtsmen who would not accept a call unless they knew who was on the line. Unfortunately for me there was one particular director, called Mr McNee, who utterly detested having to identify himself to one so lowly, and always barked in reply to my enquiry, 'Och don't waste my time, just get him to the phone.'

I probably unconsciously developed something in the field of diplomacy from my unpaid telephone answering career that stood me in good stead through my later working years where I found it an easier task than some to cool down a heated argument.

I spent just over a year under Blenchy, drawing Scotch boilers and funnels along with their contents. For each boiler drawn there had to be a book completed containing all the worked out formulae for each and every dimension and stress on plates, tubes and rivets included in the building and running of a Scotch boiler to the satisfaction of the MOT (Ministry of Transport) and Lloyds of London.

Each funnel drawing had to show that the internal staying and securing was more than adequate to prevent it being blown away and taking with it the pipes running up inside it. The funnel as seen when a ship steams past looks quite stately with the company marking clearly painted on it, but its main purpose is a screen for the boiler and engine uptakes (exhaust). There is also the important open-ended 'surplus steam pipe' running up to the top of the inside rear of the funnel from the boiler safety valves in case an excess of steam pressure causes them to lift, or if for some reason it was necessary to blow the steam pressure off the boiler to allow for some form of maintenance to be carried out. As for that ghostly sound that is heard in the cinema, coming from the ship moving slowly through the swirling fog, a steam whistle was clearly attached at the top front, backed up as a contingency measure with a compressed air horn, and each had to have their own respective supply pipe running up to them.

There was a nice working atmosphere amongst the draughtsmen, although seniority was never forgotten, and there was a lot of humour about. Smoking was not permitted in the drawing office but that did not prevent smokers disappearing into the washroom, or 'bog' as it was better known, which had a permanent pipe tobacco and cigarette smoke haze at all times during the working day. When someone was required and a quick glance showed he was not at his board, then he would probably be found in the bog; at least that would be the first place to look for him. Usually a missing person was having a puff and discussing the events since yesterday, or what happened over the weekend, or perhaps just keeping up with what the tabloids were saying that very morning.

The two draughtsmen who could be outside the building were Blenchy, who had to regularly visit the boiler shop along by Patrick Cross, and the plant section draughtsman who could be anywhere on the company property where a repair or alteration was being considered.

I can only remember one draughtsman leaving during my time there, and that was a Bob McKendrick in the Pipe Arrangement Section who, prior to emigrating to Newcastle in Australia, was given a presentation in the office by Mr Deverill, who was then chief draughtsman (Big Sanny was now a director) of a table lamp. The company's loss was my gain as Bob left me some of his technical books which he could not manage to take along with him when he emigrated.

'All very well,' I hear an impatient voice saying. 'But what were you doing when not in this building?' One of the answers to that question is that it was around this time that my group of friends and myself decided that we should properly learn the art of ballroom dancing. We finally decided, after a lot of determined procrastination to enrol in a professional school of dancing and try our hands (shouldn't it be feet) at the graceful art. Perhaps by doing this I would discover the reason why each girl I had asked for a dance and whom I had already danced with, always seemed to grimace bravely at the offer.

Let me say right away that this is not a criticism of the Alice McEwan School of Dancing when I tell you that I was once a hopeful learner there. Both Alice and her teaching staff were extremely patient and very competent indeed as many of her successful pupils can testify. I fear in my case the fault lay neither in the school nor in my stars, but in 'things' much closer to the dance floor. I enjoyed the modern dance classes. I met a lot of people my own age and we all got on well together. I was always paired off with one of the taller girls, which suited me just fine. It was a pleasant respite from night school, and a lot more fun.

Alice used to insist that the distance between two partners should be such that she would be able to slip a gramophone record between them during a modern ballroom dance, and I am more than positive she had an especially thick record made for this demonstration. These dance classes were held at the Albert Dance Hall in Bath Street, but she also had a dance studio in Sauchiehall Street. My friends and I liked the Albert and met up there on chosen nights. Making arrangements amongst young people was mostly by word of mouth as telephones were still a rarity then.

We seemed to have a larger circle of friends than later generations and there wasn't the public flaunting of intense relationships between young couples that was to appear in later years. As far as I can recall there were no serious intentions – meaning steady girl friends – until we were about seventeen or eighteen. The chances were that if a boy started to go out with a girl and meet her regularly when he was fifteen or sixteen or even start to plaster his hair down or dress too well to be true outside of a Sunday, he would earn the dreaded name of 'Jessie'.

Now we had reached the age when we knew roughly about sex

and the general gist of how it worked. Many of us were by this time aunts and uncles, which added in some way to our growing knowledge. It was about this age when the home offensive heated up with continual innuendoes about the lurking moral dangers when staying out late at night (10.30 p.m.) and dire warnings, such as 'Never let yourself get into a compromising position with a girl and have the good sense to say NO before it's too late to say it.' No doubt in the case of a daughter she was given the same treatment with only the gender changing in the warning. But it wasn't just sex we had to be careful about for we seemed to be perpetually warned about all appetites having to be curbed. The dreaded cautionary finger was wagged in your direction about impatience, temper, eating habits, sport and all other things where personal discipline was considered a necessity. This was nearly always accompanied with the worn words, 'All things in moderation,' (which certainly did not include sex).

Boys, at least the smart ones, always met the girls inside the dance hall but I must add it was more an economy measure and not meanness (there must be a difference). No one had the money to be too philanthropic with it and an evening out was usually budgeted along the lines of an admission ticket, two cups of coffee and a packet of cigarettes, plus reasonable tram fare money. There was no way one could try a particular place and then for some reason or another move on to another social spot, simply because to buy two admission tickets on the same evening was out of the question.

Occasionally our group would try a different dance hall in another part of the city for no other reason than to have a change. On a few occasions we might end up in the Locarno in Sauchiehall Street or Green's Playhouse in Renfield Street where a Dr Crock used to play. On rare occasions we would venture to Glasgow's Barrowland. Most of these places I have just mentioned were a bit too showy for us, and in any case we did not seem to fit in any too well, but as I said it was a change. It must be said that none of our parents would have recommended any of those night-spots to anyone, let alone their children, as they were considered by them to be too 'glitzy' and rather 'tough'. More than often we would go to the Plaza at Eglinton Toll or the Tudor out at Giffnock. Usually where we went was governed by either a nearby handy meeting place, or one of the mob staying in the vicinity.

What the trams did for the working people in Glasgow during the day, they also did for the young people at night. All a young man had to make sure of was whether the lass he was seeing home lived in the same direction as he did, and that they both shared the same tram colour if possible. Glasgow Transport did the rest. The alternative was a late walk home to receive the wagging finger treatment.

My next move in the DO was into the ship's pipe section where the drawings and diagrams of the total piping layout for each vessel were produced, along with their connections and attachments. The master drawing was called the General Arrangement, where all the piping in the machinery space (engineroom) is shown on one large single drawing. At first glance it looked quite confusing, but it was from this drawing that all the various drawings and diagrams were made, detailing separately each pipe requirement, and every length of pipe was given its own identifying number. This section of the office was responsible for cataloguing each separate part, regardless of whether it would be acquired from an outside source or manufactured inside the company workshop. This working area came under the pencil and province of a Mr McLure who, like Blenchy, taught and trained the young draughtsmen with tolerance and patience, two attributes necessary for their particular line of work. Junior draughtsmen watched and listened and learnt.

One of the more pleasant and easier tasks that I might be called upon to do was take part in a ship's sea trial, which usually lasted into the third day and culminated at an anchorage close to the seaside town of Gourock near to the mouth of the River Clyde. It was there that the shipbuilder's house flag was lowered and the new owner's flag was raised on completion of the final signature being written. It was very satisfying to know that another finished product had been examined, tested and accepted to go anywhere in the world where there was sufficient depth of water for her to sail safely in, and where she would meet the breadth and depth requirements to transit the international canals.

If you would like to take part in a ship's sea trial then jump into a boiler suit. (There were only white ones then to prevent any dye running in the heat and sweat of an engine room in the tropics. There was no air-conditioning either, but mosquito nets were supplied when required). Do not wander too far away in the machinery space on your own and don't be alarmed at the noise level when things start to happen. I don't think ear muffs had been invented yet. Oh! I should avoid walking under the large blowers or ventilators in the engine room as at times it can be very chilly if you have been heated up a bit, but remember, even the blowers have to be tested and I had better add here that the lovely cool fresh air blown down is not all for the staff because the more the motor engines take of it the better and cheaper they work.

Just prior to the vessel leaving her berth at Whiteinch for the start of sea trials the engine will have been turned very slowly through at least one complete revolution. This turning is achieved by an electric motor that is jacked-in to engage with the engine crankshaft and the purpose of this turning ritual is to make absolutely sure there is no obstruction in any part of the machinery. There are other signs the engineers would look for, like any cooling water leakage escaping with the air displaced by the slow moving pistons through specially located open air cocks that prevent any build up of air pressure, but we won't bother about these details at present. Suffice it to imagine that what has been done to the ship's engine is the same as putting in a car's starting handle and giving the car engine one or two turns by hand to make sure nothing has seized or jammed and that lubricating oil had reached every part. When the turn is completed and all seems to be in order, the turning gear is disengaged.

The next operation is to test the 'starting air' system. All heavy diesel engines are started by forcing pressurised air into each cylinder which pushes the piston, or pistons, away from it and starts the process of the engine running. However, with the fuel cut off the engine stops when the air supply ceases. In this manner the engine is turned a few revolutions ahead and stopped. This is repeated with a short blast of air given in the astern direction and if all is well then that is the finish of the main machinery tests. The 'starting air' test is similar to a car driver starting and stopping his car to make sure the battery is in good working order. It only remains now to raise the fuel pressure and check that it is suitable and stable in readiness to be injected into the cylinder. All is ready for the river pilot to place the engine room on 'standby' and alert the tugs in attendance that he is commencing the procedure of leaving the berth.

The pilot now has 'singled up' on the mooring lines and each tug fore and aft has a rope secured to the ship and waiting for the pilot's instructions. Soon the last rope between ship and berth is cast off and the tugs gently pull their charge out into the centre of the river, where the bridge rings down for the first engine movement. In the engine room there is the hiss of compressed air being supplied to the engine; the tone changes when the fuel starts to burn in the cylinders. The air is stopped and the engine is now powering the ship for the first time. Soon the lines attached to the tugs are released and the brand new vessel is on her own for the very first time and slowly moves down the river with the tugs still giving escort until dismissed later in the ever-widening river.

Before much else happens I think we should find out where we are to be boarded and where we can put our things. Unfortunately we don't get a cabin either first or second class but we are allocated a settee and two easy seats in the second class lounge – not bad, it could be worse.

Well, now we are approaching the 'tail of the bank' and the shores on either side are steadily growing further apart. On the river passage so far the pilot has rung the telegraph to 'dead slow ahead', 'slow ahead', 'half ahead', 'full ahead' and then back to 'dead slow ahead'. He has also done the same for astern movements, more than probably when we were leaving the berth. From now on he will ring his instructions down to the engine room at his own discretion as the trial proceeds.

The first operation when reaching a safe manoeuvring space will be to 'box' the ship's compass and this is done by the representatives of its manufacturer. This involves the bridge compass being given its final corrections for accuracy by the adjustments of metal probes by compass specialists while being given information supplied by the pilot who is navigating by known landmarks.

Following the 'boxing' process and now confident that the compass is as accurate as humanly possible, it is now time to test the efficiency of the ship's steering gear and find out just how the rudder will react to the helmsman's touch. This equipment has to be put through mandatory tests to satisfy the standards set by the MOT, Lloyds Insurance and the prospective owner. Let me cover this part of the tests by telling my readers (not wearing boiler suits) that if at any time they should see a ship performing manoeuvres such as the making of a figure eight and then turning circles first one way and then the other, do not be unduly concerned. The captain has not lost his way but is most probably only testing his steering gear.

The next part of the programme would be to make several runs over the measured mile, raising the engine power on each successive run and finishing on the maximum speed run. The 'measured mile', as the name implies is an exact nautical mile clearly identified between two white posts at Skelmorlie on the Clyde. These posts were erected in 1866 and are now listed buildings by the Scottish Office. Each and every steam or motor driven ship from that time built on the River Clyde most probably used these two landmarkers during their speed trials.

Meanwhile, in the engine room the main machinery has been partly power-loaded during the approach to the measured mile and is ready to start its first 'run' when the ship is abreast the start post and the bridge rings down on the telegraph. Stopwatches are started and engine fuel readings are noted. My job over the 'mile' was to take power draw cards which is a method used to translate the power developed inside each cylinder along with its relevant fuel pump timing. This information is shown on the card in the form of a diagram that could then be analysed and kept as a permanent record. At the finish of the run the bridge would again give a ring on the telegraph when the stopwatches would be stopped, giving the exact time the ship had taken to travel between the two posts. The fuel readings would again be noted to measure the amount of fuel consumed by the engine at that particular speed and trim. Also from this data it could be determined what the total power developed in the main engine had been for each respective performance over the 'mile', and if it had been shared equally between all the cylinders.

Successive runs would be made with a greater developed engine load (more fuel added) giving a faster ship's speed through the water, and working up in this fashion until the vessel was finally running at its full commercially guaranteed speed and fuel consumption. When all concerned were satisfied with the results and readings the ship usually then went for a twenty-four hour shake-down run at full speed. This endurance test meant the DO group splitting up to cover the whole period to take temperatures and fuel consumption readings along with the occasional draw-card. The trials usually took the ship out into the Irish Sea but, of course, it would always depend on the weather conditions at the time. The one sure thing that never changed was the trial ending at an anchorage off Gourock where the Barclay Curle and other sea trial personnel disembarked onto a tug which took them over to the jetty alongside the railway station, and the train back to Glasgow.

It's unlikely that any of my readers will have been seasick, although one or two might be feeling a bit tired (or bored?). I hope no one minded dossing down on a settee. It wasn't exactly five-star stuff but it was nice getting served in the dining saloon. Pity it was on one of these occasions when the pilot suddenly decided to change course; perhaps he was avoiding a fishing boat.

There is one thing I should mention before we leave. This will be the only time in the life of the ship when everything and everywhere will feel and smell so totally new. Rich business suits will amicably pass men in uniform or boiler suits in an unreal atmosphere of equality. It is like being on a film set that will never be enacted again.

The worst part for some of the passengers is usually at the tail-end when they have to close their eyes and jump onto the tug during the disembarking procedure. The first few times are the worst when you are hyped-up and foolish enough to believe any voice that calls out, 'Now!' It's strange how it's always easier boarding a larger vessel from a smaller one than it is when the process is reversed.

Back in the normality of the drawing office all the information gleaned and noted during the trial has to be copied and stored away under the engine number it had been given before its first nut and bolt had been ordered.

Taking part in ship trials was my first experience of being on board a ship at sea in a working capacity for up till that time the only sea trips that I can remember were two occasions on the Clyde paddle steamers, the *Duchess of Rothesay* and the *Caledonia,* and they must have been in the years immediately prior to the war. There was another time in 1936 when the family went on holiday to the Isle of Mull. It was one of the McBrayne Line boats that took us there and I remember us all disembarking at Tobermory into open boats and rowing ashore. If my guess is right it was probably because the tide was out at the time. While on this topic I will tell you that we stayed with a family called McMaster who were very kind to us. They had a son about my age and I think we shared a common Christian name. We both got on well together although I'll bet he wasn't sorry to see me leave. He found himself in trouble with his father on two occasions. Once for speaking Gaelic in front of the May family and again after the pair of us had wandered too far away into the hilly countryside where there was a danger of being bitten by an adder. I wonder if Ian (Iain) survived the war?

That particular holiday turned out to be the last one we spent together as a complete family. The following year the problems with my leg and then my ear prevented the entire family going away together and the year after that my eldest sister Clara was married.

Enough of Memory Lane and back to work. Not all the marine engines built at Whiteinch were lifted into a ship's hull alongside the engine works. Some were dispatched to other places where the ship's hull had been built, elsewhere in the country. I attended one that sailed from Burntisland over on the East Coast but what I remember of it seemed to be that we sailed out on the morning and the trial was completed the same day. It was a smaller than usual ship on that occasion. There was one that took me up to Aberdeen for the trials of a vessel built by Hall Russel and engined with a Barclay Curle Doxford type diesel engine. We were booked into a hotel quite close to the railway station, and when we left the following evening to join the ship there was a real live ceilidh going on, complete with the sound of bagpipes and kilted 'hoots' and 'hi's' coming from the reception room. On our return two days later I had doubts about it not being the same reception that was still going on in the full swing of things. (Surely the bride and groom would not still be there? No! It must have been another one.)

But back to the office and more mundane things. All the drawings were done in pencil on transparent paper and when one was completed the draughtsman added his initials to a space reserved for it in the heading legend. It was then checked by the section boss who also added his initials to it. After that it was taken to the tracing department upstairs where the drawing was traced by hand onto a heavy light-blue waterproof paper using black tracing ink. The tracers were all girls who skilfully produced a neat and accurate copy of each pencilled drawing they received from the drawing office. The tracer's copy was thoroughly checked by the supervisor, Ina Gibbon, who was in charge of the tracing department, and these tracings were kept as the originals from which the day-to-day blueprints were produced by using a moving electric arc photocopying machine. There was a special room for this process where drawings were produced by the capable hands of Johnny Cowan. There was a nice atmosphere upstairs as both Miss Gibbon and John greeted everyone with a friendly smile.

The office staff started work at 8.30 a.m., half an hour later than the workshop personnel; therefore it must have been much quieter without the hustle and bustle of the workmen making the earlier start, and who were seen to be very much in the majority in that particular area of Glasgow, but strangely enough I do not recall it being any more peaceful. I was very much aware of the change from not having to go through the gatehouse entrance any more, because I now entered through the main office entrance in South Street, and walked upstairs to the first floor where the drawing office was, and for me that was preferable.

I still came along Dumbarton Road by tram each morning and left it at the stop at the top of Edzell Street beside the convent school. It was a very short walk down to South Street and along to the office entrance. The extra half an hour I had in bed must have done me a power of good for Whiteinch now looked a better place and I had the chance of recognising people without a crowd to lose them in. Incidentally I was once told that Whiteinch got its name from the great number of birds (presumably white; or was it the mess they made?) that seemed attracted to it for some reason in the pre-industrial time.

The open unbuilt area across South Street and facing the engine works was a railway shunting yard where wagons, either singly or in groups, were continually being pushed this way then that way. I remember often hearing the sound of a steam shunter engine preparing to move a heavy static load, its huffing and puffing getting faster and faster with the familiar sound of slipping steel wheels desperately trying to catch a grip of their track. This was followed by the silence that told me something was on the move; suddenly there would be the clang, clang, clang when the free moving wagons came to an abrupt stop against each other's buffers. A busy little railway employee appeared to be continually ducking and darting about between the rolling stock with a long stick in his hand that he used to connect and disconnect the chain links between the wagons or the engine. It looked as though the engine driver was having a jolly good time and amusing himself with these wagons although I'm sure that some sort of purpose and order finally won each day.

This shunting sound went on all the time but somehow or another I was not conscious of it, even in the summer when the windows were open. For some reason if one lives with a particular background sound some in-built protective system manages to shut it out. Perhaps it's much simpler than that, with one's mind just accepting it as mine appeared to do back in Prestwick when living nearby to the airfield. I never heard the planes coming or going; nor do I recall anyone being kept awake by them. I am referring to a balanced sound only up to a certain decibel reading.

Working in an office also meant that I no longer wore old cast-off clothes, but dressed in flannels and sports jacket and I always wore a tie. Summertime lunch breaks were no longer spent looking at ships on the river, but with a group of young draughtsmen and draughtsmen-to-be in nearby Victoria Park. The sandwiches were still part of my lunchtime ritual and, of course, there was no tin can, but in its place a Thermos flask. The summers at that time seemed more reliable and allowed us to enjoy many of these picnic-styled lunches, or maybe we just didn't feel the cold. I became more involved in sport during my stay in the drawing office, spending a fair amount of time in the long evenings at the Barclay Curle Sports Ground in Anniesland where I often met with my daytime colleagues and some of the girls from the tracing office and together we played a form of tennis wearing the sportiest types of clothing we each could muster. Neither my game nor style were much good.

Quite often our group (the young ones) from the office would spend an hour in the swimming pool that was more or less on our doorstep before going home at night. Summers seemed more summery and there was always something to do outside home and workplace. I wasn't a member of the Youth Hostel Association although a number of my friends were.

Golf was always a popular sport in Scotland, and with so many council courses it meant that anyone who was interested had access to a cheap round of golf. It might not be everyone's cup of tea – many preferred football or rugby – but it was not necessary to be rich to play golf. In the few years immediately after the war the game was being enhanced with the reappearance of big names on the circuit. I remember seeing Henry Cotton about that time, as well as watching Australia's Von Nida battling against a strong wind, which was not doing his temper any good.

Let me return for a moment to the time of the crowded family days. We were not a demonstrative family, which to me was quite normal nor was there any member who craved either company or limelight; at least not twenty four hours a day. This might be unusual amongst five children. I had very understanding sisters who must have wanted to wring my neck at least one hundred times, but always finished up spoiling their wee brother. I said crowded family days because there were also the visitors. At that time I can remember an old Mr Campbell who always arrived with his two sisters, who pandered to his every whim or wish. Perhaps he wasn't well or perhaps he just had sisters like mine. Talking about funny old blokes I seem to remember Father telling of the time during his single days when once he went over to

Edinburgh for a wedding and bumped into someone (another Oldie) who remembered him as a boy and who enquired what he was all dressed up for. After all had been explained including the name of the long-time bachelor groom, he gave the reply, 'Och him! It serves him right. I never liked the man.'

The war was now two years behind me and by 1947 conditions were slowly improving, even though bread rationing, which had been introduced the previous year, was still with us, along with petrol coupons and other wartime measures. At least the Nuremberg Trials and sentences were behind us and Europe, having been completely entangled with internal bickering and jealousies, was slowly appearing as a sane and secure place to live in once again, which didn't seem to please Marshal Stalin any too much.

A habit I seem to have kept since those days is my lifelong use of and preference for margarine over butter which I tend to think is a left-over from the wartime era when the girls of the house got the family butter ration and the boys were given the marg. At the risk of an awful pun I must mention that it was a widespread practice with many families during the rationing period. It would not surprise me if there were a lot of my age group and thereabouts who have some sort of eating habit that originated from those days.

I must concede that my starting to work in the drawing office was not one of the social highlights of the year; in fact it was pretty insignificant compared with the national changes that were either happening or being talked about. The feeling I had of that time was of becoming part of a country intent on making up for lost time. Whether it was the war and the lessons learned from it, I'm not sure, but it did seem there was a genuine growing awareness and care in all areas of human concern.

In 1947 the coal industry was nationalised and the mere mention of this brings memories of stories I had heard during my evacuee days in Larkhall. I had been told of the days not so long past when pitmen, including boys no older than I had been as an evacuee, went down in the pit cage before the sun had risen, and returned to the surface long after it had set. During my stay, there had been an accident or incident at one of the local pits. The details I cannot recall but the sound of the pit siren was in stark contrast to the fearsome silence in the faces of the people in the streets and those who appeared from doorways.

It may well have been a call for help from beneath the surface of the earth to which each community service would have responded. It was a command for the sleeping miner to awake, dog-walking miner to return home, betting miner to dismiss the results and answer the call, reading miner to put aside his book. Miners' loved ones felt a terror tearing at them from the very ground beneath their feet, and the young pitmen experienced the feeling of dread known to all who live their lives out in the shadow of the coal mine cage winding wheel.

Whatever happened on that occasion could not have been very serious as I would have heard about it from Mrs Dunn, who always liked to tell me about what was going on, but it demonstrates how the sound of gunfire and exploding bombs are boxed into warfare years while other dreaded sounds remain with us unconfined to time or place.

Following on the heels of the nationalisation of the coal industry was the compulsory raising of the school leaving age to sixteen. I remember this happening very vividly because I had always assumed that no one could leave school as early as fourteen or fifteen, at least not in 1947.

The following year I was entitled to the key of the door, and for all the right reasons my birthday is a complete blank. I can remember nothing of the morning, afternoon or the evening and I can offer no explanation of why it has been removed from my memory. I contacted my sisters Clara and Joey during the time I was writing about this particular incident but neither of them could jog my memory. All I can write about it was that I was staying in Garnethill with both my parents and living a contented normal life, but something seems to have blocked that birthday occasion out completely.

I know I wasn't exactly friendless at the time and something must have been organised for the evening. I somehow or another associate the receiving of a long chrome cigarette case with an attached Ronson lighter as being a gift from someone then; perhaps only because such a present would have been bought for such an occasion. Whatever happened to the cigarette case I do not recall, but I did possess it about that time and for some years after. The case was the type that George Sanders (George who?) would have casually produced at the right moment and it must have made me feel a real suave type trying to do the same, between my catarrhal coughing bouts. I had a lot to learn.

I will mention what I do remember of that year. The railways and the electrical industry were both nationalised, as had been promised because of the common link between them being coal. However, none of these changes compared with the public interest shown over the introduction of the National Health Service in July of that year.

I had often heard Father comment since the end of the war that he thought introduction of the NHS could take place within the lifetime of a government's first term with a hard sell and high payments to change the medical profession's attitude towards the Beveridge Plan, which had been talked about quite seriously since 1942. He wasn't alone in having no illusions at all about what most of the elder members of that fraternity thought about the subject.

In retrospect I think Father would have made an excellent lawyer had he been given the opportunity for he had the gift of putting over what he wanted to say extremely well. He hoped that one day legal assistance would be offered to everyone on the same basis as the National Health, but he knew that dream would never happen during his time on Earth. One other thing he and many of his generation might well be correct about was his reply to the popular theory that if everyone received the best medical treatment when it was required, then in a very short time practically everyone would be healthy with very few people requiring to see a doctor.

'Och! If you believe that you will believe anything. If it's absolutely free there will always be these folk that will get the doctor out of his bed for no more than a running nose or a headache.'

Wartime measures regarding rationing were still with us, although bread rationing, that had been introduced in 1946, ended during the summer of 1948. I know and appreciate that rationing of everyday goods must have been hard for some, or perhaps ‘difficult’ would be a better word to use. For myself it was never punitive in any sense of the word, and in any case most people accepted the problems of feeding a country struggling to get back on its feet again and were resigned to shortages being the norm. Everything seemed to creep up unnoticed from behind. When changes are slow in coming about they are not really noticed quite so much as those that are heralded with a roll of drums. As a fully-fledged adult I had no idea what normal living without shortages was like, simply because war and its long-lasting restrictions had truly shaped me. It wasn’t all bad as life and living in general was improving and I continually heard about families picking up where they had left off and all they wanted to do now was to get back on track, pay the rent or mortgage, feed and clothe the kids and think about their education and future. I also heard of other families emigrating to one of the Commonwealth countries.

Government changes had taken place and Acts of Parliament had received the monarch’s signature but nothing had changed the habits of the old Glasgow clothes woman who still collected what she was given after knocking on the tenement doors. She had been a familiar Glasgow character to the tenement tribespeople since long before I was even thought of. I can only guess what she did with her collection and where it finished its fourth, fifth and probably sixth-hand days. Somehow these women eked out a living from their trade. They outlasted the back-green singers and their predictable sorrowful repertoire. It took no great stretch of the imagination to think of at least one reason why these pre-war jobless men had disappeared since the outbreak of hostilities.

Later the same year something of great import happened to me. On 12th November I was handed an envelope, and inside it beneath the Company heading was my indenture.

I was now a fully-fledged draughtsman and with all things being equal it looked as though I had a secure future. I had long since stopped being the office telephone answering device. The incoming calls were by then in the capable hands of an up-and-coming apprentice. As a matter of interest I will mention that the Statement of Apprenticeship Served I was presented with at the finish of my ‘Time’ was signed by the same director who did not

ON ADMIRALTY LIST

CONTRACTORS TO H M GOVERNMENT

BARCLAY CURLE & COY. LIMITED

ENGINEERS & SHIPBUILDERS

NORTH BRITISH ENGINE WORKS

739 SOUTH STREET WHITEINCH

GLASGOW. W. 4.

HEAD OFFICE:
SHIPBUILDING YARD
CLYDEHOLM WHITEINCH

LONDON OFFICE ARMADORES HOUSE, BURY STREET, E.C.3
LIVERPOOL OFFICE TOWER BUILDING, WATER STREET

TELEGRAPHIC ADDRESS:
QUADRUPLE GLASGOW

TELEPHONE Nº SCOTSTOUN 2261
CODES: BENTLEYS AND A B C

ALL OFFERS MADE BY US AND ALL ORDERS ACCEPTED BY US ARE SUBJECT TO THE TERMS CONDITIONS AND LIMITATIONS SET OUT ON THE BACK HEREOF.

12th November, 1948.

This is to certify that IAN MAY served with us as an Apprentice Fitter for five years ending 8th November, 1948, with part of his time, i.e. one year, being spent in our Drawing Office.

During this time he conducted himself to our entire satisfaction, being steady, obliging and attentive to his duties and proving himself a capable workman.

FOR BARCLAY, CURLE & CO., LTD.

Jas. B. McGhee

ASSIST. GENERAL MANAGER ENGINE WKS.

Apprenticeship commenced: 16. 8.43.
" completed: 8.11.48.

like to be asked on the phone who he was. Everything looked rosy for me as I had finally left my apprenticeship days behind me and was now supposed to be able to take care of myself financially. Let's wait and see what happens.

I was now going through a unique phase of my life. I was swinging along without restrictions and no one got hurt. I do not recall any of the family or friends slowing down in any way. There seemed to be a shortage of time. There was no such thing as someone complaining about being bored with nothing to do. Such a character would be known as a 'boring' individual, or more likely in need of a medicinal tonic.

In the spring of 1949 three friends, including two office colleagues and myself decided to plan a holiday somewhere in the south of France for our summer holidays. For us it was quite an event to even consider and for each of us it was going to be the first real holiday of our adult lives.

The train journey to Newhaven was, up till then, the longest train trip I had ever made. The first real excitement was the Channel crossing between Newhaven and Dieppe on board the French passenger ferry or paquebot *Arromanches*. It was hoped we would manage to demonstrate to fellow passengers how capable we were as sailors, but alas, the Channel was in the very best of moods and the ferry was not exactly crowded with passengers. It was easy enough writing out the pcs bought on board in a steady hand without any 'heavy weather' scrawling; well, perhaps I put a little in for effect.

Going through Customs and Immigration and holding a British passport was 'big stuff' and something to write home about. There were a lot of stateless people around Europe at this time who could not prove what nationality they held and documents of identity were very important indeed.

We saw very little of Dieppe but did witness some of its scars of battle in several of its buildings. From the seaport a train ran straight through to Paris, that was soon to be at our feet as we looked down upon it from the top of the Eiffel Tower soon after our arrival. Coming from a rather 'bumpy' part of the world, I remember thinking how flat the countryside was in every direction from where I was standing. It was in one of the crowded lifts going up a section of the tower that I had my first introduction to the smell of garlic, which I disliked then and have done so ever since.

That same evening we watched through innocent eyes that missed nothing of the extravaganza at the Moulin Rouge. Josephine Baker had the starring role of a show which to us was 'quite different' but didn't do us any harm. It certainly displayed a lot more in the way of its young ladies than was ever seen at the Half Past Eight show back home in the King's Theatre. I wondered if Glasgow would ever be the same again for me?

The *pension* we stayed at in Paris was clean and spartan which was just as I had expected it to be. Purely by coincidence and through a sister who hoarded her brother's possessions when he

LIVRE D'OR
DES
FOLIES
BERGÈRE

Mlle **JOSÉPHINE BAKER**

Top bill at the Folies Bergère, August 1949.

Je suis très ému, je vous le dis très sincèrement ! Rêver pendant des mois à un spectacle, puis petit à petit voir les tableaux que l'on a conçus prendre forme, s'animer... C'est merveilleux !

Un jour on ouvre les portes, le public entre, il va vous juger! alors on est inquiet... on a le trac

Ai-je eu raison d'essayer de modifier une formule qui avait fait ses preuves ?

On est tremblant... on sent son cœur battre fort... très fort !

Michel Gyarmathy

Non, Michel GYARMATHY, rassurez-vous ! c'est moi Joséphine BAKER, votre interprète, qui viens vous serrer la main et vous dire : soyez sans inquiétude !

Les spectateurs sont sensibles aux efforts, faites-leur confiance ! Oui, je sais on a quand même le trac... je l'ai bien moi-même ! Mais cela ne m'empêche pas de vous dire merci pour tous les beaux tableaux que vous avez réalisés pour moi ! Merci à M. Paul DERVAL d'avoir monté, à coups de millions, cette féerie de luxe pour ma rentrée à Paris ! Merci à Madame Paul DERVAL qui m'a habillée... et même un peu déshabillée, avec tant de goût ! Merci à Pierre LARRIEU, directeur de la musique, pour m'avoir donné l'appui de son grand talent ! Et, bien entendu. merci à vous cher public, vous que nous craignons un peu, mais que nous aimons tant !

Alors ? nous avons tout dit ? on peut commencer ? M. DERVAL on peut y aller ? Michel GYARMATHY on peut frapper les trois coups ? Un ! deux ! trois !.. rideau pour le premier acte de **FEERIES & FOLIES,** *le nouveau spectacle des FOLIES-BERGÈRE !*

Joséphine Baker

Antonia Derval

PROGRAMME (suite)

CARROUSEL DES FOLIES-BERGÈRE

The Roundabouts of the Folies-Bergère

A. - **Le Manège d'argent**

Les Show-Girls et les Danseuses

B. - **La Grande Parade**

L'Étoile	Mlle **JOSÉPHINE BAKER**
Les Amazones.	Les Danseuses des Folies-Bergère
Les Cavaliers	Les Show-Girls des Folies-Bergère
Les Fantaisistes	Mlles Lyne de SOUZA et Jacqueline MARCY
Les Écuyères	Yvonne MÉNARD et Pierrette KYRE
Les Rossignols	**VÉRONICA BELL** et **COLETTE FLEURIOT**
Les Cavaliers	MM. **FRÉDÉRIC REY** Jean LUTHY, Pierre JANVIER ELIO, MERLIER, HUMBERT
Monsieur Loyal	NELSON

La Direction se réserve tous droits de changements dans le programme

Ceux qui participent à la présentation de ce grand spectacle et à la bonne marche des FOLIES-BERGÈRE

- Personnel administratif	12
- Personnel artistique de la scène et de l'orchestre	126
- Personnel technique :	
Machinistes.	67
Electriciens	22
Accessoiristes	12
Tapissiers	11
Entretien	16
Habilleuses	23
Couturières, costumières, modistes	43
- Personnel de la salle	57
Soit	389

PROGRAMME OFFICIEL - PRIX : 50 FRANCS

GRAND HOTEL DU HAVRE

(en face la sortie des Grandes Lignes Gare Saint-Lazare)

Téléphone : TRINITÉ 15-93 / TRINITÉ 15-94 / TRINITÉ 15-95
Télégr. : HAVROTEL-118-PARIS
C. Chèques Post. : PARIS 1945.50
R. C. Seine 19.181
R. C. Seine 714.369

18, Rue d'Amsterdam
PARIS

Le 11 Août 1949

Monsieur May N° 61

Imp. Higuet, 227, rue de Belleville

	DÉBOURS	
apt du 11/8 au 12/8 à 450		450

NOTA. — Toutes nos locations sont faites à la journée. La présentation des notes à la fin de chaque semaine n'est qu'une facilité de paiement accordée aux voyageurs.

It would probably cost a bit more today!

NOTICE TO PASSENGERS

CONTROL OF EXPORTS

Various kinds of personal and household effects are prohibited to be exported from the United Kingdom, *i.e.* Great Britain and Northern Ireland, except under licence from the Board of Trade, Export Licensing Branch, Stafford House, King William Street, London, E.C.4.

As a concession, licences are not required for reasonable quantities of bona-fide personal effects (and household effects upon transfer of residence) exported by passengers provided that the goods are declared and produced to the Customs Officer and that they are not being exported as merchandise or for sale.

For the purpose of this concession, " personal effects " means any portable articles exported in the baggage or on the person of a passenger which he might reasonably be expected to carry with him for his own regular and private use. The concession does not cover goods carried on behalf of other persons.

The following articles are excluded from the concession :—

(1) **Foodstuffs** except as provided in Note I overleaf;

(2) **Soap** exceeding 2 lbs. in weight;

(3) **Stamp collections** of a value exceeding £5 where the passenger is proceeding to a destination outside the sterling area;

(4) **Firearms** and ammunition except as provided in Note II overleaf;

(5) **Rubber tyres and tubes ;**

(6) **Valuables** (*i.e.* broadly speaking, jewellery, furs, articles of gold or platinum or silver, works of art and antiques) except as provided in Note III overleaf.

Prohibited goods not covered by the concession or by an export licence which are brought to a port or aerodrome for the purpose of being exported are forfeited and any passenger bringing such goods is liable to penalties.

By Order of the Commissioners of Customs and Excise.

City Gate House,
Finsbury Square,
London, E.C.2.

April, 1948. Sec. 29272/1948. **Notice S.N.6. Revised**

NOTES

I. FOODSTUFFS

(*a*) *Any passenger domiciled in the United Kingdom and leaving for a temporary visit to any country abroad (including Eire)* may take with him not more than 1 lb. of foodstuffs for every two days of his stay abroad provided that in no case does the total weight of food, rationed or unrationed, exceed 15 lbs. or the weight of any one kind of food (*e.g.* canned meat of any description) exceed 2 lbs.

This concession is modified for infant passengers of two years of age and under, for whom supplies of food required for the infant's consumption and not exceeding 15 lbs. in all may be taken.

(*b*) *Any passenger who has resided in the United Kingdom for at least six months and is leaving to take up permanent residence abroad* may take with him foodstuffs up to a weight of 15 lbs. with no restriction on the quantity of any individual food taken within this amount.

(*c*) *Other passengers* may take out only small quantities of foodstuffs obviously intended for their own consumption on their journey.

(*d*) Where the food requirements of infants of two years of age and under and invalids exceed the limits laid down above, application for export licence may be made to the Board of Trade, Export Licensing Branch ; such an application can be considered only if it is accompanied by a Doctor's Certificate.

The foregoing concessions do not apply to foodstuffs exported in unaccompanied baggage and will not be allowed where the passenger fails to declare the whole of the food in his possession.

II. FIREARMS AND AMMUNITION

Export licences need not be obtained for:—

(*a*) Firearms or ammunition covered by a valid firearms certificate, provided the certificate is produced at the time of exportation.

(*b*) One or two smooth bore shot guns having barrels not less than 20 inches in length.

(*c*) 1,000 or less shot gun cartridges.

III. VALUABLES

(*a*) *United Kingdom residents visiting or emigrating to the sterling area direct* may take with them personal valuables up to a value of £2,000. Emigrants to the sterling area may also include personal or household valuables to the value of £200 in their unaccompanied effects.

(*b*) *United Kingdom residents visiting places outside the sterling area* may take with them certain personal effects normally carried by passengers, *e.g.* a wedding ring, engagement ring and one used fur coat, and a few articles of small value. *Emigrants* to such places may include in their effects (accompanied or unaccompanied) personal or household valuables to a value of £200.

(*c*) *Visitors to the United Kingdom* may take out with them personal valuables brought in with them or purchased out of their own currency.

Notice S.N.6. Revised

4 48 E2613 Wt. 16934-53 200,000 6/48 Gp. 8 Fosh & Cross Ltd., London

EXCHANGE CONTROL ACT, 1947.

TRAVELLERS' GUIDE.

This Guide, although addressed primarily to persons who are treated for Exchange Control purposes as " resident in the United Kingdom ", also contains information of use to other travellers entering and leaving the United Kingdom. Any traveller who is in doubt as to what he is required to do should consult his bank. The Guide does not apply to members of H.M. Forces travelling on official duty, who are referred to their own Service rules. **Intending travellers should, in their own interest, make their arrangements with their banks or travel agents, for the provision of exchange, in good time before their departure.**

TRAVELLERS LEAVING THE UNITED KINGDOM.

1. As from 1st May, 1948, tourist travel will be permitted to certain countries. The foreign currency to be allowed for tourist travel for the twelve months beginning the 1st May is the equivalent of £35 for adults and £25 for children under 16 years of age. Full information can be obtained from your bank or any travel agent.

2. If you need to travel for genuine business purposes a special allocation of exchange will be made available to you according to the length of time which you will require to spend abroad. A special allocation may also be given in certain circumstances for travel on compassionate, health or educational grounds. Any exchange allotted to you is for your personal use only and may not be transferred to or used on behalf of another person, even your wife or family. Full details of the arrangements may be obtained from any bank or travel agent in the United Kingdom.

3. In general there are no Exchange Control formalities in connection with the purchase in the United Kingdom of travel tickets. But if you wish to pay in sterling in the United Kingdom for accommodation in foreign hotels and, in certain circumstances for travel tickets, you will be required to produce to the booking agent a Form V issued by a bank or travel agent, indicating that you have received permission to make payment in this way. The amount of any Form V issued to you may be treated as part of your allowance of exchange. The booking agent will tell you if he requires a Form V, and for what amount, and will advise you how to obtain it.

4. There are no restrictions on the amount you will be able to spend in countries within the Scheduled Territories* and Form V will not be necessary in respect of the payment in sterling in the United Kingdom for accommodation in hotels in the Scheduled Territories.

5. When applying for exchange or a Form V you will be required by the bank or travel agent to produce your valid passport and the total cost of such facilities will be recorded therein. If you do not submit your application to your own bank you will, in addition, be required to satisfy the bank or travel agent that you are resident in the United Kingdom and not a temporary visitor.

6. Applications in respect of business journeys must be countersigned by the firm you are representing, who must declare that the entire cost of the journey will be charged to the firm. If the application is granted, the bank or travel agent providing the exchange will issue to you an " Exchange Control Card " which will be in two portions; the " outward " portion must be surrendered to the Immigration Officer on your departure and the " inward " portion given up to him on your return. You are warned that failure to produce the appropriate portion at the proper time may involve you in inconvenience and delay.

7. You should read your application form carefully before you sign it. It contains important conditions.

8. In order to meet your main expenses during your stay abroad you should take with you travellers' cheques or letters of credit available for encashment in the countries concerned. But in order to meet your incidental expenses *en route* or on arrival at your destination, you will be allowed to carry with you when you leave the United Kingdom an amount in foreign currency notes not exceeding the equivalent of £10; such notes will be treated as part of your exchange allowance.

* The Scheduled Territories comprise the British Empire (except Canada and Newfoundland), British Mandated Territories (except Palestine), British Protectorates and Protected States, Burma, Iraq, Iceland and the Faroe Islands.

[P.T.O.

9. In addition to the small amount of foreign currency notes mentioned above you may carry with you not more than £5 in sterling notes for use on board British ships and aircraft (£1 and 10/- notes will normally be accepted on board) and to cover your landing expenses on your return to this country. These sterling notes will not be charged against your allowance of exchange. **It is an offence against the Exchange Control Act to spend or exchange sterling notes in countries outside the Scheduled Territories.**

10. If you wish to take out any of the following:—

(*a*) Foreign currency notes and notes of the Scheduled Territories other than the United Kingdom in excess of the equivalent of £10;

(*b*) Gold;

(*c*) Postal orders;

(*d*) Securities and Life Assurance Policies (and documents of title relating thereto);

and you consider that there is good reason for special permission to be given in your case, you should apply to your bank or travel agent for the necessary permission to do so (Certificate C); this certificate must be produced to the Immigration Officer on embarkation. Permission (Certificate C) will NOT be granted to enable you to take out sterling bank notes in excess of £5.

11. Any notes in excess of the amounts permitted may be seized when you arrive at the port of embarkation, and you should not expect to have them returned to you.

12. Enquiries with regard to the export of jewellery and valuables (other than the items mentioned in paragraph 10) should be made to the Secretary, Committee on the Export of Valuables, Export Licensing Department, Stafford House, King William Street, E.C.4. (Tel.: Mansion House 4555.)

TRANSACTIONS OUTSIDE THE SCHEDULED TERRITORIES.

13. **It is illegal to cash outside the Scheduled Territories, cheques drawn on your sterling account or on any foreign currency account at your disposal unless you have obtained permission through your United Kingdom bank to do so. It is also a serious offence to borrow foreign currency or to enter into any other agreement to obtain foreign currency except with permission obtained through a bank in the United Kingdom. It is illegal to enter into arrangements under which you make payments in the United Kingdom in consideration for or in association with payments made outside the Scheduled Territories on your behalf (e.g., hotel bills).**

TRAVELLERS RETURNING TO THE UNITED KINGDOM.

14. You may not bring into the United Kingdom more than £5 in sterling bank notes. Any notes in excess of this amount will be seized when you land, and you must not expect to have them returned to you. Notes expressed in foreign currencies may, however, be brought into the United Kingdom without limit.

15. If for any reason you have unused sterling Letters of Credit, etc., or unexpended amounts of foreign currency on your return (*e.g.*, if you return before you expected to do so) you must immediately encash the unused sterling Letters of Credit, etc., with the bank or travel agent through whom you acquired them and should ascertain from them what are your obligations in respect of the surplus foreign currency.

EIRE AND THE CHANNEL ISLANDS.

16. There are no restrictions on the import and export of sterling bank notes or foreign currency notes as between the United Kingdom and the Channel Islands/Eire, but you should note that both the Channel Islands and Eire impose restrictions (similar to those in force in this country) on the import and export of sterling bank notes and foreign currency except in the case of travellers to and from the United Kingdom.

H.M. TREASURY,
April, 1948.

WARNING TO TRAVELLERS.

Read this carefully: it will save you trouble and expense.

YOU ARE NOT ALLOWED TO TAKE OUT OF THE COUNTRY, EXCEPT TO EIRE AND THE CHANNEL ISLANDS, STERLING NOTES IN EXCESS OF £5.

The £5 in sterling notes you are permitted to take out are intended for your use on British ships or aircraft or on your return to the United Kingdom. They must NOT be spent or exchanged outside the United Kingdom, Eire or the Channel Islands.

If you have obtained permission to purchase foreign currency for your expenditure abroad, you may take the equivalent of £10 in foreign notes. Foreign notes in excess of the equivalent of £10 cannot be taken out unless special permission has been obtained from your bank on Certificate " C ".

Certain other things are not allowed out—make careful inquiries BEFORE you start for the port.

IN YOUR OWN INTERESTS DON'T present yourself at the port with more than you are allowed to take out. You cannot leave money with the Customs or Immigration Officers, and before you embark you will be questioned. You may even be searched. Any excess money will be detained, and you are unlikely to get it back—so **leave it behind.** And don't be tempted to make a false declaration, which may lead to arrest and prosecution.

THESE RULES ARE IN EVERYONE'S INTEREST. YOUR CO-OPERATION WILL BE APPRECIATED.

ISSUED BY H.M. TREASURY PURSUANT TO THE EXCHANGE CONTROL ACT, 1947.

March, 1948.

Money laundering hadn't yet been invented.

went off to sea I still have the original receipt from where I stayed in Paris. It also confirms that I paid the bill.

The following morning the three of us left Paris on an early departure train from St Lazare Station bound for Nice via Marseilles. At the station we were each astonished by some of the antics of the intrepid French travelling public. First of all the whole of Paris had turned out at the station and none of the three of us thought it was for our benefit. The crowded part was not unlike our own main railway stations which were now taking the brunt of being part of an outdated and geriatric system due to the war years. What was new to us were the passengers climbing on board the trains through the windows, followed by a fellow passenger or helper who after passing in their luggage to each other, blocked the corridor with it. Seemingly it was quite permissible to do this. Human arms that did not have a case at the end of them or were not being used to hold a child kept waving about in the air as though to attract someone's attention.

I am sure it will not come as a surprise when I tell you that of our four booked seats each had someone sitting in them. There followed our explanations about redeeming the seats given in very broken French and their individual reasons, spoken in very good French and in obvious detail, all speaking at the same time to substantiate their claim for sitting in them. However, it is well-known that British people have a very high and well controlled 'foreigner tolerance circuit' which has saved Europe on so many occasions and which they attempt always to turn or should I say twist to their advantage. On this occasion and thanks to four fair fellows (I'm dark) a happy compromise was reached just as whistles blew and the train shuddered through its first painful movements. We had all managed to squeeze onto the bench type seats and honour appeared to have been satisfied by all in the compartment. By their condescending smiles our fellow/female French travellers gave the impression that flaws they may have, but no-one could say they were not generous to a fault with foreigners. It would have been funny if we had been in the wrong carriage. It has been known to happen.

A good proportion of the passengers were Algerians with both men and women wearing their traditional loose flowing robes as did their matching children. Along the length of the corridor there were family groups of them squatting down in their own customary manner amongst their belongings. I had never seen anything like it outside the cinema.

Up till that time the highlights of my holiday had included leaving and entering a country, the smell of garlic, a taste of Parisian theatreland, and now the dress of the North African families. Very slowly the door to the big outside world with its other cultures was opening for me.

I remember sister Joey once telling me that for many people the first foreign nationals, and I include Europeans, that they had ever seen were the servicemen of other countries staying in Britain during the war. It might just be that the war made our world that little bit smaller.

Before reaching Marseilles some of the carriage doors had been opened while the train was still speeding along. This again seemed to be the done thing to get more air into the compartments when it became over-warm and stuffy. By now there wasn't much more that could happen to surprise us. Our immediate travelling companions each ate their fair share of the French grape crop, and in all honesty to them they did manage to spit out the seeds without one landing on any British-bought brogues.

At Marseilles an exodus from the train meant it was then possible to move around and go to the toilet without standing on anyone unseen on the floor amongst the sea of battered suitcases. We also each had a whole seat to sit on through to Nice. The pleasant heat in the South of France seemed like a heated hothouse, and the flora of the countryside took on the semi-tropical look which made my holiday something very special. It was all so absolutely new to me.

A lot of French sailors left the train at Toulon which meant that we were allowed to travel along the Azure Coast in five star comfort amongst grape seeds to Nice station.

The original plan was to stay at the Garden Hotel that night, but (here we go) unfortunately for some reason or another there was no accommodation for us, and I think it was because we apparently had arrived a day too early. This seemed to trouble the hotel personnel more than it did us. As far as we were concerned it would have been no bother if we had to sleep outside for a night in our new-found warm climate. However it was not to be because after a few telephone calls by the hotel we were dispatched by taxi to another hotel for the night.

The taxi drove us to, and then along, the sea front promenade where everything looked rather expensive; then, horror of horrors, we turned into the most magnificent hotel driveway that I had ever seen in my life. The hotel itself was surrounded in beautiful tropical gardens with sprinklers spraying all shades of coloured water that had been caught in the hidden lighting. Our frantic attempts to tell the driver that he had made a mistake did not deter him from taking us right up to the main entrance, and then insisting that we, along with our four worn cardboard-like suitcases, accompany him into the very extravagantly furnished and marbled reception area. There then followed a conversation between our chauffeur and the receptionist with exceptionally few words spoken between both of them. Our persistent friendly driver than left us and returned to his taxi after a two armed wave as if conducting some part of an imaginary symphony accompaniment to his '*Bonsoir Messieurs*.'

The receptionist had what appeared to us to have a covert word with one of the staff who beckoned us towards one of the lifts. The lift took us up as far as it could go, after which we climbed some stairs, to somewhere in or near the attic, where we thought the staff rooms were. Our guess was right and the four travellers spent their first night at Nice in the penthouse suite as we now called it, and it didn't cost us a penny or should I say sou? What a super address to give if at some later date I was ever asked where I stayed when I visited Nice. Unfortunately I have long forgotten the name of the hotel, but perhaps one day I will return where I'm sure I could find it. After spending the night in the Penthouse Suite and eating a Continental breakfast we were taxied back to our own Hotel Jardin, no doubt to the relief of both hotel staffs.

The three of us managed very well during our stay on the Côte d'Azur, even though we each looked like someone's poor relation. We had of course to economise for only one of two reasons; the first being we had to economise and the other being that even though we had the money at home there was a government restriction allowing only £35 maximum to be taken out of the country. Eating out wasn't too expensive and it is worth a mention that we were not in the least too proud to eat an offered sandwich. French picnickers about our own age were always generous and we would make light of it when accepting by deliberately translating, '*Oui, j'ai une grande faim*,' into '*Oui, j'ai une grande femme*.' So instead of saying I was very hungry, I told them I had a fat wife and that broke the barrier and earned something to eat. We did fairly well using these tactics, but we had to be careful about patting our stomachs and saying we had fat wives in case anyone got the idea that there were also four pregnant girls to feed as well. Perhaps that's why they shared their food in the first place.

Quite early on during our sojourn in Nice we met up with a couple of English girls who were both from London and doing exactly what we were doing. They were called Joy and Irene and were staying at the same hotel as we were. They were good company with a cheerful sense of humour. It must have suited them to be with us during our few days in the sunny South. Heaven knows why. We didn't exactly fit the role of idle playboy types. Incidentally, having mentioned such persons I must now add that we thought we recognised a few Hollywood faces with one in particular who always played the good cowboy part; however we could not recall any of the names. They were obviously celebrities but I suppose even in these days there would be look-alikes.

One morning we took the bus along to Monte Carlo and although clean and tidy we still had the feeling of being cast in the role of poor foreign travellers rather than casino table players. Three of us had taken our kilts with us for this holiday but I don't think we were wearing them that day; therefore we must have been wearing something else. It was during that outing that I saw for the first time the excellent idea of tearing a number from a roll of tickets at the bus stop instead of having to stand in a queue. Coming from a country where queues seemed to have a method of multiplying, this method the French had was a pleasant change.

As it turned out we felt a bit out of place in Monte Carlo. We felt it was geared up only for people with money to spend. The two girls had joined forces with us on our sight-seeing trips and were still with us. They were now part of our group and we all enjoyed each other's company.

The Principality of Monaco is about the same size as Hyde Park and I was surprised just how small it was; yet its geographical positioning placed it in a unique position to have witnessed the comings and goings between what we know now as Italy and France centuries ago and right up to modern times. It did not take us very long to walk about and see the palace from the outside and part of the casino from the inside. Unfortunately the girls were deemed too young to be allowed into the gambling den and they waited outside in the sunshine for the male section to reappear and tell the what they had missed. It was more like a visit to a museum with stately stairways and lavish furnishings and large windows and marble steps leading here and there. We were most amused at the serious faces of those people working away with paper and pencil on their own system that would give them the winning number. They were doing this whilst seated beside the gaming tables during the actual play. Most of the players doing this seemed to be moneyed more-than-middle-aged women. Our two young ladies didn't seem unduly bothered about not going in. There were also stories about suicides and a gun but I just cannot remember the details or whether it was just blarney, and in any case the girls were not really interested with that side of it. We had time for another stroll through its gardens and along its streets looking at the houses and few shops, that surprisingly seemed to have been there for some time. Soon it was time to collect our bus passenger numbers and bus it back to Nice.

It continually surprised me that amongst all this wealth and the popularity of the place there was a pebbly beach stretching along the coast between Nice and Monte Carlo. We were all fairly good swimmers, including the girls, and although we didn't swim on our visit to the palace and casino we made up for it each day at Nice. Swimming in a tideless sea made little difference to us. It was the getting out part that started us staggering because of a tideless sea continually pounding a ridge along the length of its coastline. It was like wearily climbing out of a hot bath. Back home the first step into sea water is the worst but at Nice the last step was the hardest, especially if you were fairly exhausted after trying to keep up with two healthy females and trying not to show it.

Our last night in Nice, and just by chance, was La Nuit Blanche. It was an annual carnival with a parade of flower floats along the seafront that culminated in a sky exploding with fireworks. It was at that point that Joy, who was a London girl, suddenly broke down in tears and was absolutely terrified by the noise and brilliance of the display.

It didn't take too much to reason out that the fireworks had triggered off some vivid memory of the London wartime 'blitz' that had left a scar on her mind which she may well be carrying to this day. I took her back to the hotel and remained with her until she was certain the carnival was over. There was no such thing in those days as 'counselling.'

The following day we said our goodbyes to the girls with the hope we would meet up again. The four of us were sorry to leave them for they had been good company and shared our sense of humour.

I returned home with happy memories of my first real grown-up holiday, along with photographs and souvenirs. If there were a few garlic bushes that have since sprouted up along the beach at Nice from around that time they are probably at the spots where I planted a sandwich that contained a little too much of the stuff in them for my taste.

Back home in Glasgow I was soon into the swing of things again. There was always something to do, but I wasn't to forget my first holiday abroad and neither were my three companions.

It was back to work again and there was plenty of it. Every shipyard had the makings of a vessel on all available stocks, and the clatter, bangings and riveting were familiar sounds at almost all hours. Familiar shipyard sounds now reflected the intense activity that was taking place. Shipowners were investing heavily to build up fleet numbers which the war had depleted and it was not unknown for vessels to change potential owners before they had even entered the water. Such was the demand for ships.

The temperament of the people of one city is pretty similar to that of another. When I was both a boy and a young man this often showed up on the pavement in any part of the city. It wasn't uncommon to hear an elderly lady suddenly come out with 'Oh dear, dear. Have you ever seen the likes of that?' THAT of course being anything from someone dropping a piece of litter to another rudely pushing or even a child cycling on the pavement. However it never ended there because the call was taken up with other grown-ups and echoed around the immediate area. The guardians of morality were everywhere, so in a sense I wasn't totally shaped within my own home. There was a strong underlying factor held by a lot of staid people that if one did wrong in public, it was very wrong. Now, the one characteristic that did not go down at all well was arrogance whereas another one that was readily acceptable was independence and it doesn't take much to know that one can very easily overlap the other. In answer to the unspoken question I can only say that in some way or another people living together and practically on top of each other with all the problems endemic to large families and differing natures, managed in general to live out very private lives with the advantage of having close and friendly neighbours with a good measure of tolerance had by all.

The independence I write of is the type which resents very much being spoken down to or being treated as an inferior. I can remember a time just before the outbreak of war when a motor car driver impatiently and thoughtlessly honked his horn at an unfortunate pedestrian who was hindering him. I could sense at that young age the feelings of all the nearby people against the honker and his unnecessary noise. A horse could neigh until it was blue in the face and providing it wasn't in any pain no one would have dreamt of complaining. I do not think for one moment that Glasgow invented the mental 'friendly brick' (a spin-off from the power of prayer) but there were strong vibes of a common wish directed towards the ill-mannered driver that he would be very soon repairing a flat tyre. The feeling would have been the same had he behaved similarly to a horse and cart; perhaps more so as a startled horse could have dangerous consequences. Thinking back I cannot but reflect how the drink and drive laws have, albeit much too slowly, changed for the better since those days.

Strangely enough, in later years my car was fitted with a horn only to keep within the law. I do not think I even tested one to find out if it worked when I bought a car. Will my French readers (hope burns eternal) please note! The brake is much more of a life and face saver with a lot less noise. My attitude is probably a left-over from those early years when consideration to someone at a disadvantage was expected.

We all have to experience unhappy milestones in our life but this particular decade demanded much from many people. Another ship's trial was due from the North British Engine Work's river berth and I was listed as one of the DO staff to go out with her. I think it was a Tuesday morning, 10 a.m. departure from the berth, but whatever day it was, Mother had taken ill the day before.

I left home for the sea trial on the morning, fully intending to join the ship, but when walking down Edzell Street I met up with a colleague from the DO and I suddenly told him I was returning home and briefly explained to him that my mother was not well, and asked him to give my apologies to the chief draughtsman along with the explanation for my absence.

I returned home wondering just exactly what I was going to say in order to explain my unpredictable return. Sadly it wasn't necessary for her condition had worsened considerably and she died that same afternoon from what was generally accepted as a heart attack. She was sixty three. That afternoon she last spoke to me through fading handgrip signals in a fashion I was to experience only once again forty five years later and which was to revive this memory.

That evening I momentarily saw my father cry when he suddenly stood up in the kitchen and quickly made for the door. Father was not the emotional type, and these tears must have been the rarest tears in Scotland, but then, the one he was shedding them for was well worth them.

On my return to work the chief draughtsman, Mr Deverill, told me how sorry he was about my sad loss, and how we all must strive after adversity to get on with our lives, and back to normality. I was reminded that the recent ship's trial was carried out with one person short and how the staff had coped. The last part was to put my mind at ease, yet at the same time to take the hint not to make a habit of causing any office upsets. Such advice I could have done without, but it was usually given to junior staff from the men at the top under such circumstances. It was probably more of a Victorian left-over than pomposity. Mr Deverill was a good man to work for and well respected in the DO. When I think what it must have been like when he was my age under a similar incident makes me shudder.

That same year Father had his sixty fifth birthday and was due to retire from Scottish Oils & Shell Mex where he had spent all his working life. He had started work at the age of fourteen with the Pumpherston Oil Company at Grangemouth where oil was extracted from shale. At the start of the year both he and Mum were looking forward to his retirement as an event which could have been so happy, but it was not to be and his retirement day arrived without any plans having been made. It passed as a low key pleasant family affair.

Happily my sister Sybil, along with her husband Frank, had come home from Rhodesia on leave a few months before Mother died, something I knew she had been looking forward to very much. Thinking back, all the pieces seemed to fall into place as though in answer to a prayer. They spent the main part of their stay with us. There had been an addition to the family the year before when they were overseas, and my niece Maureen was now the proud sister of a little African-born brother called Ian.

Frank had already returned to the Copper Belt at the end of his leave, with the intention being that Sybil would follow later with the two children. However, that was not to be. He left two weeks before Mother died and at the same time the Mau Mau terrorist threats and attacks were being stepped up with more European families becoming the soft targets for their atrocities. Sybil, like most of the other wives out there, had never been far from a loaded revolver during the day when she was alone; it rested at night beneath Frank's pillow. He decided that politically it would be too dangerous to expose his family to the increasing dangers that could be awaiting their return, and resigned from his job, returning home at a time agreed with his employers.

When Frank finally came home he first held a job as engineer manager for a short time in Kircaldy over on the east coast with a linoleum company before taking a job in London and in the latter part of 1949 Sybil, Frank and family moved down south to live in their very own first house in Surbiton. During the months before she left the north Sybil had taken over Mother's role in the home with Frank staying as often as he could. This meant a lot of travelling for him to and from Glasgow and Kircaldy. He bought a new Austin car which he had to wait for but it was a family priority in order that he could at least get home for each weekend, and when possible at any other time. The public were always being told that things in general were returning to normal but public transport and accommodation were two things that were far from normal. The former still did not have sufficient rolling stock and what it had was old, outdated and very cold. The latter was extremely difficult to find. Everything of a personal nature, such as a telephone or a car, still had a long waiting list.

One thing I managed to get out of all this was the use of a car to practice my driving in. I attended a proper driving school and probably through that and because the roads were relatively quiet, though with still plenty of trams and horsedrawn traffic I gained my licence. There were no government license testing centres at that time and I was put through my road test by a representative from the Automobile Association.

The government apparently had no intention of changing from driving on the left hand side of the road to the right hand side, for if it had, and there was some talk about it, then immediately after the war would have been the best time to have achieved it. Many of the returning servicemen had plenty of experience of driving on the right hand side of the road in jeeps and other left-handed vehicles. The roads at home at that time were very quiet and the opportunity for such a change under these conditions will never come again.

When Sybil moved south it was agreed that Father would go with her and apart from any bits and pieces my sisters wanted all the household furnishings were sold off. I went to stay in Giffnock with sister Clara, brother-in-law Charlie and niece Elizabeth. I will add here that some years later I was given, amongst other things which appear in this book, some personal family things kept by my mother, but not until I finally married and had a place of my own. Up till then they lay in sisters' lofts and trunks awaiting for that day to arrive.

Meanwhile, the last of the big service industries was taken over by the government; this time it was gas. There was also better news for the shopkeepers and shoppers when clothes rationing came to an end. Now we could all wear what we pleased, provided we could afford to buy it.

My brother-in-law Charlie had his own business which kept him fully occupied getting it back on the move again, even though it had to do with the building industry. Like everyone else he had a difficult time during the war years and was only now coming out of the doldrums. He had been a keen tennis player as a young man with a silver trophy bowl to prove it. Charlie was determined business-wise to get back into the swing of things again.

I probably kept late nights which would not have mattered with Clara. She, like her father, was an owl and at her best at night, whereas I on the other hand was a lark, like my mother. I have no idea how those family differences come about; perhaps it has something to do with the time of day or night one is born.

Staying out at Giffnock meant that I had much further to travel each day to and from work. In the morning I caught a red No. 8 tram from Giffnock destined for Bishopbriggs or Springburn into the city across the Glasgow Bridge to Argyle Street, where I would change to a blue No. 6 Dalmuir West from Riddrie or a No. 9 to Dalmuir West from Auchenshuggle. These were two of several tramcars that would take me the length of Argyle Street and on to Dumbarton Road, then along the north bank of the river westward to Whiteinch. I had to allow myself at least an hour for the whole distance and even that was running it pretty tight.

I had met Marjorie many times at the Tudor Dance Hall when I stayed in the town centre, but somehow we moved closer together at the time I went to stay with Clara.

Up to that time the girls I mostly danced with were those I had met through the Alice McEwan dance classes where, at the risk of repeating myself, I was always paired off with a tall girl. It was probably the only time in my life when I could say I had an advantage as a skinny six footer. I have happy memories of my dance classes at the Albert, although when I think back at my tangoing I would love to recall that I pushed George Raft out of the picture. However, I fear that neither Alice nor any of the tall

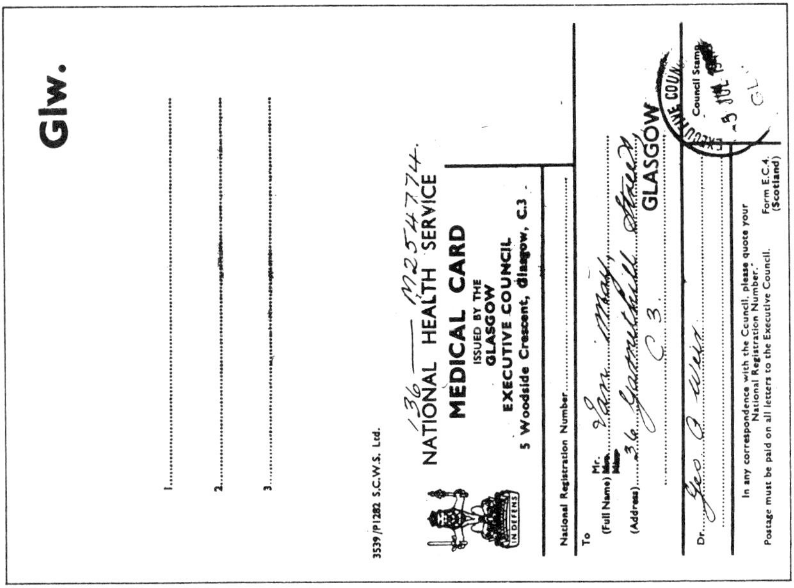

Glw.

1. ....

2. ....

3. ....

3539/P1282 S.C.W.S. Ltd.

136 — M254774

NATIONAL HEALTH SERVICE

MEDICAL CARD

ISSUED BY THE GLASGOW EXECUTIVE COUNCIL

5 Woodside Crescent, Glasgow, C.3

National Registration Number..

To Mr. (Full Name) Sam. M. May

(Address) 36 Garnethill Street

C.3. GLASGOW

Dr. Geo. O. Weir

In any correspondence with the Council, please quote your National Registration Number.
Postage must be paid on all letters to the Executive Council.

Form E.C.4. (Scotland)

Council Stamp

EXECUTIVE COUNCIL -5 JUL 19

2

GENERAL INFORMATION

1. This card shows the name of the doctor who will give you general medical treatment under the National Health Service. It should be shown to him if he asks to see it ; if it is not produced the doctor may charge a fee. He will give a receipt for the fee on a special form, which contains instructions for the recovery of the fee.

2. **Day Visits.** Please do not ask the doctor to call unless the patient is too ill to attend his surgery. Attendance at the surgery should be during surgery hours. When the condition of the patient does require a home visit, please try to give notice, if at all possible, before 10 a.m. on the day on which the visit is required.

3. **Night Visits.** Please do not call in the doctor between the hours of 8 p.m. and 8 a.m. except in emergency.

4. **Accident or Emergency.** If neither your doctor nor his deputy is available, immediate attention in an emergency can be obtained from any doctor giving general medical services under the National Health Service Act.

5. **Medical treatment when temporarily away from Home.** If you are away from your usual address for a short time, you may apply for treatment to any doctor giving general medical services (see 7 below).

6. **Change of Doctor** (see opposite). If you wish to change to another doctor, take this card to the new doctor. It will be returned to you by the Executive Council. You may change at any time.

3

7. **List of Doctors.** A list of doctors giving general medical services can be seen at the Post Office.

8. Any enquiry or complaint should be made to the Clerk of the Executive Council at the address shown on the front page of this Card. A complaint should, wherever possible, be made within 6 weeks of the event which gave rise to the complaint.

CHANGE OF DOCTOR

To be filled in if person wishes to transfer to another doctor.

I wish to be placed on the list of

Dr...Date...............

Signature of applicant
or authorised person ....

Address..

....

....Date...............

Signature of doctor.

*Drugs	†Mileage

* If doctor is to supply drugs he should enter D in space marked*

† If doctor claims payment for mileage he should enter the number of miles in space marked†. If there is any special difficulty of access, details should be given on a separate note.

Who is going to worry about a running nose now?

girls will have such cherished memories. Incidentally, when I talk of girlfriends I should make it clear I mean girls that I knew. The number of the opposite sex I could claim to have had as steady friends were less than the number of fingers on any one hand.

Marjorie would have been considered a taller than average girl and resided in the district of Shawlands, being only a short tram ride from Giffnock. She was the eldest of the four Niven children, having a sister and two brothers. Her mother was a very friendly type of woman. Her father had a small garage in nearby Nithsdale Road that specialised in repairing and caring for the vintage cars of his customers. He was a keen racing enthusiast who would periodically drive down in his old Lancia to Silverstone where he would be in his seventh heaven amidst the dust and fumes of the race track, and would follow this up with an evening amongst his friends, discussing the performance and track timing of the various cars.

Marjorie worked in Timothy Whites, the chemist, in the city centre, and usually managed to catch the same tram that I was in when she was going home in the evening. She had to do her fair share of baby-sitting for her younger brothers; one night was allocated to 'do' her hair, which she wore in a pony tail, and she may have had to attend her church repertory club of which she was a keen member; but that still left us with plenty of time to visit either the Elephant, Embassy or Waverley at Shawlands, well provided with cinemas. We also enjoyed a weekly jaunt to the Tudor for a night 'at the dancing'.

After the first few weekly dates we started to see a lot of each other and became quite attached. We spent a holiday together at my sister Joey's home down in Walton-on-Thames in Surrey, taking the train down and driving back by car a week later. I had now become the proud owner of a two-toned dark blue and maroon coloured Morris 12 H P saloon car. Both the side steps had been removed to streamline it and make it look a bit different. I bought it from Bob, my brother-in-law, on special pay-back terms. He had now achieved the lifelong ambition of an Allard car, albeit second-hand. It looked all bonnet to me.

It had been on the cards for a while that Bob would sell his Morris to me when the time came for him to get rid of it, and when it did, Marjorie and I arranged to make a holiday of the occasion. At that time I did not have much experience as a driver (her mum probably thought the same), and even allowing for the quieter roads of the late forties the journey took us the best part of twenty four hours. We started our journey late at night in order to clear London and the south during the quiet hours of darkness to save time on the busier roads in that area and for me to accustom myself to the car. Life was certainly picking up in the right places for I was now a car owner with a perfect passenger and an all-night drive ahead of me.

One of the main problems during that drive was when a lorry would become permanently stuck in front of me because it usually took ages before an opportunity arose to overtake, due to both the winding and narrow roads of the forties. In any case it wasn't long before I had to pull into a quiet spot, and amongst other things, clean the windscreen and lights from the muck thrown up from vehicles travelling in front of me. One point I do recall was that lorry drivers were extremely helpful in those days with clear and helpful hand signals, and would encourage you to overtake when they knew the road ahead was clear. Both my passenger and I arrived back safely in Glasgow tired and stiff in the morning, more or less on schedule. How true it is about the last mile being the longest! It seemed to take an age from the time we passed the city limits until we arrived on our own doorsteps.

It was about this time that I saw less of the group I normally went around with as they themselves were meeting other people and going their own ways, just as I was doing. The number of friends I was keeping in contact with was sadly diminishing. Of the first group of friends of my own choosing, made at school, I had only managed to keep one. The next group of friends were those I made in my teens since I had started to work. There then followed what could be called the 'big bang' in friendships when courtship started. Now there was no longer just my group of friends but the girlfriend's as well, which included her family. Somehow or another that particular period for me was the apex of the 'group' time of my life and numbers started to taper away as permanent relationships were formed. I now found myself living in a more private and personal style, involving work or study or courtship, which probably meant a combination of all three. Slowly each of the pack I had moved around with drifted off to start on their own in whatever direction their career or loves led them. I kept in touch with some 'old faithfuls' through letter and pcs but slowly and surely the apprentices of my vintage were spreading their wings and joining various shipping companies or taking jobs elsewhere. I still have a letter from Ian Hunter that somehow survived the years.

Both Marjorie and I were cigarette smokers, with me being the heavier of the two. I would not be very wrong in saying that the whole world smoked then. It was sociably acceptable and no one said it was healthwise a bad habit. A foolish habit, an extravagant habit, but not one that would kill. The subject of cigarettes steers me back to my case-cum-lighter and perhaps I did get it from Marjorie. I was never the gigolo or romantic type, being far too lazy and lacking in sentimental enthusiasm, and I certainly did not buy it myself, but enough of that – subject now dropped. Well, not quite. I do remember buying Marjorie a cigarette lighter with 'Goofles' inscribed on it.

Marjorie once asked me in a sombre moment what colour her eyes were when she had her back towards me, and of course I didn't know and replied along such lines that they were her eyes, therefore she should already know. The last thing then and thereafter that I would note about any female was the colour of her eyes. There might be a few budding opticians who could have answered such a question but there was no one I could think of. I seem to remember going through the colour range of the May family, but I should have guessed that it was the one colour hers wasn't. Hers were green, and as I did not get the right colour I can only put up the same defence for not remembering who gave me the cigarette case. But whatever I said must have worked as all things romantic between us carried on as usual in an ordinary fashion.

I was still staying in Giffnock with Clara and family when the decade ended. It was a nice area to live in with its own little shopping centre. The Tudor cinema with its ballroom was right on my doorstep, and just across the street from it on the opposite corner was a cafe. Traffic-wise it was entirely different from the streets of Garnethill. It was on a train, tram and bus route.

Elizabeth, my niece, like most girls at her age, desperately wanted a dog, or she would die from a broken heart, and in order to avoid this contingency, her mother did some phoning around, asking her friends for advice about buying a dog. I was not therefore surprised a short while later when Clara asked me to go to a certain kennels with her to collect Morag, a two-year-old golden Labrador bitch, now being sold to a good home because she was gun-shy. I appreciate full well that there is probably no other way to train a dog to the sound of a gun than the method whereby the animal is tethered in an area where guns are fired off around it. Morag was one of the casualties, which showed when she cowered and shivered at any sudden noise. To me every picture tells a story.

Elizabeth was overjoyed with her new four-footed friend and fortunately very sensibly decided not to die after all. Morag turned out to have a lovable nature as well as being a good watch dog which wasn't much help to me when I returned home later than I should have. I always forgave her rather noisy and active reception, which did nor take much effort on my part. The main thing was that she made her young mistress very happy.

The ten years that were almost past seemed to have flown. During that spell of time I had been evacuated from a city to a village and from there I moved again to live with my family in a small seaside town. Near the end of my schooling there followed another break from my parents when I was placed in digs at Prestwich and from there I went to stay with my sister Sybil and brother-in-law Frank in Largs before returning to live with my parents in Glasgow where my travels all started from in 1939. At the end of the decade I had lived under eight roofs and had attended three day schools in almost as many years, and had completed a five year apprenticeship, leaving me as what was termed a 'journeyman draughtsman', and a job for life.

In the great outside world a new hope, or perhaps a dream would be a better word, was just beginning. In New York there was now a permanent meeting place where every country in the world could speak their thoughts and discuss their problems in the optimistic expectation of preventing future wars, and give

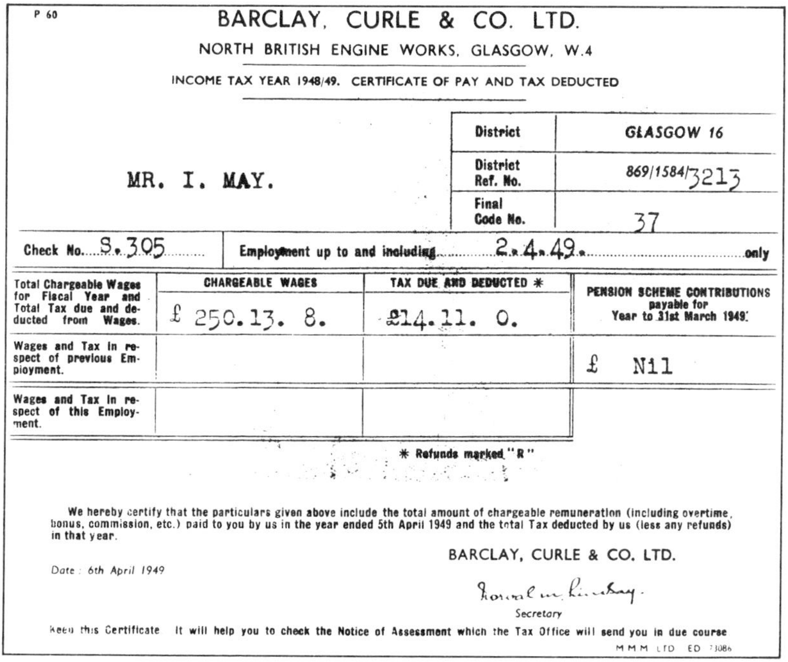

P 60

BARCLAY, CURLE & CO. LTD.

NORTH BRITISH ENGINE WORKS, GLASGOW, W.4

INCOME TAX YEAR 1948/49. CERTIFICATE OF PAY AND TAX DEDUCTED

MR. I. MAY.

District	GLASGOW 16
District Ref. No.	869/1584/3213
Final Code No.	37

Check No. S. 305 Employment up to and including 2.4.49. only

	CHARGEABLE WAGES	TAX DUE AND DEDUCTED *	PENSION SCHEME CONTRIBUTIONS payable for Year to 31st March 1949.
Total Chargeable Wages for Fiscal Year and Total Tax due and deducted from Wages.	£ 250.13. 8.	£14.11. 0.	
Wages and Tax in respect of previous Employment.			£ Nil
Wages and Tax in respect of this Employment.			

* Refunds marked "R"

We hereby certify that the particulars given above include the total amount of chargeable remuneration (including overtime, bonus, commission, etc.) paid to you by us in the year ended 5th April 1949 and the total Tax deducted by us (less any refunds) in that year.

BARCLAY, CURLE & CO. LTD.

Date: 6th April 1949

Secretary

Keep this Certificate It will help you to check the Notice of Assessment which the Tax Office will send you in due course

M M M LTD ED 73086

This will give some idea of how much a draughtsman earned in 1948/49.

economic assistance to the poorer countries. Meanwhile back in Europe the people of West Germany were being helped in a practical way by the Marshall Plan which was proving itself worth more than a thousand pitiless and vengeful Versailles Treaties.

The time I have written about covered a phase in our history where even at the time of writing I still find it hard to comprehend how all the mass violence and horror that took place then could have come about with so many ordinary decent people in the world. But no government could not have known a war was inevitable since the Spanish War days when arms and tactics were blatantly being tested. It seems quite incredible that human sanity could have steered itself straight into the foaming reef of another European war. Such an outcome had to be coldly planned and orchestrated in full tactical detail. I cannot think back at the suffering it produced without damning the dispassion, fearful passivity and ineptitude and all the other reasons that were intertwined together that contributed towards the lack of united international action until it was too late.

My world was now ten times older and ten times bigger, yet I did not seem to have grown up very fast in worldly ways, for I was still living, if not a boyish existence, then a very youthful one which meant constantly reassuring myself that I would soon decide what I was going to make of my future. I felt all I had to do was wait until the correct time, when all would be revealed to me. I had so much to learn about myself and the world I was living in.

Those of my generation living across the whole of Europe who survived this decade without visible mental or physical scars, did so through the ability of their own genes, likened to that of the endurance of a weed, vulnerable and insecure on the surface, with roots desperately wriggling beneath the surface in search of some sort of stability on which to anchor. Across the whole of Europe we had been infused into partings, loneliness, hurt and loss of familiar faces that must have created some degree of insecurity and uncertainty, albeit in varying degrees somewhere inside each of us.

We know that in this world we live in, suffering and sorrow are no strangers during times of war and what it leaves in its aftermath. They are busy attendants, covering all the heartbreaks in their differing ways and degrees. Whoever they touch, whether child or adult, they leave a very special effect that is without logical mathematical foundation, as no hurt or disappointment can be multiplied by ten, nor divided by two, to give a known result. There is no immediate balm for loss of love and understanding. It has to tear its way through bone, muscle and skin and painfully shed its way patiently from its inflamed seat in the mind to rest forever amongst the chemistry of memory. When it subsides there will remain perhaps the most unjust part of all, for it removes the blame and anger from the source of the cause, leaving a silent clinging guilt for doing so. The best that good people who survived unaffected can do in years to come will be to tolerate and understand and remember.

I can reason that in order to experience true sadness then one has to know what pure happiness is like, and the same applies to fear and bravery; therefore, if any good can come from a war – and there must be if the bad that caused it is done away with – I pray that this good is distributed in a just fashion with no exceptions. I hope that those who have suffered the nightmare of comfortless abandonment will enjoy the ecstasy of sanguine dreams, and those who have plumbed the depths of sadness will ultimately draw comfort from the greater heights of happiness.

That decade had divided itself almost equally between violent war and unruly peace, for such was the world's political posturing and military threat overlap during the time when the one stopped and the other started. It would have been difficult for any stranger to place an exact marker between the two. There were, of course, signatures on documents at first in the West and later in the East, but there was certainly no great crashing sound of cymbals from the sky, and it was still not a very peaceful world to live in.

In that decade's tenth year I was bouncing along in my usual lifestyle, although something that must have been developing within me for some time was apparent now. I now divided whatever I did into various secure mental compartments. It was probably all part of the maturing process. Let me try and tell you how it showed. What I did when I was at work and whom I met there were kept metaphorically in one compartment. I cannot ever remember returning home from my employment and telling anyone what I had been doing all day or whom I had been speaking to, but if I did, in the answer to a question, it would have been in the most casual sort of way and without detail. In another cell there would be the family and family matters. I am certain that amongst all my friends, except from the two or three close ones who had been to the house, none of them were aware I had a father. I doubt very much if those who were aware I had a father had any idea what he did for a living. Likewise I would never have asked what their father's business was. My mother and sisters had known the few close friends I had brought home; otherwise it was a vague 'someone I knew', or perhaps I would meet a person who later, in answer to a query, became 'Thingamabob who I just bumped into by chance'.

There was no solid reason at all why my family knew so little about my outer circle of friends, but then, I knew very little about their's, and in any case whatever the reason was for that behaviour pattern most families I was in contact with all seemed to live in this pleasant fragmented way. I must in honesty mention that this behaviour trend was in no way derived from devious intentions or deceit, but rather something in our crowded upbringing, plus a dangerous dose of shattered wartime dreams that unintentionally taught us that some parts of our life must be our very own. Another seclusion zone was the opposite sex. In answer to the inevitable questions I would give the girl's first name and the film we had seen, then the lid came down.

Family, religion, politics, study, work, play and romance were all kept apart and that generally was the way the latter years of the decade passed. Maybe girls chatted more about their lives than boys did but in general that was the normal pattern the younger men followed at that time. Marjorie and I were going steady then and I would like to think we were a fairly average young man and woman of our time.

Looking back and seeing the faces of the few girlfriends I once knew, and trying to remember what I could of some common denominator each shared, two facts emerge. The first one was their sense of humour and the other was that none would have been out of place in the precincts of a university. Not one of them had a graduate training, but no one would have known. I can't honestly say the same for all the males I knew, for some were a lot more practical than academic. Looking back it was strange how so many parents from all walks of life did such a good job in producing sensible children without any apparent training; it just seemed to happen.

One belief we all held was a sureness that young lives would never be destroyed on any battlefield again. That was what we thought – and our city thought. Sadly, events since then have proved our young intentions were good but not achievable.

I have mentioned humour and a city. Let me couple them together and tell you that this place I have mentioned is the only city that I know where its residents can identify themselves with a password or pass-sentence. I first learnt of it as a wee boy and much later on, in places across the length and breadth of the world during a seafaring lifetime, I have humorously identified myself to other Glaswegians and they to me. For obvious reasons it is strictly classified information. But for you, a good friend, I will just whisper that it has something to do with what the tram conductress shouted in pure Glaswegian to potential passengers crossing her tramcar boarding/departure area. I must say no more, my lips are sealed. At the time of writing I have been away from Glasgow for a long time, yet I do not want to risk the city gates being slammed in my face for seditious scribbling.

The whole way through this book I have been writing about my city and not giving mention to anything regarding any similar place that would have been of more concern to the reader. All I can say is that back in those days that I have been reliving, other cities and towns in the land were faraway places that I had no reason to visit. I hope most can identify with some of my memories and thoughts of the time. If people are more or less the same everywhere then I shouldn't think their cities and what goes on in them really differ very much. Talking about cities, I have often thought that nothing can happen in any city that hasn't been at least thought about in everyone's mind at sometime or another. If we all have such a place within us, mine would probably be as follows.

THE SOMEWHERE CITY

Twin inner eyes blinked full ablaze, and I found myself widely awake,
Where my past and present motley met, in a mad mixed-up time mistake,
First my veiled city self demanded that I this instant come and see,
And stern staring bade I must enter, where fading fingers pointed me.
Then dream-drawn towards this inlet, a ghostly door that bore a name,
I hopeful prayed it mere by chance and not fate spelt mine the same.
Next I found myself fearful floating, lightly lifted from the ground,

Gazing over life's satired see-saw, and its tinselled merry-go-round.

Self-scenes choked each busy bridge, pulse pushing worn worries along,
In a busy mode-mad ambered arena, with good green arresting red wrong.
And calm-cooling latent alchemies of temper traffic and fervent fires,
Each secret hid and active feared, at differing depths of deep desires.
But what humbled me the greatest, when seeing the lean labyrinth lanes,
Was rusted time tied up in bundles, and lost effort ebbing down drains.
And taunted a lake of salt sweatlets, life wrung from ambitious allure,
That fertile field with fat cattle, bloom-blinded the bare barren moor.

Top surface gilt grazed smileful skies, tinting-touched its casual view.
Like the flowing falls of every excuse, that mirrored all I meant to do.
Then my somewhere's park breath-breathed, soft singing its poetic ponds.
As feathered friends did freedom flaunt, dash-dance to flee their bonds.
Its wishing well lilt lusty laughed, as smile's spell spiced each drink,
Made cloudless-clear such simple things, were designed to make me think.
For taking there in day's cool quiet, the rued regret from heated night,
Would give sane shift to one same thought, when seen in different light.

My thinks and thoughts of honeyed hopes, ideals and ideas
slight frayed,
Feelings felt and environ's effect, all helped shape the city
they made.
With hallowed health its river flowed, with ruby and milk
stained craft,
That loyal helped me live and love, from good in its salt taste
draught.
Now I saw the unmarbled cenotaph, clearly unpolished and
unkempt forgot,
That told neither of merit or valour, nor virtuous battles stout
fought.
But was written of self-importance, and its myth of an
unfillable space,
Like any thumb pulled from water, leaves a hole fill-gone
without trace.

Material milestone matters still haunt, 'midst memory's
truths and trust,
Tight trapped in old homespun cobwebs: cage-cloaked in
past dreams dust.
I was given the city's freedom, with the chance to redress my
past role,
Near as having a preluded preview, of a glimpse of my own
shrouded soul.
Then this tour was sudden judged ended, with no further
time granted me,
Though when leaving the exit portals, one last scene I was
meant to see.
Under self hewn stones of each found fault, on an untidy
grave of green,
Slept my peace-perfect somewhere city, and the dream it
could have been.

At least by the near approach to the fifties all the original surviving war conscripts and volunteers were back living normal lives with their families and no doubt working and aiming for their respective future hopes and ambitions now that they had one to look forward to. The Commonwealth boys had returned to their homes, the Americans by now had gone and the French, Poles, Norwegians and other Europeans had long since left our towns and cities and the POWs from our farms. There were still a lot of displaced unfortunates who for one reason or another could not return to their native countries and who were to remain as human flotsam across free Europe for some time to come.

There were those who would never lead what could be said to be a normal life again. They would live out their remaining years with a perpetual legacy from the war. I only hope that it makes those healthy people who are perpetually paranoid over their own physical well-being think again, and that it shames those who have never given in the whole of their lives towards anything outside their own selves, and have no intention of doing so.

When the forties finally slipped away during the celebrations of a decade, passing away amongst the hustle and bustle of a New Year's Eve, my thoughts hovered around the two empty places at the table. I wondered what advice they would have given me that night. There must have been thousands of young men and women of my age group thinking along the very same lines in more than a dozen languages. It was a very rare time when language barriers were removed and doctrines shed, leaving us all with something to share.

The war-weeds had at last matured.

I was now a resilient young man with little or no idea just how fortunate I had been since the day I was born. I was now trained for a job that I liked, though still not sure whether to start a sea-going profession, for I knew I would not impose on my sister indefinitely. I had an adequate education given me in a patchwork fashion and which I still intended to further. I was confident that I knew practically everything about Life, or more correctly about living. After all, I had a fairly safe future as a draughtsman and by nature neither hurtful or cruel. I knew all about the Baby Boom and shared concern over the future social planning that it would require. Yet the hard reality was that I was very naive and knew very little about the world I was in or who lived in it. I had no idea that there was such a thing as a bad mother or father, and believe it or not, I still thought the very worst thing that could happen to a child was to be stolen by gypsies.

I was fortunate indeed to have reached manhood with a healthy body and sound mind, both of which were mainly shaped during the years leading up to and including the time between 1940–50. I was lucky in that the worst I might have to carry into my maturing years from the turmoil of this ten year mould were only unseen blemishes, scratches and scrapings. Many young men and women of similar age to myself fared much worse and were condemned to carry more hurtful and more deeply hidden wounds than I.

Having very nearly reached the end of what I have to say I would like to add that I have not told you everything. There is nothing that is evil or wicked, but whether it concerns me or someone else they are the memories that are absolutely mine. Remember what I said about my father and who should be given a second chance on this Earth? Well I think in this matter he would be quite proud of me. Like him I have no intention of coming back.

It wasn't a decade that the human race could proudly display over its rosy fireplace, but it certainly will not be forgotten because it was such an important part of history. There were so many personal photographs taken and letters written during that decade that were posted and carried to practically every country in the world. Some day they will show the ageing background, the unfashionable clothes and a smile or glint of an intrinsic style, or of someone's known and remembered handwriting that tells of personal events. In time they will all fade; then, with the passing of their keepers the stories each held will mostly disappear.

I will leave the reader with a glimpse into the city of Glasgow where I spent my early happy and contented years. You will visit four tenement homes around the time of the early thirties, and the postwar forties. If a theme or scene jogs a remote memory or strikes a chord in some sentiment or feeling then I can only hope it can be enjoyed. Whatever we retain from within the confines of our existence one thing is certain – it is people and what we remember of them that really count in the end.

7

FOUR TENEMENT TALES

THE RIGHT THING

Scenario One A ground floor tenement situated in what is considered a good district in Glasgow. There are two spacious public rooms with each having ornate plaster ceilings with intricate patterns. Suspended in the centre of these rooms is a chandelier type light, one of which can be raised or lowered by hand. These fittings are in contrast to a long ornamental and tiled open fireplace with a marble mantelpiece carrying a large Germanic clock with an Italian red glass figurine on either side of it. There is abundant natural light from the two bay windows, containing in their surrounding woodwork hidden balance weights to allow for the easy opening and closing of either the top or bottom window. A window pole is nearby for easy handling. In this, the larger of the two rooms, there is a copper coal scuttle at one end of the fireplace that balances with the set of polished brass fireside poker, tongs, shovel and brush. As in the other rooms there is a wooden picture rail about nine feet from the floor running round the whole length of the wall. In this particular room there are several oil paintings displayed in gilt frames hanging from the rail. A heavy rich-looking wallpaper is between the picture rail and the skirting board at floor level. An expensive carpet that matches the tone of the heavy curtains leaves a two foot border of polished wood, apart from the window area that has a larger polished floor area. There is a large mahogany dining table with leaves that can, if necessary, be removed. An upright piano is set against the wall not far from an old spinet that is still playable. On the mantelpiece there is a long decorative marble eight-day chiming clock. There are eight padded upright dining chairs and two comfortable heavier matching fireside seats. The dining chairs are methodically placed around the empty table almost as though waiting for guests. A tea-trolley matching the table is positioned near the door. A tall lampstand with what looks like a large oriental-type shade has been positioned beside one of the fire-facing seats. Around the room can be seen several framed photographs and house plants. Slightly out of place is a picturesque display cabinet positioned near the windows that clash slightly with the neat twin tables separated in order for one of each to be in front of a window and carry an identical Chinese vase.

The other public room is similar, though a little smaller and has water-colour paintings hanging against the heavy tasteful wallpaper. There are two large bookcases stocked with a large variety of literature. Two easy chairs rest in front of the fireplace. This one has a large gilt-framed mirror running the length of the mantelpiece that reflects the chairs on either side of it and a comfortable matching sofa between them. In what could only be described as the centre stands a polished table with four seating chairs around it. Not far from the bookcase stands a chess table with black and white marble pieces positioned and ready for the next game. As expected the thick carpet matches the colour of the curtains and there is the repetition of framed photographs and house foliage.

The family bedrooms are smaller than the public rooms and all the same size. There are three such rooms with their own tiled fireplace, large curtained window and fitted washhand basin. Each has an expensive wallpaper on the walls and a good quality carpet. The furniture consists of a double bed, a large and small wardrobe, a chest of drawers and a dressing table and in a corner there is a washhand basin. The bedrooms are furnished for a comfortable night's sleep.

The flat has a family-sized bathroom complete with WC and cast iron bath, having its water discharging from a lion's mouth and legs ending on the floor in the shape of a lion's paw. There is a large washhand basin at the frosted and coloured designed window. The whole floor is tiled to match the wall tiles that rise seven feet on each wall. The washroom door has a glass in its upper half that matches its window pattern.

The flat contains a large and easily run kitchen with double porcelain domestic basins fitted in front of a large window overlooking the back green. There is a family-sized gas oven cooker and a larder press suitable for a large family requirement. There is the usual type kitchen grate and side oven with a fire that supplies a more than adequate amount of hot water. The coal bunker is in the kitchen and totally enclosed and concealed as part of the dresser running the length of the kitchen. A solid shelf runs round a good part of the kitchen wall and a four battened clothes pulley runs the length of the kitchen and is suspended from the ceiling and rope operated. There are call-bells attached to the end of their respective spring which in turn is connected by a wire to one of the bell-calls fitted into the wall at the side of each fireplace in the flat. By design they appear like a Byzantine ceramic handle which the user rotates, causing an agitation along the concealed wire to the spring in the kitchen.

Each window in the flat is well recessed into the wall with full length folding wooden shutters concealed at either side and giving a cupboard appearance blending in with the rich woodwork that surrounds each window.

Just inside the entrance and off the long light oak panelled hallway with polished floor there is a good sized cloakroom with WC and washhand basin. it is in here that the gas and electric meters are situated and there is a small high barred window opening out onto the stairway. Next to the cloakroom there is a single and adequate maid's room with its own small fireplace and wash-basin. The floor is laid with linoleum and a small bed-side rug. The walls bear a cheaper wallpaper. There is a single bed and a small chest of drawers with a mirror on top of it and next to it is a small upright chair.

The hall has wooden panelled walls and a decorative plaster ceiling with polished oak block flooring. A long narrow expensive carpet runs along its length. Near the main door stands a tall mirrored hallstand and about midway there is a large house plant flourishing in a wooden designed holder that has four shaped legs and a swan-like neck and head rising from each of its upper corners. Facing this from the opposite wall is a grandfather clock, having a bright lustre and loud ticking sound. At the far end of the hall, wisely placed close to the kitchen is a large press (cupboard).

At the front of the tenement there is a narrow garden that is mostly grass and is separated from the public pavement by wrought iron railings. The entrance into the clearly numbered close (tenement entrance, passageway, stairs and landings) has several steps leading up to it and its spacious interior is tastefully tiled along the walls up to the height of an average person. All parts above the tiled area are painted in a warm off-white colour. The big window between each flight displays a design in coloured glass. The handrail running the whole length of the stairway and landings has a hand grip made from hard red wood with a rich polished lustre. There are also small blunt brass studs strategically spaced along its length to deter a child from sliding down it. Each landing has an adequate gas light that is lit every evening and turned off in the morning by the glaslighter. In this particular close the landings and steps are cleaned and whitewashed each week by paid washerwomen. The landing and the immediate flight of stairs leading downwards is the responsibility of the two flat dwellers and neighbours who share the cost of the cleaning between them.

To the rear of the close at ground level and past the two front (flat main entrance) doors the direction divides either up the stairs or down a few steps into the basement leading into the back green (garden for the common use of tenants). The basement is where the heavy washing is carried out in coal fired boilers but outside laundry services have made this area redundant. There is ample space for parking prams or bicycles. The back green is of ample size and well kept by the property owners. Steel upright washing poles are positioned on the green for the convenience of the

> residents. There is a covered-in area where the dustbins are kept and situated beside the back door leading into a lane. Normally the only people who use that door are the binmen.

Worry showed visibly on the grandmother's face as she continued to blame the modern society, as well as her husband for encouraging Andrew to climb that particular peak.

They had done everything for the boy, bringing him up as a son. Good schooling had produced a worthwhile academic sportsman, with the proper type of friends which, as far as they were concerned, was of great importance indeed.

The grandparents had seen to all his needs, and up till now they had been very pleased how he had turned out at the end of his school years. All that remained now was to see him through Glasgow University, and live to see him graduate.

It had never been easy for them and there were times when he required an amount of shoving and pushing in the proper direction. They had never expected it to be easy and often over the recent few years they had agreed that he was an exact replica of his father. They had both put a lot of effort into the shaping of their own son and their grandchild and it hadn't been easy in the days of continual sliding family values. At least no-one could ever point the finger at them with accusations they had not done the right things in bringing them both up when they were young. A certain amount of discipline was necessary, especially with boys.

Their only son had made a fine choice in the girl he married. She had come from what they had considered a nice family and a good home. (They had made sure of that.) It had not gone unnoticed that their first and only child was born seven months after the wedding. No-one had made any comments regarding this event, which was not unexpected. Their social group lived under the golden rule that if a suspected near miss turns out all right then in the end it is best forgotten. Anything of a sexual nature was never openly discussed and that included marriageable daughters disappearing for an extended holiday abroad to a friend of an aunt's.

Their new daughter-in-law had been a thoroughly modern

young lady, and of course some things could well be overlooked with the younger generation even when she had stated quite publicly that she intended to share everything with her husband, including his love of mountain climbing. At first they had put it down to girlish talk, but later changed their minds when she bought climbing equipment along with the necessary clothes.

It certainly came as a terrible shock to both parents when they found out about the dreadful accident that had occurred near the end of the climb when an unexpected rockfall had taken both their lives.

From that time the grandparents had steered young Andrew well away from climbing as a pastime and when he reached the age when, as guardians, they had to choose an acceptable competitive sport, they put his name down for swimming.

It had been a good choice. He won several medals and two silver cups. He captained the Inter-Schools winning team three years in succession and was the custodian of the heavy, highly prized shield during that time. He was a popular student and the school was proud of his prowess in the sport. His grandfather had seen to it that his academic studies were not neglected and he had satisfactory examination results.

His godparents had been chosen by the grandmother and they also were pleased and proud of their sporting godchild; therefore it did not come as a surprise when shortly before the then widowed godmother died she gave him a piece of furniture as a gift. She couldn't remember where they had got it from, as it had been such a long time ago, but she wanted the boy to have it as a memento of both of them. The display cabinet was, of course, to show his past and present achievements. One object lesson the lad had learnt from that elder generation was that time should never be wasted. When one had accomplished one objective, then the time had come to strive for something else. What one gained in this world had to be manifestly exposed, but in the most tasteful of ways; otherwise it might be considered as common.

It had come as a very unpleasant jolt to both of them when just before his eighteenth birthday he suddenly said that he was joining a student's team to climb the same mountain that had claimed the lives of both his parents. The choice of the climb had not been his but a mere coincidence. The group of climbers would have experienced guides with them and the climb would start from the same small hotel at the side of the lake where his mother and father had commenced their fatal climb sixteen years before.

It had now been four days since his phone call from the village post office, affirming that all was well for commencing the climb and giving the reassuring news that the weather conditions could not have been better. All this had been said and repeated between fade-outs and loud hissings which, of course, was brushed aside at the British end as the fault of the Swiss because only foreigners could create such poor telephone reception. They had, however, made out quite clearly the promise to phone back in two days' time.

By now they both knew that once again in their lifetime something else had gone terribly wrong. Their marriage had first produced a son and then two years later a daughter. They had lost the boy in a mountaineering accident and the girl they had lost through pride. Now both were sure they had lost a grandchild.

Wendy had always rebelled against her parents' belief that to be a responsible member of the family one had to strive for success in all things and the attainment of status in society through superiority in either business or profession was the measurement of one's success. She had argued in vain with them on many occasions, accusing her parents of pushing young Andrew in the same fashion as they had done to both her and her brother. Had it been the attitude of only one of her parents it would have been easier for her but both parents on this subject were of the same opinion. It wasn't long after she had happily married – in fact a fortnight after the honeymoon – that she told them tenderly but firmly that unless they adopted a more modern attitude on certain human values she would never permit them to influence any child she might bear in the future.

Both her parents were well aware that she missed them both just as they missed her. There was little doubt that it was only a foolish family stubbornness between the three of them that had caused the slow burning of the bridges between the two generations.

There was a sudden, heavy, official knock at the door and they heard the maid leaving the kitchen and opening the main door. It was only a matter of seconds before the neat figure, dressed in her uniform of dark skirt and white embroidered apron, wearing her maid's tiara type hat, told them in a hushed voice that a policeman would like to talk to them. The grandfather nodded his assent and in moments the policeman entered the room and saluted.

He respectfully enquired if he had come to the correct address and when that was confirmed he asked of the grandmother if she would like to sit down. Her husband moved towards the drinks cabinet, asking the visitor if he would be allowed to take a wee drink. The policeman declined and waited until the host had poured himself a drink, then moved over to stand behind his seated wife.

The man in uniform informed them that the police had received information from the Swiss Consul regarding the death of their grandson Andrew. It had been a tragic accident, he told them, and then paused to make sure that both had fully understood what he had told them.

The old man nodded and directed him towards the display cabinet and Andrew's smiling photograph displayed on top of it. He gave a tired gesture with his right hand, not meaning to indicate the silver teaset and the several small objets d'art but apparently to show the late young man's collection of swimming trophies. He even pointed out the scars in the wood, and one in particular on the middle shelf, explaining how they had been caused by the heavy shield that he had kept for three successive years. The official visitor murmured that such a loss must come much harder to bear under the circumstances.

It was then that the grandfather politely enquired if anyone else had been killed in the fall.

The policeman looked at him rather quickly before replying that Andrew had been the only person who had lost his life, but he added it was not caused by a fall. He had died through drowning.

He then continued by telling them that when the weary and tired team of climbers returned to the hotel after a very successful ascent on the mountain Andrew had shown bravado in telling his friends that the best souvenir he could take home with him would be to tell his grandparents that their grandson had been the first man to both climb the mountain and swim across the lake immediately afterwards. The policeman continued saying that the young man had told his friends that the Alps region was several hundred miles south of his own Cairngorms which should make it easier for him. He concluded by saying that as far as he knew no-one had ever made such a climb and then immediately swum across the lake before; at least that was what they had gathered from the Consul.

Later the same day, both the grandparents had a long talk together after which the grandmother said that she thought they should move house to be closer to Wendy. The grandfather agreed.

Andrew's trophies were packed away and the display cabinet was amongst several items of furniture later sent to a furniture sales room to be sold.

'WHAT FOLK DON'T SEE?'

Scenario Two A four-storeyed tenement two room and kitchen top flat in which everything to do with the family life is centred around the kitchen. It has an alcove recess bed (box-bed) where the parents sleep and beneath it is a 'wheelie' or 'hurlie' (a low portable pull-out bed on wheels and usually used by the youngest of the children). There is an open fire grate that supplies the heat for both the built-in side oven and the domestic hot water. There is a sink in front of the window with hot and cold taps. The usual net curtain covers the lower half of the window and a full-length curtain that would be pulled across when someone was having a sponge-down. To one side of the grate on top of the oven is a gas appliance with four small gas rings. The sideboard and bunker run along the wall facing the fireplace and the traditional heavy kitchen shelf runs around as much of the wall as it can. Overhead is a clothes pulley and a permanent feature beside the fire was the wooden clothes horse that is never without something wet or damp draped over it. The flooring is linoleum and there are two chairs facing each other on either side of the fire. One of those chairs is a make-up bed and beside it on a small painted table is a wireless. The centre piece of furniture is the well-scrubbed plain wooden kitchen table with four plain painted chairs around it. A child's comic page from a newspaper lies in a discarded fashion on the table. Over the grate is a heavy looking wooden mantelpiece with a clock taking pride of place at its centre.

There is no bathroom or WC inside the flat. (Residents usually went once a week to the Corporation Public Baths for a hot private bath, or, where older children were concerned, several at one time regardless of sex and supervised by an economical mother.) There is a 'cludgey' (WC) on the outside landing that is shared by the immediate neighbours.

In the close there are four flats to each landing. What one can rub against or what one walks on or what one looks up at is all whitewashed. There is no sign of paint or wall tiles to be seen. Everything appears smaller even down to the landing windows (half way up each stairway and always looking out onto the back green and, having a deep sill, often used as a resting place between landings). The close entrance is directly off the pavement with the usual passage leading to the ground floor flats, stairs and dunnies (cellars, WC and wash-house with coal-fired boiler facilities), back green and rubbish bins.

There is a very small hallway that is barren of any furniture apart from a lino flooring with a small rug at its centre.

A small back room backs onto the kitchen and contains two threequarter beds, a painted chest of drawers, a narrow basic type cabinet with a mirror on top and an enclosed lower part storing a chamber pot. All the furnishings stand on linoleum. The walls are neatly covered in a pink water-based paint. Like all the other ceilings in the tenement this one is plain and whitewashed with an electric light suspended by its own cable hanging from its centre.

The other room is the parlour at the front of the building. This is the place where formal visitors are ushered into and welcomed. The walls bear a standard type of decorative paper up to the height of the dark brown painted picture rail. There are two rural scenes hanging on opposite walls. A dark, well-polished table with a crochet-fashioned cloth lies over it, on which stands an empty vase. There is a small rug lying in front of the open fire with the usual brass fireside tools lying in its vicinity. The neatly sewn, tasteful curtains had been made up on the sewing machine standing in one of the corners and discreetly covered with a refined looking cloth made by the same expert hand that produced the curtains.

Bella was typical of the district she was born into and brought up in. Although not quite thirty she was already both tired and worn out long before her time. It didn't take much intelligence on anyone's part to see that these two and other reasons, in this damned area where she had her home, had shaped her outlook on life and her temper. The tragedy of such normality was both its general acceptance and the slowness of its change; therefore Bella knew that nothing could possibly happen that would alter her present way of life, nor did she hold any silly expectations of an unburdened and carefree future.

She was by nature quiet and had a fondness for reading, when she possibly could, though perhaps it wasn't a good thing to know that there could be a better and easier life. There seemed so much in this world that was unfair. The political pamphlets that her father gave her to read at one time had really made her quite bored with and about politics. She often thought of her two dead children but never mentioned them to anyone, not even to Jim, although by some means she knew that Jim did the same. Perhaps it was part of the local environment not to burden others who also carried the same memories of hurtful losses.

She still had three children to cope with and the demand on her time and energy seemed endless, especially when there was illness involved. One of her girls was coughing continually and flecks of blood were to be seen on her pillows each morning when there weren't any newspapers brought in from the litter bins to act as covers. She knew the child had TB and she had reported it to both the school authorities and the local medical surgery which, as far as she was aware, was run by some charity supported by several church organisations. As a younger woman she could never understand why the various churches, that all seemed so against every mortal thing that didn't think the way they did, could get together and run a clinic for any and all denominations. Maybe, just maybe it was the beginning of something that boded well for the future. It was from the clinic she collected the bottles of cough mixture for Wee Jeannie.

TB was common enough in this part of the city. In fact there were few families who couldn't claim to have knowledge of a relative or friend who was either suffering from it or had died of it. Local children caught chickenpox, scarlet fever or meningitis, although she had often heard that it was mostly the children from richer homes who caught those diseases. It was often said that poorer children flourished like weeds and somehow seemed to be better protected in some ways from disease than children from better homes. Bella knew what the first child died from but she wasn't sure what the little boy was taken away with because no-one had bothered to tell her what exactly had occurred to cause his death; nor had anyone even attempted to at least understand an impoverished mother's grief. She recalled one lady visitor who seemed to have no feeling at all for her and Jim just after that terrible period when they lost a four-year-old daughter from that awful cough and a two-year-old son from a sudden illness within six weeks of each other. Jim had thought the lady was a health visitor nurse or maybe a doctor or perhaps she was just a kind lady visitor from some department of the Corporation. She must have got their name from the school list for no-one in any official capacity ever said who she was or why she had come. Looking back at her own personal contact with such people, Bella was sure it was part of some conspiracy to tell people as little as possible. Thinking back she supposed at times it might have been through Jimmy that there were health visitors coming to the house at all for he had been fairly well-known at one time. She had been married to Jim now for six years, but so much had happened since then.

Jim had always been a very fit person who had taken care of his body when he was young with constant exercise and careful eating habits. He was comparatively small in stature but very active and agile. He had never been anything more than a labourer only because he never had the opportunity or the means to advance himself. Bella made a slight movement of her head to one side when she remembered that marrying someone who at least had a job was considered then to be the first step to a wedded paradise. He had been a good amateur boxer and a keen member of a harrier club and very, very fond of Bella.

At that stage in his life Jim had never known defeat in the ring. He knew the rules and always abided by them. The one surprising feature about him apart from being such a fine boxer was his good nature. There had never been any money involved with his sport. Though there was lots of talk about how much he might win some day, in the meantime he had been presented with several little items from both the running club and the gym. There was the occasion when he was given a belt that he was allowed to wear but never own.

When he finally moved into professional status all the items belonging to the clubs had to be returned, that being the usual procedure. Jimmy did not seem to mind as there were still several mementos to remind him of those early years and Bella wasn't really interested one way or another.

This change happened a mere two months after they were married and Bella saw no reason to worry over whether it would be better being married to a labourer or a good boxer. In the ring Jim looked small yet he was so quick on his feet that at times some spectators thought their eyes were beginning to play tricks with them.

The money earned in the fight game (winning of course) was much better than what a labourer earned at the best of times. It was sufficient for Bella to comfortably keep the home going, and when the first child arrived Jim was a very generous and caring father. In fact the first two years were financially good ones as he made more money with his ever growing number of professional contests. It was sometime during the first year that the pair of them bought a rather nice display cabinet from a second hand furniture shop, not particularly far from where they lived. It bore a scar near the centre of the middle shelf and there were lesser scratch marks in the same vicinity; otherwise it seemed to be in excellent condition. Soon there was a framed wedding photo, along with mementos of various successful bouts with well-known boxing names. There was also a thick file of newspaper comments that had been removed from the sporting section to join the growing number of souvenirs. On the bottom shelf were a few second hand books.

In this particular district it was very difficult in general to be a success and not share it with one's whole family and friends. It was proving rather expensive – but what else could they do? If trouble and sorrow were shared only amongst a few close people then so should prosperity. That was how the community that Jim and Bella lived in thought and somehow they never managed to move into a bigger flat with their own WC. It was something the pair of them had often talked about but with so many of their own families caught in the web of recession the matter was constantly shelved.

As the winning fights continued so the number of mementos grew in number.

Bella's concern started shortly after the birth of her fifth child when Jimmy came home late one night and was quite drunk. She didn't know why and she didn't ask him, but it wasn't so very long after the incident that he lost his first fight and it seemed to be all downhill after that. Jim started to talk about his luck changing back to what it once was, and it never did. The sad thing about such a wish was that no matter how bad one's luck appeared to be, it could always get worse.

The first items to be removed from the cabinet were the little periphery mementos of lesser fights but as food became more of a priority then something else had to be either sold or pawned. It was not surprising when they flitted. They moved only a few streets away but the rent was cheaper because of the rundown condition of the place. It consisted of only one room and kitchen. It was not a desirable street to live in and most of her new neighbours seemed to have a lot more children than Jim and Bella had, but perhaps the cramped living conditions merely gave that effect.

Bella now had to economise on household items, which included food and disinfectant. There were the expectant complaints about the former and the predicted vermin visitation because of the latter. Beetles could often be seen in the close scurrying into cracks in the public stairway and soon they were to appear with the woodlice around the kitchen sink when the last of the strong carbolic solution was finished. The flat grew darker and colder as less coal was bought and less money put into the gas and electric meters. The common toilet they shared with neighbours no longer smelt of Bella's cleanser but of the stale smell of urine. The neighbour's man and at least one of his sons returned home regularly the worse for drink and contributed to the lavatory's stench. It was a district where anything could happen. Young men fought in gangs yet had nothing really to fight for. A lot of men got drunk and so did many women and when they finally managed home it was to collapse wherever they could. In the morning the tell-tale traces of sawdust from the nearby pub floor that led to the kitchen sink could be seen before the smell of stale beer and stomach contents attacked the nostrils.

They had their own rules, which were strictly adhered to should a wife or child be seen to carry a bruise brought on through an assault by one of the family. In this district nothing ever ended with the first blow as so many of the same family lived nearby or, more likely, directly below or above. It didn't take long before a wife abuser was severely beaten by the brothers and uncles of the battered wife or child. He was also harangued in public by women. Families did their own policing, judging and sentencing, and in a patchwork way it worked for it deterred some and gave satisfaction to others. The police never interfered unless their enquiries took them outside this area of the city.

During the past year Jim had slowed down and was now not at all as he used to be. He had retired from boxing eighteen months before; that was the year after the two children had died. By that time he had already lost his adoring boozy retinue who only liked to be seen with winners. He was now losing his eyesight and taking more time to think out something that he could have done in the past in the time it took someone to snap their fingers. He also slept a lot longer that was usual for him. Bella had thought that for some reason she had been allowed such a little time to grieve with so much happening. She was fully aware it was expected of her to quickly get over the upsets and return to normal. Outsiders said that poor people, and more especially the ones from her district, were hard and cruel. She denied the cruelty charge, and being hard was a necessity for survival or had to appear so for such a façade had to be a good one.

Item by item was slowly removed from the cabinet and either sold separately or taken to the pawn shop, never to be redeemed. What amount of money received by selling their personal articles and most of the dole money went to the factor (rent manager) or ended up in one of the meters. Some of their friends had their meters broken into with all the subsequent heartbreak made worse by the knowledge that the money would only be spent on drink.

There wasn't much left in the cabinet now. Only a worn pair of child's shoes, a photograph of Jim in boxing shorts, wearing a large ostentatious belt, various boxing match bills and newspaper cuttings. Bella remembered, when she removed the cloth from the top shelf, that she had put it there herself to cover the stain caused by the contents of an accidentally spilt cough bottle lying overnight on the shelf where it had been kept. The incident had happened three years ago and she remembered that even in those days it would have been financially impossible to have it restored. Sometimes she would look at the only picture that showed all the children. She had never seriously considered abortion, although she knew that some of her friends had paid a woman to carry out whatever it was she did. No-one ever spoke about the details; such things seemed irrelevant. She started to feel guilty about what she was thinking. There were so many other women with more weans (children) than she had who managed to cope. She noticed amongst the cuttings in the cabinet a Communist pamphlet and thought it quite ridiculous and out of place. Her father was a Communist, as was one of her brothers. The rest of the family were divided between socialists or being nothing. Now and again there was a political rally that always finished in a fight somewhere and if the police didn't take them away it was on to the local pub to spend what they had in their pockets. She often thought it was an awful way to earn your self respect.

Hearing Jim in a restless sleep and one of the children coughing she knew she had to go down again to see the lady for more free medicine. She opened her own door just as the man from the dole office arrived. She knew he didn't like calling and couldn't leave quick enough, as TB had been reported from the house.

She was quite right; he didn't stay very long. Only long enough to spend about four minutes with Jimmy and tell Bella she had married a man who liked to spend most of his time in bed. He could not have made it clearer what he thought about people on the dole expecting free medicine and blankets but someone had to work, and to emphasise what he was saying he repeated that they had to work very hard for their money. He reminded her about the Means Test, then told her that the following week's dole would be withheld and reassessed after she had sold her display cabinet, which he could see absolutely no use for in this sort of home. Then he left.

The next morning Bella removed the few simple remaining items from the polished shelves: a few pieces of paper, two photographs no longer framed and an almost empty cough bottle. The cabinet was then returned to the same shop it had been purchased from. It fetched for the family the amount of 3s. 6d.

On her return home with the money Bella heard some talk about an impending war with Germany, and wondered what anyone in this world had that was worth fighting for.

'THERE'S JUST NO TELLING'*

Scenario Three A middle storey tenement flat situated in what is considered a nice locality in Glasgow. There is a large comfortable lounge with a plaster pattern encircling the wooden rose for the light fitting in the centre of the ceiling. A plaster frieze also runs round its perimeter, giving a classical look. The room has a comfortable fireplace and a large window area with folding wooden shutters on either side of it – not normally used because of the growing preference towards using heavy curtains. (However, the war had halted that trend during the enemy bomber raid period and a cautious spell that followed it.) The room has a large carpet laid in the centre, and around the edges nearest the walls linoleum has been laid over the exposed floorboards. The main feature is the grand piano that looks even larger in the direct light from the nearby windows. An oak-leaved dining table that has been wound in to its smallest size, stands in the centre of the room with four matching chairs placed around it in an orderly fashion. Two easy chairs and a small settee are strategically placed in front of the fire. Against one of the walls there is a high well-stocked bookcase with some of its contents appearing to have been placed in a neater fashion than others. A tasteful though not luxurious wallpaper shows on the walls and because there are neither picture nor mirror suspended from the picture rail the room appears larger than what it is. There is a Spartan hint to the room, perhaps because there are no standing lamps or ashtray holders.

There are two double bedrooms with each containing a small tiled fireplace and a wash-

*Scottish expression when no other words seem to fit the occasion.

hand basin. One is carpeted and the floor of the other is completely laid with linoleum where two small rugs have been added for comfort. The carpeted room has a double bed and in the other one there are two single ones, otherwise the usual basic furnishings are the same in each room.

A single room near the entrance area has a small plain fireplace and the floor has linoleum on it. There is a narrow bed with a small rug at one side of it. A little dressing table is placed in front of the window and a matching wardrobe stands against one of the walls. The usual net curtain covers the lower half of the window and heavy window-length curtains have been drawn to each side for such curtains are necessary during the long light summer nights and early mornings in northern latitudes.

There is a comfortable sized kitchen with an adequate larder press, gas cooker and usual open fired range. There is the standard kitchen wall shelf displaying the heavy dinner plates and china utensils, sideboard and coal bunker. On a wall can be seen the row of long-redundant room service bells that no longer work and there is a recess bed that is not in use but proving functional as storage space. There is a family-sized bathroom with WC, and a cloakroom that is large enough to take a single bed. It has a high barred window looking out into the outside landing and the gas and electric meter are situated there.

The hallway runs almost the length of the flat. It has a covering of linoleum with a narrow carpet running along its centre. The only furnishings are a traditional hat and coat stand and a slim polished barrel containing umbrellas and walking sticks.

The front of the tenement has a small fringe garden with wrought-iron railings running along its length. Like all Scottish tenements it is built from quarried stone with a slate roof and erected to last a long time. The close is entered at pavement level and inside is painted in a pale yellow colour. A tiled strip runs along the wall at shoulder height. Just past the two front doors of the bottom tenant the passage divides into the stairway leading upwards and continuing through to the back green. There have never been any additional washing facilities in this building.

Since the death of their mother six years ago Anne and her brother Robert had remained together, sharing the same flat. Their parents had never been wealthy by any stretch of the imagination, but on the other hand, their father had never been out of work and the pension he had accumulated for his widow when he died three years before the war started had been well managed by her. Robert, at the time of his father's death, had just completed his medical degree. He had proved to be a late developer where medical knowledge and expertise were concerned. At school he had been an average pupil, but later, when it had come to matters medical, he had soaked up his studies like a sponge does water.

During the war he had distinguished himself in the RAMC as well as specialising in the study of the human eye, on which he had written a number of medical articles.

Anne had trained as a teacher, although her first love from an early age, had always been music. Anyone hearing her play the piano knew immediately that her fingers had a very special touch. Her mother had been a school teacher before she had married. In these days there had been no such thing in the Scottish education system as a married lady teacher. She had been an educated mother who had made sure that she would have educated children.

She did not have much in a material sense to leave her children when she passed on; just a few pieces of china she had treasured over the years and a silver box handed down from her parents. It had been a family joke for some years before she died as to how the pair of them were to share this family legacy.

Helen came twice a week and sometimes at the weekend to help with the housework and perhaps do some shopping. The war had produced part-time-this and part-time-that and Helen had become a part-time housekeeper. She was older than both the brother and sister who employed her. She had a refreshing personality as well as being gifted with both a pleasant singing voice and a talent for painting in water colours. She had soon become as much a friend as she was a good housekeeper to them.

Helen's daughter was a qualified teacher who worked at a small school that specialised in children with a speech difficulty. One proven new and popular method in helping them to overcome their impediments was to encourage them to sing, and through this particular approach in the classroom teaching Helen had volunteered for several hours a week to give what assistance she could. Perhaps her willingness to be near her daughter stemmed from the time when she nursed her through meningitis, that left the child with a slight irregular heartbeat.

Anne and Robert had moved into the flat only on a temporary basis, at least until the war had ended and Robert had been able to find out where he would be working. Because of these uncertainties, plus the fact that the flat was rather large for the pair of them, it had been furnished with no more than the bare necessities. Robert considered that collecting pieces of furniture for the home was his department, and his sister thankfully did not argue against him on this point.

One day, not very long after they had moved into the flat, Robert arrived home with a friend, and in between their puffing and huffing they produced a piece of polished furniture that turned out to be a display cabinet. Robert proudly declared he had bought it at a sale room. It had been the first time he had taken part in a public auction and his friend told Anne how excited he had become during the bidding up to the time the auctioneer accepted his bid. Robert, of course, denied being anything other than deadly calm.

He explained to his sister that it was second-hand and added that there were minor marks on the middle shelf and a woodwork stain on the top one. Anne ran her fingers along the scratched surface and remarked about them being deeper than mere marks, but she said brightly that it was just what was needed. As soon as it was cleaned and polished (a job for Helen) every piece of china and oddments that had belonged to their parents, along with other little items which had been collected since, were put on display in the cabinet. The silver box that Robert had so often told his sister that he enjoyed looking at, because he found the intricate design quite fascinating, was strategically placed over the scars on the middle shelf. The top shelf stain remained and was duly hidden from sight under a decorative cloth.

Robert could be heard in a quiet voice going over each item that had been placed on the various shelves. Anne waited patiently until he was finished and said that there was still room for two more items and each of them should have a choice as to what one of the final two items were to be. Robert laughingly agreed.

Anne produced a silver framed photograph of her favourite uncle and as she placed it on the shelf her mind wandered back over several years to one of the many reasons he had endeared himself to her...

Uncle John wasn't much to look at, being rather too theatrical to be true, but to really know him and see past his eccentricity was to find a loveable person. She always laughed when recalling the incident about the glove. He had a pair of knitted fawn-coloured gloves that he wore each winter over a lot of years. His lady dog, Katy, had a lifelong habit of gnawing the wool on the right hand index finger with her small front teeth – a habit that her master for some reason seemed to encourage. This particular glove index finger had been darned and darned and darned. On several Christmases and birthdays Uncle Andrew kept receiving presents of hand-knitted gloves of differing colours which were never seen to be worn. One late autumn he and Katy had been invited to Crieff for a week's visit to an old friend, who happened to be the station master. Over a few whiskies the topic of the glove came up between the two old pals when the station master had an idea and suddenly said that there was a box at the station where all the lost property was kept and it was decided that the following day the box would be checked to find out if a similar glove or gloves were to be found in it.

The following day at the station the box was searched and, believe it or not, there was a single right hand knitted glove of the proper size although it was not quite the same tone. Uncle John beamed with excited pleasure when he saw it and made it quite clear that the lost glove was exactly what he wanted. The station master then informed his visitor in a serious way that each item was labelled when found and after six months any unclaimed item was still given to the local orphanage where, if it could be used by them it was gladly accepted and if it could not be used by them, it was gladly accepted and put aside until auctioned off on a particular day of the year with the proceeds going towards the orphanage upkeep.

The label on the glove showed that its six month period had already expired, as had several other items. This usually predicted that the Widow McPherson was due to collect them in her voluntary capacity and deliver them to the home.

It was now the time of day when a cup of tea arrived, as did another visitor. Sergeant Neil of the Railway Police was a well built middle aged man who kept himself fit by being careful with what he ate and in what he did. He originated from the Western Isles, and believe it or not, was teetotal – well, almost. It was said locally that he and Mistress (Mrs) McPherson had been seen together on quite a number of strictly social occasions.

Perhaps it wasn't a complete coincidence that the lady in question arrived to enquire about the lost property box and take away what items she could from the collection. Permission, of course, was immediately and politely granted along with the invitation to join them in a cup of tea.

By this time the policeman had removed his gloves, rolled them together and placed them in his coat pocket before hanging the coat up in a small cubby-hole just outside the office they had gathered in. Katy had noted every move he had made and when he returned she went over to him and nuzzled her mouth into his hand before he shooed her away and lifted his hot cup of tea to his lips.

'That's a right daft dog you have there. She must think I've got something to eat in my hand,' he said between sips.

'Aye,' said Uncle John slowly. 'Like all her sex she has a few funny wee ways.'

As though to tell them something Katy left the room.

The conversation then centred around the orphanage and the comings and goings around the station, especially on Friday and Saturday nights. The station master introduced the subject of the glove and spoke in such a manner that the lady became quite concerned. 'Of course,' she said, 'you poor wee man, you must have the glove.'

A phone call complaining about a railway horse destroying someone's front garden sent the railway's upholder of the law, still buttoning his heavy overcoat, off to investigate the matter and he totally failed to notice his pair of gloves lying on the floor.

The lady also decided to leave when she recognised the gloves as belonging to Mr Neil. She picked them up, saying, 'Seeing as it's a bit cold I'll just wear them myself until I can return them to the gentleman himself.' (She thought, as did the station master, that perhaps they had been left behind deliberately.)

She put the left glove on first and it fitted fairly comfortably but when the right hand glove had been pulled on a bare index finger was clearly exposed.

'Och,' she said, 'some men will wear anything. They widna know how to darn a thing if you didna do it for them.'

She waved a goodbye to the two old friends, and still muttering about the ineptitudes of some men, she headed towards the station exit with her bag of treasure for the orphanage.

A week later the same lady received a parcel via the station master containing eighteen pairs of hand knitted gloves. There was a simple written note amongst them that said, 'For use at the Childrens Home from a Poor Wee Man and his daft dog. P.S. Perhaps the dark blue pair might be of some use to Mr Neil, at some later date of course.'

When Uncle John had told Anne the story he was wearing the glove in question and added that all he wanted to do was to wear out the left glove before throwing it away. As regards the difference in colour it didn't really bother him. Anne could not help laughing with him, for to be quite honest it didn't bother her either . . .

Anne's thoughts returned to the present time and she stepped back to let her brother place something in the cabinet.

Robert looked at the photo of his uncle with satisfaction for he too had happy memories of him. He had heard some of the stories that had only been made possible by a very unusual person. After all, it was he who gave him a pet dwarf rabbit on his eighth birthday which grew and grew and grew.

The choice he made was his porcelain tramp . . .

He liked the great outdoors with the call of birds and the sound of waves rolling shorewards. He enjoyed attending a weekend football match and hearing the roar of an excited crowd. On more than a few occasions he had managed to dodge away from a classical leisure event with the blessing of his sister, who knew full well he would be off to some sporting activity.

It was after his medical studying time was well behind him and he had started to specialise that he met quite by chance, on one of his long walks, a gentleman of the road. The tramp had come from a good family and was well educated by any standards. Both of them had chatted amicably for a few hours before their paths divided. Later on, during the same day, he felt compelled to purchase a figure of a tramp, which bore an uncanny resemblance to the traveller he had recently been talking to.

Later on in life Robert always thought that it was from about this time that he realised that an important part of general education was to be found outside the lecture hall . . .

Shortly after the ending of hostilities there was a strange coincidence for within the same week the brother and sister each received an official letter of thanks, though from differing sources. It was also the same week that Robert accidentally caught his full weight on the display cabinet door, which was open at the time. This caused a woodwork joint to slightly open out in the vicinity of the upper hinge. The damage made it harder to close and lock the door without giving it a final hard push. He was adamant that he had not been celebrating at the time.

Anne's letter of thanks was for her war efforts with piano recitals and in the helping of dispatching Red Cross food parcels. Robert was being thanked for his medical services in the field of optical research. Both the letters were placed in the silver box which their mother had hoped they would somehow manage to share.

The sister would sometimes take the silver box out of the cabinet, run her fingers over the design and gently open it. She would think of Robert when he had something on his mind, and of his dreadful habit of humming some popular tune hopelessly off-key, and she had to smile.

It appealed to her sense of humour when she thought of the intricate work he could carry out on the human eye, and the pleasure she could give through the human ear. She would smile again thinking it really quite strange that he should have been born tone deaf and she should be born blind.

The following year the pair of them moved to a comfortable home in another part of the city and the display cabinet found its way back to the sale room.

Scenario Four A top storey two room and kitchen flat in what would now be considered a good working class district. The kitchen has the usual kitchen/scullery fittings and appliances. The grate fire supplies all the required domestic hot water. As only one person is staying in the flat the kitchen has a neatness almost matching the scene from a picture post card. One of the rooms is entered only from the kitchen. It is small with most of the floor space taken up with a double bed. The floor is carpeted and the wallpaper has a look of quality. The ceiling and its surrounds are plain and clean. A small dressing table fills the curtained window space. The front room is entered from a small hallway and is kept as the 'best room' or the parlour. It has a small fireplace with polished brass utensils within the confines of its fender. On one of the walls are the doors of the press-bed (almost a three quarter bed recessed into the wall and concealed behind wooden doors). A carpet almost covers the floor and that part of the flooring that can be seen is polished over in a rich brown wood stain. A large plant in its own stand holds the best view from the centre of the window space. A small polished table with chairs is positioned in the centre of the carpet. One gets the impression that all the wooden furnishing throughout the flat has been chosen with taste and treated with care. There is no bathroom, only a small space entered from the hallway, containing a WC and washhand basin. Since the war and with full employment it is now considered a suitable flat for a single person, or a young couple as a starting home.

The coalman, who looked to be in his mid-twenties,was sitting on the edge of the moving cart, holding loose reins in his hands. Beside him sat a young lad, and between them they gave the appearance that they were without a care in the world. The big Clydesdale horse seemed to know exactly where he was going as there were no visible signs along the reins or audible instructions that he was being told what to do or where to go. Now and again they had to stop to allow tramcar passengers waiting at the stops access across their cobbled path between tram lines and pavement. Alex had finished his last delivery for the morning with his young helper, Jack, and was doing a little something extra that always helps to further future business and perhaps put a couple of shillings in his pocket at the same time. He glanced over his shoulder to the rear of his cart and mentally checked the empty coal sacks folded in four neat stacks in front of the board with the price 3s. 2d. chalked on it. The display cabinet that they had collected from the sales room looked heavier than it was, at least from a robust coalman's point of view.

Alex had been most surprised when, of all people, Mrs McCann had asked him if he could collect and deliver it for her. She was known to be very canny with her money and he could not for the life of him guess what she would want such a piece of furniture at her age for. Mrs McCann was one of those terribly independent types who would never consider getting into debt and would insist on knowing exactly what her money was going to buy her. He recalled quite clearly several lectures with the allegorical theme about everything one gets in this world having to be paid for one way or another.

A few weeks prior to the purchasing of the cabinet she developed a slight tickly throat cough and guessed it was about time she had a business call from Alex's uncle. She would insist that a total job was done and it all had to be costed, then paid for before it was the time for her to leave.

Alex's uncle had originally started up in business around the same time as his father had become a Coal Merchant and from that beginning the brothers had shared the horses and stables. His father had been humping (carrying a heavy load) coal since he left school and his uncle had started out as an apprentice carpenter and ended up as a carpenter-cum-cartwright before starting his new business. All this happened about ten years before when Alex was about eight or nine years old.

He didn't mind working with coal but having two businesses in a close family meant that he had to work with his uncle when the occasion demanded and he did not like it the slightest bit. He could never tell whether his uncle had a strange sense of humour or was eccentric, though sometimes he appeared to be just plain daft. Alex had been reminded on more than a few occasions that a coalman had to sell a product into a home, whereas he was always sent for to attend to the 'final product' as he metaphorically put it, adding that every house and home needed his services at some time or another. Unlike his brother he always spoke in a sombre voice and never direct to any particular person but to the surrounding general space when whatever was being discussed. He would assure his client regarding any questions about cost, care and circumspection. He always reminded them that he had never had one complaint about his work since he entered the profession. By now he had long since dispensed with horses, being completely motorised.

The coal cart turned into the street where Mrs McCann stayed and stopped outside her close. The young coalman wondered if she would pursue her original enquiry about his uncle.

The pair of them carried the display cabinet up the three flights of whitewashed stairs. He gave his usual hefty knocks on the door to the accompaniment of his loud 'Coal' call and the door was opened by a small wiry elderly woman. She told them to place her purchase against the wall beside the kitchen cooking range as that was the only available space she had for it at present, with constant reminders to the two men to be careful. The cabinet was finally sited where the lady of the house wanted it, although she was careful not to show it. She gave Alex 3s 6d. and then dismissed both men with a wave of her hand. Her manner was not offensive but more that of casually dismissing a faithful servant.

The reality was that she had known the young man since he had left school. Mrs McCann had known his father before he had started his business and knew he would make certain that his son would learn the trade as he had and that meant humping coal from the street into the kitchen bunker and leaving each empty sack on the stairhead so that the housewife knew how many bags she was paying for. This his son and heir had done since he had been demobbed from the Navy three years before.

As Alex was closing the main door behind him the old lady started to say something when she was overcome with a bout of coughing and had to sit down. The coalman hastily returned and asked if she would like a glass of water, but she only looked at him through watering eyes and shook her head vigorously. He glanced around as though looking for something and at the same time wrinkling his nose as though sniffing something. He already knew what her answer would be to his next question, which was whether she was still interested in an appointment with his uncle at some time convenient to her. Recovering from what was now a gentle throat clearing she conveyed her intention to still see him, but not until nearer the end of the month, at which time she would know how much money she had in hand to pay for the clean removal of the 'final product'. As though to change the subject she commented that she had paid too much for the delivery of the cabinet and Alex got the distinct impression that the time to take his leave had arrived. Mrs McCann gave him an order for one bag only to be delivered in one week's time, emphasising, 'Not the usual three.'

As soon as the main door had closed behind the coalmen Mrs McCann locked it and immediately went into the kitchen to take a long satisfied look at her display cabinet. The peculiar stain on the upper shelf and the deep score and scratches clearly seen on the middle one did not bother her the slightest bit, nor even the slightly damaged woodwork in the vicinity of what she thought was a strained hinge. Well pleased with her inspection she wiped every inch of wood and glass before applying polish with an expert hand. Finally she went into the little room off the kitchen and from a large cupboard known as the 'wee room's press' she collected several items and placed them in the new cabinet. Amongst these articles were three photographs, a child's crayon drawing and a porcelain teapot. With the latter she appeared to be particularly careful and even gave it a slight caress before placing it over the scarred area on the middle shelf. A china teaset found its way onto the top shelf between the drawing and the photo.

Other pieces of bric-a-brac were placed inside in a manner that finally produced a tasteful and balanced scene.

Everyone who knew Mrs McCann was well aware of her canny nature regarding money, which may well have stemmed from the time her father had been on the 'buroo', or dole. Yet in all fairness to her each would agree that her fashion in handling money showed her to be a careful manager, not a mean one.

She very rarely paid a bill in one amount, no matter how little it was and usually insisted in making several prior payments until the total money was paid before receiving any goods or service. Her friends, neighbours and tradesmen alike knew of her strange little ways where money was concerned, but they also knew that with this system all her bills were paid in full. Hence the reason for the young coalman's tactful sounding out about his uncle's business.

During the following week the lady fully enjoyed the luxury of having a display cabinet in her kitchen showing her dearest possessions. She had planned this since the day almost two weeks ago when she first saw it in a sale room. Now she was savouring the pleasure of the happy memories these several items behind the glass brought to her mind. Periodically she would dismiss with annoyance the tickle at the back of her throat and the occasional cough that went with it. Fortunately a few sips of water soon made her forget about it.

The night before her bag of coal was to be delivered had been very cold and Mrs McCann had remained in bed a bit longer that was usual for her the following morning. She had put off lighting the kitchen fire until a little after nine o'clock. Once it was burning bright she banked it up with the remaining dross from the bottom of the coal bunker and then decided to have a cup of tea. Half way through her cup and after a lengthy look at the display cabinet and its contents she picked up the poker that had been lying against the brass fender and prodded the fire into a comfortable blaze. She then sat down in her chair to finish her tea. She thought back to her recent chance visit to a furniture sales room and how her eye had been instantly attracted to that single piece of furniture. She had instantly noted the rich rosewood beneath the heavy dark varnish along with the solidly carved scrollwork on either side of each half door. All the characteristic telltale traits of lines and traditional workmanship were reflected in this piece of furniture. She recalled vividly the many times her late husband had told her what to look for in classical furnishing. A closer look showed the bevelled glass in the doors and windows with the finely carved pattern around the top and the whole thing standing on four beautifully carved legs.

She dozed off before finishing her cup of tea.

She heard the fire engine a matter of seconds before someone pounded on her door. The policeman asked her if it was her chimney that was on fire, and as the thought of a court fine flashed through her mind she told him that the fire had not yet been lit. The constable remarked how strange it was that no-one in the close had lit a fire on such a cold morning and reminded her that the fireman on the roof would set off a water fire extinguisher down the burning chimney, then drop down a few pebbles as the sound of the falling stones would tell him if the chimney was clear. He added in a kinder tone that firemen would be on hand to check each flat in the close to make sure there was no further danger.

Mrs McCann rushed through to her kitchen, scarcely knowing what to do but keeping the presence of mind to pour a kettle of water into and over her fire. The dousing created much steam that carried a lot of ash with it but at least the fire no longer burnt. This exercise would be taking place in each of the neighbours' kitchens, a fact that would be known to the firemen who accepted it as part of the daily scene.

She was just composing herself when an excitement grew within her and she heard a voice telling to quickly push the display cabinet in front of the fireplace, then crouch behind it.

This she did and only just in time for it to block the path of a heavy fall of hot soggy wet soot from her chimney. She opened the cabinet doors and grabbed the photographs, crayon drawing and the teapot, and was still clutching these items when the fireman came in and sprayed the hot soot and fireplace with a small portable extinguisher. When he was satisfied that there was no further danger he told her with a comforting smile that it was probably spontaneous combustion that had caused the chimney fire and added that she might not have the cleanest kitchen in the neighbourhood but she did have the cleanest kitchen chimney. Tapping the woodwork of the cabinet he remarked how fortunate it had been that the fall had been stemmed with hard wood as some timbers ignite at a lower temperature than others, but not with what the cabinet was made of.

When she was alone she took a good look around at the mess. it would not take too long to clean the place up and mercifully the cabinet had limited it all to the area in front of the fire. If necessary she could easily rally round a neighbour or two who would be only too willing to offer any assistance she might require.

As for the display cabinet, she would clean it down and give it a quick polish. She had already found a home for it when she had first laid eyes on it. Her plan was that some day her son would get it. As a cabinet maker and restorer of fine furniture he was amongst the best. It was not to be unexpected as he was trained by his late father, and they couldn't come better than he. She replaced her husband's photograph in the cabinet, along with her grandchild's drawing attempt. Before replacing the teapot she removed the lid to peep at the mixture of five pound notes and one pound notes which were going to pay for her return trip to see her son, daughter-in-law and first grandchild who had been born abroad the year after his parents had emigrated. The thought of meeting them again was exciting and it was now only ten days before her departure.

The door sounded again but this time she heard the familiar call 'Coal' with it. She opened the bunker lid, then let the coalman in. He tipped one full bag into the storage space, then looked at the mess with one of those 'I told you so' looks. He wasn't quite prepared for a smiling Mrs McCann standing beside him, and even more astonished when she asked for another bag of coal from him. After he had completed delivery of the second bag and helped her to replace the display cabinet against the kitchen wall he said on his way out that there would be no point now in saying anything to his uncle, and with a cheery wave he closed the door behind him.

No, thought the lady, she would not be requiring a chimney sweep for at least another six months. The air seemed a lot clearer after the fall of soot from the chimney. No doubt that probably accounted for the sudden disappearance of the tickle from the back of her throat.

She looked at the cabinet, wondering if she really had heard a voice telling her to move it in front of the fire and crouch behind it. She shook her head, telling herself that a display cabinet cannot talk. Then she had a sudden thought: 'If it could talk, what kind of tales could it tell?'

SOME TIME LATER IN A COMMONWEALTH COUNTRY

Four sturdy children are playing in the garden of a pleasant middle-class home when one of them suddenly pipes up, 'My Dad received a big present from my Gran this morning. I'll ask Mum to show it to you.'

The mother was obviously quite used to questions and requests from her youngest offspring and showed it by the lack of any surprise at the young innocent's interest in the newly uncrated pieces of furniture.

There were the 'Oh's' and 'Ah's' as the young eyes took in every detail of the display cabinet.

It was explained to the children that it had belonged to a grandma who had died nearly a year ago. Then followed what it had been used for, and finally they were told it would be taken to the workshop the following day to be restored.

'What does restored mean?' asked one.

'Will it be put back in its crate?' asked another.

'Will it be put away for a long time?' came another question.

'Will the shelves be changed?' asked a concerned voice. 'I like them the way they are now.'

The mother calmed them down and explained in detail how it would be examined carefully all over and any damage would be repaired and all marks and stains removed. She assured them that when the work was finished the cabinet would look the same as on the day it was made.

'Please can we check it first?' came the excited questions in unison.

Permission was immediately given.

'There's a deep scratch on the middle shelf,' said one young expert.

'And a nasty funny stain on the top one,' cried another.

'The back seems sooty and singed,' said one with a competent thoroughness.

'One of the doors is tight,' came from one in a very professional manner.

'Mum, how can all these things have happened to it? Please try to tell us.'

'Let me think.' The mother started, knowing full well that stories of some sort were now fully expected. 'What was the first one? Oh yes, it was the deep scratch on the middle shelf. Right! Just give me a moment.'

The children knew she was thinking and waited wide-eyed for her to start. She didn't disappoint them.

She started. 'A long, long time ago in a big busy city far far away from here . . .'